2007

# Sanity Savers

# Sanity Savers

### Tips for Women
### to Live a Balanced Life

## Dr. Dale V. Atkins
## with Barbara Scala

**AVON**

*An Imprint of* HarperCollins*Publishers*

HarperCollins books may be purchased for educational, business, or sales promotional use. For information please write: Special Markets Department, HarperCollins Publishers, 10 East 53rd Street, New York, NY 10022.

FIRST EDITION

*Interior text designed by Elizabeth M. Glover*

Library of Congress Cataloging-in-Publication Data

Atkins, Dale V.
    Sanity savers : tips for women to live a balanced life / by Dale V. Atkins ; with Barbara Scala.—1st ed.
        p. cm.
ISBN: 978-0-06-124295-3
ISBN-10: 0-06-124295-0
1. Women—Psychology. 2. Women—Conduct of life. 3. Self-help techniques. I. Scala, Barbara. II. Title.

HQ1206.A85 2007
158.1028—dc22                                                    2006036888

07  08  09  10  11   JTC/RRD   10  9  8  7  6  5  4  3  2  1

For Rob,
the love of my life.

There is not a woman alive who can't use a bit of sanity saving. We often do too much. We think a lot about what we do, care what others think, and wonder how our actions affect everyone else in our lives. It's tiring just thinking about it.

Years ago, *many* years ago, I began thinking about the idea of Sanity Savers in the context of just getting through daily—make that hourly—life in healthy ways. It seemed to me that the women I met in my life and in my psychology practice were often out of balance, unaware that they were even seeking a way to find equilibrium in their lives. When they came upon a plan that worked it was temporary—it worked till their kids came home and began arguing, till their boss was fired and the office environment shifted, till they were diagnosed with cancer, till their mom became scarily forgetful, till their partner was laid off, till they could not juggle their work commitments and social life.

Is it possible to have balance in your life no matter what you are dealing with? I've found that the answer is yes. Picture yourself on a seesaw. There's a delicate balance as you and another shift ever so slightly this way and that. You marvel at the achievement. Then one of you sneezes or suddenly jumps off, and the momentary balance is gone. So it is with life.

When life and the people in it (including yourself) change, we tend to hang on tight to keep things familiar and safe. Not gonna happen. Instead, learning to sway from time to time, keeping center within your reach so deviations won't be as long or as difficult, is the way to go. It's all about balance. It just takes the willingness and awareness to want to stay balanced and a formula to put into place when life gets off kilter.

So I came up with five manageable but essential things every woman at any age needs in her life to maintain balance. I call them *the Five S's of Saving Your Sanity* for whatever life is throwing at you.

Can't get along with your partner? Friends judging you for having a gay son? Feeling alone at the holidays? Need to split from your business partner? Received a scary health diagnosis? Don't like your son-in-law? Need time away from a spouse with a chronic illness? Feeling too old to get back in the dating game? Trying to get pregnant? Sharing custody and cannot have a civil conversation with your ex? Job getting stale? Discovering your spouse cheats? Caring for ill parents? Needing to spice up your sex life?

If any of these life situations rings a bell or if you have a few of your own that send you up and down the emotional seesaw, incorporate the *Five S's* into your everyday life and see if you stay more even keeled:

1. **SELF.** Maintain a healthy body, mind, and spiritual connection.
   *Ask yourself:* How is my body reacting to this situation? Is this "good" for me and my well-being?
2. **SUPPORT.** Be with people in your life whom you care about and who care about you.
   *Ask yourself:* What do I need to do to get the help I need to get through this situation? Are my resources being drained or filled through interaction with this person?
3. **SURROUNDINGS.** Connect with nature and create a peaceful place for yourself.
   *Ask yourself:* How can my environment nurture and create calm? Am I keeping a fresh outlook by staying grounded in the natural world?
4. **STIMULATION.** Live a life with purpose, curiosity, and passion.

> *Ask yourself:* Am I keeping myself mentally engaged and challenged? Is life interesting and fulfilling?

5. **SAVOR.** Take time to be, have fun, and appreciate the gifts in your life.

> *Ask yourself:* Am I reflecting on the essence and joys of what this situation can bring? Am I doing the best I can do to be aware and appreciate what's happening today?

You will find that if you keep the Five S's at the forefront of everything you do, you can survive anything that comes your way. You'll become more balanced and pay more attention to what's lacking and what changes can be made. You can transition more easily to what is next in your life. You can build up your resilience. You will be better equipped to move on to more stable ground rather than getting stuck in a place you don't want to be. And you can be stronger, more fulfilled, and lead a happier life.

But what happens when you are suddenly jolted by something? When the awkward double stroller smashes your toe and cell phones seem to be ringing wherever you are, you have a choice. You can either become a conduit for passing the irritation and aggravation you are experiencing on to others, or you can become aware of your reactions and make other choices. It's up to you.

Start by paying careful attention to the details of the present. Become aware of your breathing, how your body feels, and how you are moving through space. Intentionally slow down, carefully focusing on details, and take deep, full breaths to calm your thoughts, emotions, and body. Despite how simple this sounds, it really works. Scientists have established that among the many benefits of simple, slow breathing, we can influence our heart rate and lower our blood pressure. After you center yourself, keep working on the Five S's.

Remember, living a balanced, sane life is a process, not a fixed state you can achieve and then forget about. The point is, to have and maintain a life in balance, you must be able to be flexible and adapt. As long as you live, new people and new circumstances will come in and out of your life. If you believe that balance requires keeping all the balls in the air at the same time and doing so brilliantly, you are requiring yourself to be a master juggler who never drops a ball. But everyone drops the ball sometimes. Maybe, instead, you can put a few balls down or appreciate that when they fall on their own, you may need to leave them there for a while to keep your sanity. Sometimes putting down a few balls is the wisest, healthiest thing you can do for yourself and for those around you.

Balance is something that should be on every woman's list to achieve. It helps save your sanity! Sometimes you'll hit areas on your life path that are particularly rough and difficult; other times they are relatively smooth and not too steep. In this book I present situations that are both serious and light . . . just like life. You may feel as if you are losing your sanity when you are driving in traffic. You may also feel as if you are losing your sanity when you hear that your daughter must have emergency surgery. One event cannot be compared to the other. But you need healthy ways to maintain your sanity and balance as you walk through the hills and valleys of life.

You can use *Sanity Savers: Tips for Women to Live a Balanced Life* in several different ways. Each day (Monday through Friday, and one for the weekend) involves a situation that can strain your sanity. These range from lighthearted to life-changing events. The readings, like life, are not in any particular order. Some days a situation may seem taken from the pages of your personal diary. Other days may present a circumstance you will never encounter. But your sister, best friend, or mother is dealing with that very issue. Despite the fact that you may never have to fire someone or raise a child on your own, the Sanity Saver could be worth pondering—or not. You decide.

You may, however, prefer to read several situations at once instead of one every day. Or rather than going in order, you may wish to select Sanity Savers that fall into one of the categories identified by the leaves at the top of each page—Well-Being, Parent, Single, Midlife, Work, Community, Partner, Family, and Friends—and read one of those each day. Then you can switch to another category. Whatever way you choose to use this book, the situations and the issues for each Sanity Saver will give you insight and guide you to maintain your balance and sanity whatever comes your way.

Can you commit to balancing your life and preserving your sanity? Many people claim to want balanced, sane lives, but refuse to move from words to reality. You've begun reading this book. That's a start and tells me you want to do more than just imagine living life differently. You're ready to begin and move further along the path toward greater balance. I can't tell you how much I respect and applaud you. If you allow the ideas in this book to help you, you will not only improve your own life, you'll improve the life of every person you encounter.

I hope I have helped you come one step closer to saving your sanity every day of your life, and I wish you a life filled with health, peace, and balance.

# *Monday*
### *Well-Being*

## A "New" New Year's Resolution

New Year's resolutions are often about committing to an exercise program, losing those extra twenty pounds, or quitting the smoking habit. While all of these are likely to be terrific for your health, offer great promise, and are made with the hope that your life will be better, the funny thing is that often our New Year's resolutions from one year to the next are exactly the same.

Ring in this New Year by changing your attitude about something or someone (including yourself). So often our attitudes remain unchanged and unchallenged and we become stale in our outlook. Take a refreshing approach and question whether your perception serves you well or restricts you, holding you back.

How many times have your own or other people's opinions prevented you from doing or trying something? "I always wanted to go skydiving but my friends will think I'm crazy." "I would like to take an art class but I can't draw." "I would like to learn to play the piano but I was never very good at it when I was a kid." "I would like to travel but I don't have a companion." "I would like to dance but don't have a partner."

- **No Challenge, No Change.** If you don't give yourself a challenge, there can be no change, and without change, there is no growth. Ask yourself, "How can I be continually challenged?"

- **Meet People Who Are Different from You.** Step out and don't limit yourself to your usual group (age, culture, race). Find people with similar interests but from different backgrounds. Meet

and be with people who are both younger and older than you. Learn from their experiences.

- **Be Conscious and Present.** By being fully aware, we can accept, reject, or change that which we don't want into something that can be helpful and productive.

- **Be Eager for Personal Growth.** Seek knowledge, adventure, and friendship. Do not confine yourself to a familiar road, traveling along paths others have gone or mapped out for you. Leave the familiar path from time to time. Be adventurous. Find your element; never stop searching. Continue your quest in life. It is all about growth!

By changing your attitude you can try things you thought you were "unable" to do and have experiences that will open your mind to incredible possibilities.

# Maintaining Friendships When You Are in Different Life Circumstances

You are a longtime single woman and your best friend is married with three children. Or you're divorced and your college roommate is about to get married.

Whatever the circumstance, it is easy to believe that you no longer have anything in common. Just because what is so important to one hasn't crossed the radar screen of the other doesn't mean the friendship is over. Some of the best friendships are enhanced when both watch, learn, and appreciate what is happening in the other's life. Friendships can grow from the foundation of a shared background, similar values, being yourself, and good laughs rather than solely from similar experiences.

- **Make Room for Differences.** Try not to fall prey to adult cliques and being exclusive with certain types of people. Think twice about joining the private club of "only moms with young kids" and letting go of your friends who don't have children. Why not say yes to a family barbecue at your girlfriend's house if you are single? Even though you think your working friend just doesn't have a clue about what it's like to be an at-home mom, give the relationship a chance to absorb your different lifestyles. Evaluate whether you can rearrange your friendship for now (and now can be a few years) and stay in touch, relate, and connect. Friendships ebb and flow with life circumstances. Who knows, your single friend might be a midlife mom one day, and

if the bond is maintained, you might be the person she'll seek for support and guidance.

- **Don't Assume There's Nothing in Common.** Not having life experiences in common doesn't have to mean there's disinterest. When you spend time with your friend, pay attention to what you talk about and what you don't talk about and why. Are you hiding the issues you have with your children because she doesn't have any and wants them? Do you know for sure that she is uncomfortable hearing you talk about your kids' school, or is it possible that she gets a kick from being close to your children as a surrogate aunt? Many women who do not have children love to be with their friends' kids and can develop unique relationships with them, which benefit everyone. Address the differences as well as the similarities that still remain intact.

- **Live Vicariously.** Ask about your friend's life and realize that your differences can allow for a closeness that is not possible when there is similarity. Enjoying your friend's single life when you are dealing with moody kids and a cranky husband can give you a moment of escape. You might giggle together over her "courting" stories and have fun helping your girlfriend select an outfit for her next blind date. Talking with her about what she is experiencing is something that can make both of your lives full.

Don't write friends off just because their life path is different from yours.

# Healthy Communication with Your Significant Other

We all know that good communication is essential if you want a good relationship. But many of us don't quite know exactly what we need to do. "Life" gets in the way, and we seize communication shortcuts or take the person and the relationship for granted by communicating in a way that is not healthy.

Among the many ways you can tell whether you are communicating effectively to your partner is by feeling respect for him and for yourself during the interaction. Recognize that all interactions either hurt or enhance your relationship, so consider wisely how you are communicating what is on your mind or in your heart.

- **Empathize.** Discover ways to see your partner's point of view in a sensitive way. Listen, without interruption or judgment, to what she or he is saying and how she or he is saying it so you can recognize the feelings behind questions and comments.

- **Timing.** If this is not the "right time" for a serious discussion or confrontation, let him or her know before he or she begins and tell him when you will be available to pay attention, cooperate, and participate. Gather your wits about you and mentally prepare for being open and vulnerable so that you are more able to work through a problem than resist. Heavier discussions that are too lengthy will stress out both of you. Try getting your important points out and allow for comments in a fifteen-minute segment. If there's a need to go on, ask whether he or she's OK to discuss it for another few minutes. Try and be clear and brief, but thorough.

- **Try Something New.** If your partner suggests a new approach to an old problem, be open. Perhaps it is time to change a long-standing pattern that gets in the way of your ability to communicate effectively, particularly during times of crisis. Your way may have worked in the past but may not in the future.

- **Be Conscious of Body Language.** Rolling eyes, sighing, shaking your head no, sitting with your arms folded across your body may send a signal or message to your partner that although you say you are "there," you do not appear to be listening with a joint solution in mind if you are problem solving, or interested in what he is saying. Nonverbal communication is generally more convincing and believable than verbal.

Communicate with your significant other as if this person is a precious blessing in your life.

# Treat Yourself Well as a Single Woman

Think of how much more interesting your life will be if you make daily decisions to live it fully.

Whether married or single, it is better to depend on yourself to do what interests you rather than wait for others to invite you to participate in something that may or may not suit you. Sometimes single women feel as if they are third wheels and are uncomfortable being with married friends. And some of their married friends don't ask them to join in events that are family oriented but fun for all. And let's not even talk about those dinner parties where if you don't have a partner, you are excluded completely.

Stop waiting for the phone to ring for the next date, delaying plans to buy your own place, or looking to others to fill up your social calendar. It's your life to live, so enjoy the independence that many would envy.

- **Don't Wait for "Him" or Anyone Else.** If you would like to meet someone, do not put your life on hold while waiting for a partner to show up. Become involved in living your life. Plan a fun vacation to an exotic and interesting place. Spend at least part of a holiday with people you enjoy and who value you in their lives.

- **Create Community.** Become involved in an organization that you believe in and connect with a network of other people who are dedicated to its mission. Become immersed in doing what you like. Volunteer.

- **Buy Yourself Gifts.** If you see a nice necklace, art, something special, and you can afford it, buy it. You deserve it.

> It's up to you to fill your life so it's a
> fulfilling life to have.

# Gaining Control of Your Life When Your Child Has a Disability

When you thought about having children, you probably expected that they would be well and healthy. Most parents-to-be never think (except for a fleeting fear) about the realities of raising a child who has extra needs. You had an image of the child you were going to have. Now you have a child who is different from that one.

Living with and raising a child who has a disability can challenge your sense of yourself as a competent person and parent, but it can also give you enormous opportunity for growth and discovery. Understand that much of your life needs to be changed. Decide what can be changed and change it. Life with a child with extra needs means constant adjustment, and having a sense of humor helps.

- **Let Go** . . . of the child you had expected as you come to terms with the appreciation for and adaptation to the child you have. During this process you will likely experience internal discord and discomfort, feel jealous of your friends or family whose children seem "OK," wonder what you did to "deserve" this, blame yourself, or be angry. This process is difficult and it takes time.

- **Create Your "New Normalcy."** It takes time to set new expectations and to discover creative ways to maximize strengths and minimize weaknesses in both yourself and your child.

- **Learn as Much as You Can** . . . about the disability and what is realistic to expect regarding its progression if applicable, treat-

ment, and life adaptation. Identify supportive people (other families who have children with similar issues) and organizations (national organizations, support groups, information sources), and use them.

- **Identify Areas of Stress** . . . for everyone in the family, and discuss decisions that need to be made with everyone. Set attainable goals to help reduce stress (manageable ones over which you have control). Differentiate the long-term problems from the immediate ones and create *flexible* plans for dealing with them. The most effective ways of employing direct stress reducers when living with a child who has special needs is participating in activities such as exercise, work, time-out, prayer, and meditation.

Children who have disability differences may not be the children we expected, but that does not mean they are not the children we want.

*Well-Being, Friends*

# Is Your Reservoir Dry?

Are you on track? Are you running on empty? Do you feel over-whelmed? Are you spending too much time with people who deplete your personal resources—not to mention your patience? Is it hard for you to say no? If you can answer yes—even grudgingly—to any of these questions, you may be at a point where it's impossible to give of yourself. This bottom-of-the-barrel feeling lets you know that your reservoir is dry.

Right now, this minute, relax and imagine a reservoir full of water. Then imagine it empty, but with hordes of people trying to get the water they need. You'll see panic, fear, anger—and an empty reservoir. Consider what you need to do to refill it so you have what you need to stay full and giving. Then prepare a checklist of activities and attitudes that will help it remain full. When you sense that your reservoir is dropping to scary levels, refer to your list to keep yourself healthy.

- **Keep Your Own Needs High on the List.** What would it mean if you said no to people so you could gather your own wits about you and have more time to think or simply be still? When asked to do something that you really don't have time for or interest in, think of this response: "Sounds great, but this is not the right time for me." Or "Let me think about it and I'll get back to you." Do as you say you will, and get back to them. But say what you mean. Always consider the pros and cons when you have to invest time and energy.

- **Don't Keep Up with the Joneses . . .** or anyone, for that matter. When you talk to people, are they comparing their busy lives

with yours? Is there a subtle jealousy regarding who is doing more or has more on their plate? Identify those with whom you feel competition and determine how much energy you want to give to that dance. Try sitting on the bench and observing rather than running the I-want-what-you-have race—which nobody ever wins, by the way.

- **Limit Your Time.** Are you spending a lot of time with people who deplete your personal resources? If so, do something about it. Determine ways to limit or restructure the time you spend with them so that your experience is enhanced. It sometimes helps to bring along a neutral friend to relieve pressure.

- **Replenish.** Put aside or totally remove something from your daily tasks that doesn't benefit you. Turn the ringer off on the phone and sit quietly, even if only for a few minutes. Drink a cup of aromatic herbal tea as you relive a wonderful visit to a park, a great family party, a summer vacation. Play with a pet; attend to houseplants or your garden.

Your reservoir will only be full when you
take time to fill it!

## Aging Successfully

Aging is about change, and change is about loss, adaptations, and new beginnings.

There are some things over which you have no or little control that influence your aging. But there is plenty that you *can* take charge of so that you can fully engage in the aging process and benefit physically, spiritually, psychologically, and emotionally.

- **Have a Life Plan** . . . that is meaningful and purposeful, and keep adapting it to your situation. Rely on your own and outside resources to fill your objectives.

- **Enhance Your Reserves and Strengths.** Always grow and learn. Stretch your body, your mind, your attitude, your circle of people and interests. Focus on experiences and people that give you deep satisfaction and a sense of personal control. Engage people of all ages and walks of life.

- **Expect Adversity** and appreciate that it is part of a life in balance. Understand and adapt to loss, and compensate so you can benefit from what remains.

People who grow old well focus on the growing
and not on the old.

## Back-to-Back Meetings All Day

So you have back-to-back meetings all day with incredible demands on your time. All that you read and hear about taking breaks and time for yourself during the day seems totally out of reach. Yet you know you need to take care of yourself while being the consummate professional.

Try these tips for keeping your sanity while achieving your goal.

- **Room with a Different View.** How about taking a walk in the courtyard instead of meeting in an office or conference room? For more informal discussions, gather in the office break room over tea. Each time you come in and out of your office, take a different route and say hi to people as you pass so you're not an automaton.

- **Drink Tons of Water.** Guzzle lots of water and stay hydrated, which will also give you lots of restroom breaks.

- **Complete Tasks.** When several phones ring, multiple files are open before you, and people are knocking on your office door, breathe in one long inhalation followed by one long exhalation. Breathe with focus. Then finish one thought, task, and project at a time.

Create space for health in your
back-to-back schedule.

## Tone It Down

More important than what you say is how you say it.

If you were reading a transcript of conversations you have with your parent, child, lover, or coworker, you might not have any idea about the real meaning of the words. The emotion behind the words is set by your tone.

Think about it. If you are angry, fed up, sarcastic, impatient, intimidating, bored, accusatory, excited, enthusiastic, supportive, or loving, your tone gives the listener a lot of information. However, you may be one of those people who have no idea that your tone is often harsh, mean, or even insulting. Maybe it is what you heard when you were growing up or acquired from frequently being on the defensive. Whatever the reason, it is not OK to continue this negative tone just because it is what you heard or you proclaim it to be "the way I am."

To keep your sanity when trying to communicate with someone, try these:

- **Push the Rewind Button.** What is your style of communicating? When you talk, pay attention to whether you have a threatening or demeaning tone. A quick test is to tape record some of your conversations (legally, of course) to really *hear* the way you talk. Focus on yourself and take responsibility for the way *you* sound.

- **Watch How Others Respond.** Stop yourself if you see others react in a way that demonstrates they are turning you off, tuning you out, becoming defensive, etc.

- **Don't Accuse** . . . them for responding in a certain way. Think about looking in the mirror and seeing what they see. How do you look? How do you sound? Rather than push forward, ask, "Is there something I am doing or saying that is getting in the way of you being able to hear me?"

Pay attention to how you sound when you talk to someone. Your tone is what people believe.

# Thursday

*Friendship*

## Friendships When There Are Three

What is it about threesomes? Girlfriends, I mean.

Problems form when two women out of three (or more) pair up against the other. You can easily see this dynamic in kids when a nice game of hopscotch is somehow turned upside down when the third friend arrives. One of the three may become manipulative and sets up the other two against each other, which leads to real problems.

The feelings are the same when little girls grow up. Trouble brews and competition escalates when someone feels left out and uncomfortable with the way the friendship is moving. She'll want to get one of the friendships back to where she thought it was, which may cause unnecessary tension among everyone.

Is there a way to coexist with the "girls," not take sides, and just have some fun? Here's how girlfriends can get along when three is usually a crowd.

- **Confront the Instigator.** Gently confront your friend who seems to pit the group against each other. Ask her if she is aware of what she is doing. Suggest that she think what she might be afraid of, angry at, or missing, and see if she can find another way to get her needs met. She may or may not know what you are talking about, but give it a try anyway.

- **Suggest a Three-Way.** Suggest that the three of you get together to discuss *your* perception of what is going on. Be careful not to accuse, but rather bring up your concerns about how the friendship is shifting and behaviors are changing.

- **Don't Take the Bait.** When you experience the manipulation, don't respond to it. Take a moment, feel what is going on in your body, and say, "I am not comfortable and need to have us all talk about this together."

- **Create a Pact.** Ask each other how to deal with situations when someone feels disappointed, threatened, left out, or concerned about something rather than resorting to previous behaviors.

A friendship of two is not the same as three.
You have to accommodate.

# Friday

*Parent*

## Take Good Care of My Baby

No one should be an isolated caregiver to children. You need the support and occasional company of other adults. Whether a parent or a caregiver in a daycare center or family child care home, everyone needs support, because at times caring for children can be lonely, frustrating, and challenging.

If you are a mother, grandmother, aunt, or friend, save your sanity and the sanity of those you love as you chip in and help parents and other caregivers look after the next generation. When you search for child care:

- **Choose with Love.** Focus on a person who has a warm and affectionate manner with your child. Look for a low ratio of children to caregivers. If your child is an infant, the person who cares for him may be able to care for two other children and that's it.

- **Check Out Credentials.** Feel comfortable with the experience of this caregiver. Although many people overlook it, a person needs to be sophisticated and responsible when caring for young children. Always watch someone with your child. Focus on how your child responds to that person upon leaving and arriving.

- **What Are Your "Must Haves"?** Discover what is important to you and to the caregiver in providing good child care. A warm and loving person who does not read, talk to, or sing with a child may not be able to provide the kind of stimulation your child needs.

When you think about having someone care
for your child, be mindful of matching
your child and the caregiver so your child thrives
and the adult is fully engaged.

# Finding Time to Meditate

You hear over and over again how valuable meditation is for your peace of mind, emotional stability, and physical health. You don't deny it, you just don't feel you have the time to do it.

Images of sitting cross-legged in a mountaintop retreat for three days are relaxing but just unattainable. So how can you begin to allow yourself to even think that meditating is available to you in your hectic life?

- **Welcome Calm.** Meditating brings clarity and peace. It's like plugging into an energy source of calm. You can begin to meditate by focusing on your breath. Just be aware of breathing in and breathing out. Slowly. Calmly. Now who can be too busy to not want calm? Invest in meditation time, and your rushed, hurried life might actually get into balance.

- **Give Yourself Permission** . . . to *think* about meditating for at least ten minutes every day so you are not put off by the thought of "one more thing to fit into my already too busy day." If your life went more smoothly because you put in ten daily minutes, wouldn't you do it?

- **Get Up, Meditate, and Then Get Going.** Once you commit to trying, meditate first thing in the morning. It will help you keep your balance throughout the day. Before drinking your morning coffee, reading the paper, or responding to late-night e-mails,

find your chair (so you don't fall asleep as you begin to relax) and begin your "practice."

Regular meditation soothes the soul and protects you from the negative effects of stress.

# Moving from Your Home

You are about to move. If you are like many other women, you are and have been a nester. Over the years you likely have made your home into a sanctuary for yourself and your family, and as you anticipate a move, you may have a desire to cling to what is familiar, safe, and loved.

So how do you tear yourself away, emotionally, from a home you've loved for so many years? A place that has been your haven, your comfort through difficult times—a place you and your loved ones have filled with so many memories? The house is, in reality, nothing more than a building. But it is the place that has captured so many memories that now might be left behind.

- **Be Hands-On.** In the process of making this move, try to literally touch everything that is there. Every item has a memory that will come back to you as you pack it or decide where it must go. As you handle things, allow yourself to relive each of those memories, one at a time. This is, in itself, a very important "journey" for you to take . . . one that you will carry with you as you move into the next chapter of your life.

- **Let Go.** Give yourself permission to let go of things that are no longer useful to you and can enhance someone else's life. Things that have outlived their usefulness for you can be donated if still in good shape or now belong in the trash.

- **Others Feel the Loss.** Remain aware that you are not the only one who will be feeling sad as this house transfers to new dwellers. Your children, family, and friends have loved being in your home, and it has been a cornerstone for all the people in your life. They, too, have their memories, which they may be reluctant to give up. Your children especially may have difficulty comprehending the "why" of it all (needing to leave a home because of a divorce and inability to maintain the house financially, downsizing because of age or illness, etc.). Understand their struggle with the move.

- **Say Good-bye with Grace.** Attempt to put on a happy face and forge ahead, and grow from this life lesson. Be determined to make this move with grace. Accept the moments when your heart is filled with sadness. Do some of the moving by yourself so you can say a proper good-bye to your home and take with you the cherished memories.

Moving forces you to look at your life along a continuum. You are about to start a new chapter. Close this one in the way that is most comfortable and complete for you.

# One-on-One Parent Time

Every child needs to know he is special. But finding the one-on-one parent time each child so justly deserves is a tall order, especially if your schedule is tight and children have the same school schedules. By making the effort to do special things with each child separately, without dealing with sibling rivalry, dominant or submissive personalities, or the inability to focus on each individual, you will benefit your child's emotional and mental health. While family time is terrific, it does not replace focused, uninterrupted time with one child at a time.

- **Schedule "Mom Only" Time.** Arrange a special date with each child and put it on the calendar. Give the children the option of selecting their special activity on their own among two or three choices. Talk with the family about the importance of having one-on-one time so each child knows that he'll get a turn with Mom (and Dad) and that this special time is something that you value.

- **Focus** . . . on that child when you are together. Stay away from distractions when you are together. Pushing your child on the swing while talking with your friend on the cell phone is not "quality time" together. Use these special days to be with your child, listen to him, walk at his pace, talk about what interests him. If the child has a problem he wants to talk about, use this time to help him problem solve.

- **Enjoy Your Child.** Do your best to make this a positive experience. Pay attention to the wonderful qualities about your child and talk with him about how special he is. This is not the time to chastise your child for misbehavior in school, poor grades, or other disciplinary issues. Make this child the center of your attention and have fun.

- **Seize One-on-One Opportunities.** When your son goes to his friend's for a last-minute sleepover or when you drop off your daughter for an extra softball practice, ask the other child to come along for the ride and carve out a few minutes to do something special. Squeeze in a few precious minutes from doing errands so you can turn it into a special mother-child opportunity. Stop for a sandwich at the local deli, spend a few minutes at the pet store looking at the puppies, or visit a nearby pond to feed the ducks.

Special things happen when you make time
to focus on each child.

# Seriously Ill and Working

You are sick but no one at work knows. You may feel that you want to try to keep your diagnosis a secret so that it doesn't interfere with your work and you can brush it under the table if you recover.

For so many women however, the illness does tend to take over their lives. Try to maintain your sanity and your job as you manage your illness.

- **Keep Working.** It can be a healthy escape from your illness, medications, and treatments.

- **Decide Whom You Tell.** Your immediate supervisor should know if your treatment schedule and illness will affect your work performance. It's your personal choice to remain quiet if you don't want to be the topic of conversation at work, or you may choose to have your work friends be your support group. Some may be able to pick up the slack when you are feeling less than stellar.

- **Get Support** . . . outside work with family and others going through similar illnesses. Find out how they are coping with work life.

- **When You're Better.** It's healthy to celebrate your health with coworkers whether they knew or not.

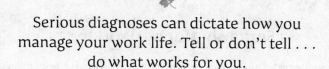

Serious diagnoses can dictate how you
manage your work life. Tell or don't tell . . .
do what works for you.

*Thursday*
*Well-Being*

# Too Much to Do

Does this sound familiar? You cannot sit still and relax. You are always doing something and feel as if you are wasting time when you're not doing something. You have a really busy week ahead with lots of things planned and you're already getting stressed. Even if there are fun things on the agenda, it's packed, and you're wondering how you're going to do everything.

There is such a thing as relaxing. You just have to find it. Change your attitude about being busy and maintain your sanity while keeping yourself in check.

- **Rethink Busy.** Do you equate "busy" with "worthwhile"? If you are not busy, does it mean you are lazy, not contributing, not making a difference? Only you can change your perception of what busy means. Everyone, even the busiest people, needs to kick back and relax to restore herself to balance.

- **Plan Fewer Things.** Attempt to lighten the load in your schedule and just do things as you feel like doing them . . . or don't do anything.

- **Do It When the Spirit Moves You.** Participate in activities because you want to and not because you have a list of things to do. When you look at your calendar, allow there to be "holes." Deal with these breaks by breathing deeply, telling yourself those are your health pockets of time to restore . . . and that's why they're called breathers. Try to destress as you attempt to empty your busy-ness.

### Busy does not equal worthwhile.

# They're Back . . . and Broke

You thought you raised your child to be responsible about money. And then she appears at your door, expecting to live with you, with credit card debt and not a penny in the bank.

Discussing the financial arrangement before your adult child moves back home will help you to keep your sanity as well as help your child become more financially accountable.

- **Blaming Backfires.** What result do you want? If you want to badger your kid for getting into another "money mess," think long and hard about whether that will serve any positive purpose.

- **Let Them Contribute.** If your adult child moves in, she becomes part of the household now. There are errands to do, dinners to prepare, laundry to fold, a garden to weed, rooms to paint. And the list goes on . . .

- **You're Not Being Cheap.** When your adult child begins to earn money, you can ask her to contribute financially to your household. Let go of guilt by holding the money in a bank account and returning it to her when she is ready to move out.

The way you handle money is not necessarily the way your kids will handle it. Your way may or may not be better, but if they live with you, you can offer to be helpful as they get back on their feet.

# Volunteering: What the World Needs Now Is You

Everyone everywhere can use a helping hand. At some point in your life, someone was probably there for you at a difficult or lonely moment. If someone wasn't there, wouldn't you have appreciated it if someone *had* been? Why not become that person you most wanted and needed, and then be available for someone else?

Volunteering to help others, especially when you are older (a time of life when many people focus on what they either no longer have or can no longer do), can be an enriching experience that will give you an immeasurable sense of self-worth, as well as an iron-clad defense against feelings of isolation and loneliness.

- **Do What You Like to Do.** Do something or be in a setting that suits you and your personality. If you like to be around babies, there are plenty who would love to be held and cuddled, and who need affection. If animals are your thing, offer to take some of the shelter dogs for walks. Tutor a child at the local clubs or youth organizations. If you have musical talents, offer to play the piano at the local nursing home or church social.

- **Don't Look for Anything in Return.** When you are older—and hopefully wiser and more mature—you understand that the returns are often not what you thought they would be. Allow yourself to be surprised by what you experience.

*Week 3*

- **It's a Real Job.** Think of your volunteer job as "your" job. Focus time and energy into your work and realize that you're helping other people in a profound way.

- **Don't Get in Over Your Head.** Get to know the routine of the job and the environment. Find a schedule that works for you and when you are at your most energetic and alert. You can always do more; what is difficult is jumping in too soon and having to cut back on your commitment. People will soon be dependent on you and grateful to you, so get off to a good start by being realistic about what you can do.

Share your gifts.

*Well-Being, Community, Work, Friends*

## Shyness

Why is the word *shy* often preceded by the word *painfully*? Because it is painful for you to be in a situation in which you fear interacting with people. You wonder if you will have something interesting, intelligent, and appropriate to say. Many women are misunderstood and assumed to be aloof or stuck up when in fact they are shy.

Some people are, by nature and experience, more at ease with new people. Others cringe at the thought of entering a room full of people they don't know. Facing a cocktail party, fund-raiser, back-to-school night, or fellowship hour after a church service may cause you to stay home, break out in hives, or clam up altogether. Sometimes going to an event with someone you know helps, but then you may stay attached to that person and not branch out.

How can you melt away that frozen feeling when you're out and about?

- **Practice with Strangers.** Sounds strange but it works. Practice approaching someone by making eye contact and saying hello. Offer to help someone who is struggling with packages. Ask a retail clerk her opinion of the outfit you're trying on. Attempt to mingle at functions. Meet one new person a day, two a week, or whenever you're walking around town. With each connection, say, *Hello, nice to meet you,* in your mind so your face will soften and you may have a hint of a smile. Give yourself chances to change your perception of yourself as shy.

- **Engage by Asking Questions.** When you are introduced to people, ask them about themselves. Most people enjoy talking about their own lives, so ask about their interests or what their connection is with the event you are attending.

- **Keep the Conversation Going.** When talking, use the person's name, as it reinforces your memory of the name and demonstrates that you are interested in him as a person. Say something positive about what was said or an idea that was offered. This breaks the ice, and can make the other person feel important.

- **Visualize.** Before you walk into a room, breathe deeply and visualize yourself talking with one person. If you need to, practice a few key phrases in front of a mirror.

- **Assess Your Level of Anxiety.** If it is five or over on a scale of one to ten, walk around, breathe, and do not go over what you said and tell yourself you should have said this or that. Focus on the positive aspect that you talked to someone you did not know. If your score is less than five, give yourself a pat on the back for being courageous.

Shyness can be addressed by giving yourself
the courage to try to interact with someone
you don't know.

# On Opposite Ends of the Pole with Parenting

You read volumes of parenting books, and you are convinced you know what to do, but your partner is not on the same page. His or her approach is exactly the opposite of yours, and your relationship is strained while the kids become more confused.

You know that your son's bedwetting is directly related to his fears of beginning a new school, while your partner thinks he is being a baby and you are treating him like one. Or your teenager is going through a rough patch with friends, and her dad is convinced she needs to put herself into more clubs and social situations. Big dispute: overloading her schedule is not what you want to encourage her to do.

When you and your partner are raising children together and have different perspectives on how to handle a situation, how do you keep your sanity and your parenting confidence intact?

- **You're Both Trying to Do a Good Job.** Affirm with your partner that you respect him or her as a parent and believe he or she has your children's best interests at the forefront of his or her mind. When you decided to have children together you believed your philosophy about parenting would be similar. Find a time, away from your children, to discuss what your concerns are about your children and what is behind your approach. Ask your mate what his or her concerns and goals are regarding his or her parenting.

- **Listen to the Reasoning.** Share what you feel. Tell your partner that if you determine certain disciplines to be detrimental to your child's well-being, you will not sit by. Let him or her know you are willing to work toward a good compromise that will benefit the whole family.

- **Work Through Your Differences.** Quietly reflect on what you are trying to accomplish with your child. Discover if this is in line with or opposed to your partner's goals and expectations as a parent, and whether you can compromise. Suggest you talk with someone who has some expertise in parenting and explore some of the ramifications of different approaches, given who your child is.

Keep discussions about how you will approach certain child-rearing issues between you and your partner and not the kids, and work toward becoming a united front.

## Running a Small Business

While there are risks of running your own business (and this is exacerbated if that business is run out of your home), most small business owners wouldn't have it any other way. You may like the freedom of being your own boss, having flexibility in your schedule, and the challenge of doing it on your own.

You may also know the feeling of constantly being under pressure. As a sole proprietor you put on a balancing act every day as you juggle providing services and products, administrative duties, and sales. And if you're a small business with employees, you are responsible not only for yourself but also for those who work for you. Even though you may try hard to delegate, much of the work falls on your shoulders, especially when you establish your business. Hiring more help can be a good solution but may be out of reach because of financial constraints. For better or worse (usually for better), small businesses can take on the feel and function of a family. And you know how that goes—"a mother's work is never done."

While enjoying the perks of making their own schedule, most small business owners agree that their business is in their lives 24/7. Day-to-day operations are time-consuming. Creative thoughts materialize at different times of the day and night. So how can you be open to new ideas for your business without feeling a slave to it?

- **Work Time and Me Time.** Create your work hours and stick to a schedule. Before, during, or after work, do something that clearly separates you from work. Whether you exercise, meditate, walk the dog, stop at the corner café for a cup of tea, transi-

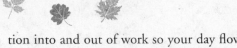

tion into and out of work so your day flows. If your business is in your home, be conscious and careful about mixing the two. Don't procrastinate delving into a project by folding laundry. Leave your household chores till after work hours.

- **Plant Destressing Seeds.** During the work week cultivate ways to destress. Notice a sale at a store near your office and go at lunchtime to buy a treat. Exercise at midday or turn off the world by listening to some favorite music. Listen to a chapter of a book on tape during lunch. Check out the lecture schedule at the local community center. There may be something inspirational that you would enjoy and may give you a place to turn off work while keeping your creative juices stimulated. Shifting the mood and your attention can help you appreciate that things are not as serious as they seem at work.

- **Nurture Something Other Than Work and People.** Plant a garden and shift your focus off work by watering and weeding in the fresh air. Watch your garden grow and get satisfaction from seeing quick results in contrast to your work, where results often take time. If you are indoors, buy a "simple care" plant (try some herbs to clip when you prepare a meal).

- **Think and Jot.** Keep a notepad or micro tape recorder, or record a voice note to yourself on your phone or PDA whenever you have a thought that relates to work. Some of the best and most creative ways to deal with business issues will come when you are outdoors, after meditation, engaged in something creative like painting, writing, playing music, playing with children. Why? Because you are using different pathways and opening yourself up for alternative ways of thinking.

- **Get Out.** Being out of the office can enhance your ability to think out of the box and create solutions to problems that were inaccessible within the familiar four walls. Listening to others describe how they approached a problem may give you hints and ways to deal with what you are facing. You have something to learn from everyone.

Working around the clock will only exhaust you and make your small business less productive. Instead, give yourself a break and recharge; you'll experience an increase in productivity (yours and the business's).

# New Mother Fatigue

You're a new mother and you're exhausted. Instead of getting more run down, cranky, and overwhelmed, think of yourself as a marathon runner. You need to reserve your strength for this race and many more to come. You need endurance.

Of course, we all know the Golden Rule: sleep when your baby sleeps. But, that's not always easy to do. Here are some pointers for surviving the infant stage.

- **Short but Sweet Sleeps.** Gone are the days of eight-hour restful nights. Instead, go for as many uninterrupted sleep hours as you can possibly squeeze in. You'd be amazed at how even four to five hours of undisturbed sleep can feel like a lifesaver as compared to a mere two to three hours. If you have a spouse or partner, start early with sharing those nighttime feedings. Someone else can be in charge of supplementing late-night or early-morning feedings with formula or stored breast milk.

- **Alternate Nights.** You can share every other night with your partner—one on and one off—so that you can be sure you get a full night's sleep at least half the time. If you can't do this on a regular basis, try doing it on the weekends so you can get at least one full night's sleep each weekend.

- **Rock-a-By Baby.** Rock your baby in a cradle that you can reach from your bed (without having to get out of it). Visualize yourself and your child rocking to sleep.

- **Late-Night Snacks.** Whenever you are awake in the night, reach for some healthy food. Feeding yourself nutritious food will help you find the strength you need in the morning.

- **Develop New Housekeeping Standards.** Don't spend all your waking moments cleaning house. Enjoy your baby and new family life and create a new standard for a clean and tidy house. Remember, clean doesn't have to always mean tidy.

Sleep, even interrupted sleep, restores the body, the mind, and the soul.

# Surviving a Weekend with People Who Disturb Your Peace

Sometimes there's no way to avoid having people over for the weekend who, well, frankly, get under your skin. Not only are they inconsiderate guests, your best friend's husband downright annoys you, and your partner's old roommate from college grates on your nerves. And let's not even get into mandatory time spent with in-laws.

Whatever the reason, you find your inner sanctum of peace and quiet is disturbed. In fact, you realize that one of the major stressors in your life has taken up residence in your guest room. What to do?

- **Plug Into Your Peace.** When alone, do something that you enjoy; find something relaxing, restorative, or nurturing. Make time at both the beginning and the end of the day so you can treat yourself to a relaxing meditation, a quiet walk, some time in the garden. Restore yourself and recharge your batteries.

- **Stick to a Schedule.** Changing activities and venues allows you to be engaged with your guests while alleviating some stress. Plan events when you are together in small doses. Include others who are easy to be with to take away some of the pressure and who can "entertain" your guests so you don't have to all the time. You will benefit if you let them feel like part of the household and be useful by pitching in with some chores.

- **This Is Your Refuge.** If they criticize your space, your interior decor, or the fact that the plumbing sings when the shower is on, remind them that this is your castle and you like it as it is. Understand, however, that your home is a comfort to you but may not be to those who are not used to it.

You *can* endure the not-so-perfect guest. Clarify the space by lighting a sage candle and breathing in the scent before and after their stay.

## Laugh

Why is it that so many of us stop laughing?

It's great to howl at the moon and giggle with girlfriends, but so often we stifle our laughter, even though nothing feels quite as good (or is as good for you) as a true belly laugh—you know, the kind that makes you cry. Laughter keeps you young.

If you have not had a good laugh today, now is the time to make that happen.

- **Get into the Mindset of a Child.** Play on your own and allow yourself to have fun.

- **Experience Sheer, Unadulterated Joy.** Do something that makes you smile and feel really good. Watch your pet play and get on the floor and engage together. Buy a couple of your favorite comedies and watch them (even ten minutes at a time) to remind yourself what fun it is to laugh.

- **Silence Your Inner Critic.** Nobody has the right to shut you up or shut you down—not even you.

Whatever it is, someday you will laugh about it . . .
so why not now?

*Monday*

*Well-Being, Family, Partner*

# Too Tired to Care

Caregiving has the potential to be the most exhausting of all jobs. If you are caring for aging parents or an ill spouse, raising children, and holding down a job, you are for sure not getting enough sleep.

Save your sanity by dealing with your physical, mental, and emotional exhaustion so you are not in a state of constant fatigue.

- **Sleep and Recharge.** Without sleep, it's difficult to concentrate, problem solve, and use good judgment, all of which you need to give care. Use a friend or employ a respite service a few times each week so you can sleep undisturbed for the night shift or take an afternoon nap.

- **Have a Sleep Ritual.** Every night, enhance your chances of going to sleep and staying asleep by listening to soothing nature sounds or quiet music, turning off the news, reading inspirational passages, praying, or doing progressive muscle relaxation exercises while breathing deeply and calmly.

- **Exercise Every Day.** Walk as often as you can. Strengthen your back, arms, and legs, since so much of what you do is bend, lift, twist. Do whatever you can in small increments and drink lots of water.

Get the sleep you need to recharge your personal batteries so you can care for yourself as well as the person who depends on you.

# Afraid to Get Help for Your Child

When your child needs help—get it. If you feel embarrassed or ashamed, although it is a common response, it is not a good enough reason to deny your child needed help. Your self-esteem may be hurt if you learn something is amiss with your child, but trying to deal with the issue alone will only make it more difficult.

Remember that your child is separate from you. You may feel that your parenting is lacking or that something is wrong with you if your child is in some sort of need. Keep your pride under check and get the help you and your child need.

- **Don't Run Away** . . . from the people you can rely on for help when you need it. Problem solving is best done with a fresh perspective, and your eyes may be cloudy. When you are sad and feeling alone, that is the time to ask for help.

- **Find Your Personal Style** . . . to ask for help. Your child deserves to have the help needed to deal with the problem as early as possible. Do the research, find the sources, and be as direct as you can to get what you need.

- **"They" Could Judge** . . . but you know who you are and what you have to do. People may judge you as a bad mom if there is something wrong with your child. Stay strong and firm and do what's right.

**When your child needs help, put your needs aside and realize it is about your child and not about you.**

# Wednesday
*Partner, Friends*

## When You Don't Want to Hang Out with Your Partner's Buddy

Having a partner can be one of the most gratifying experiences in life. Having someone to whom you are committed and with whom you want to share your thoughts, activities, and friends . . . well, maybe not all friends.

What happens when you don't like your partner's friends or he or she doesn't like yours? Do you stop seeing that person? What about when you don't care for the mate of your partner's best bud? How do you handle it?

- **See Through Your Partner's Eyes.** Attempt to get to know this person who is not your favorite and open yourself up to the fact that there is a reason your partner feels close. Keep in mind that because your significant other has a deep friendship does not mean that you will or that you have to also.

- **Three's a Crowd Anyway.** Discuss openly and honestly that if you choose not to accompany them, you are not rejecting anyone. Instead you're giving them the opportunity to enjoy each other's company without having you around as a third wheel.

- **Be There When It's Important.** Ask when it is imperative that you attend an event with or for your partner's friend. And then do your best to show up with a smile and an open heart.

- **No Trashing.** Whenever you are together, be careful not to talk poorly about the friend afterward. That is not your role and it will not be helpful.

Your partner's friends may not be your friends, and spending time separately can enhance each of the relationships—yours with your partner and your partner's with the friend.

# Thursday

*Family*

## Adult Sibling Rivalry

Are you and your sister still in competition for who has more? What do you do when your big brother still calls you "squirt" (and you're over forty and not a petite)? Have you never forgiven Sis for going out with the guy you had a crush on? Do you treat the baby in the family as if he is still in a highchair?

Sibling rivalry is all about competition and is rooted in the past. Come to terms with your brothers and sisters and let go of rivalries, competition, and favoritism, and allow your relationships to mature and grow. After all, you all are adults now.

- **We're in the Twenty-first Century.** So get out of 1975, 1955, or whatever year you conjure up when rivalry strikes. Look at your siblings as adults and not children (although they may act like children at times). Establish a new order or respect for one another even if you have to take the high road and go first.

- **Don't Dole It and Roll with It.** Respect your sibs and don't go into autopilot when the usual teasing begins. Joking and humor about "when we were kids" is fun, but not at the expense of someone's feelings. If you set the example, hopefully your siblings will follow. If they don't and you're the recipient of unwelcome comments, try to let it roll off your back because, unfortunately, some things (and people) never change.

- **Honor Accomplishments.** When your brother or sister excels in something, are you able to acknowledge it with sincerity? How about celebrating with them when they get a raise, run in

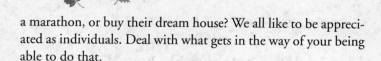

a marathon, or buy their dream house? We all like to be appreciated as individuals. Deal with what gets in the way of your being
able to do that.

As you rethink your sibling relationship, consider
trading in competition for cooperation.

*Friday*

*Parent, Well-Being*

## Losing Control with Your Children

What is it about parenting that can put us all so close to or over the edge?

When asked, most mothers would respond that having and raising children is a blessing. Yet how is it possible that mothers are often so upset, frustrated, and angry, losing their perspective, patience, and temper with their children, often to the point of verbally abusing them?

When you lose your temper with your kids, you probably feel awful not only about what you said but about how your child feels in response to what you said. Once they are out of our mouths, we can't take words back. Since most children believe what their parents say they think about them, it is better for us and our children to learn to step away and keep quiet until we get ourselves under control. This way we can talk with confidence and don't have to feel embarrassed, ashamed, or sorry for saying the wrong thing.

- **You've Lost If You "Lose It."** When you feel yourself approaching the feeling of "losing it," make sure your child is safe, leave the room, and collect yourself. We lose our children's respect if we can't control ourselves. If you do lose control, be sure to apologize for saying what you said and take responsibility for going over the line of decency.

- **Calming and Redirecting Exercises.** Breathe slowly, hit a pillow, count backward from one hundred, move around, and swing your arms in big circles. Stay away from your kids, pets, or anything breakable. Recite a prayer that brings you comfort and

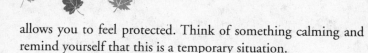

allows you to feel protected. Think of something calming and remind yourself that this is a temporary situation.

- **Think Before You Say.** Think of ways to say what you want to say while stating your feelings without demeaning, demoralizing, intimidating, or scaring your child. Instead of "You don't deserve to have anything since you are an ungrateful slob," try "I am angry that your room is not clean. I know you can straighten it out and have it look just fine. You are capable of doing that." Remind yourself of the qualities your child has that you admire and love.

- **Give Yourself a Pat on the Back.** When you avoid the exploding point, tell yourself you are a good mother for protecting yourself and your children from saying hurtful and destructive things. Recognize that you are no longer acting like the type of mother you don't want to be and the type of mother you don't want your child to have.

Before you say anything to your child, think of whether what you say will make you feel as if you are the mother you want to be.

# Keeping the Faith

You may have had situations in your life when the only thing that got you through was your faith. Many women find that as they get older, their faith becomes stronger. Relying on that faith becomes a cornerstone of your life.

At times you may encounter people who don't believe in your commitment and challenge it and you as they question their own faith. How do you stay strong and still keep the faith?

- **Faith Is Personal.** Understand that your belief system and faith does not require anyone else's approval or acceptance. Similarly, if someone in your life is not committed to your faith (or any faith), you do not have to perceive this as a threat to your ability to fully believe what you believe. The way you feel comforted in your soul is what matters.

- **Faith and Prayer Require Practice.** Find time each day to reaffirm your convictions and your beliefs. Use it as an opportunity to ground yourself and accept that there is a force larger than you who is watching out for you and keeping you safe.

- **Faith Is Always There.** Call on your faith when you are dealing with things in life that may not make sense. Birds don't get up every morning and worry about finding worms—they just do. Trust that no matter what you are going through, you are being guided by your faith to a higher learning.

Hold on to your faith and nurture your spirit.

# When Your Child Accuses You of Loving a Sibling More

"You love him more than me." Did you ever hear those words from your kids? Worse yet, did your child ever announce to a captive audience of friends and family that you, his mother, clearly love his younger brother more than you love him?

With those very impressive eyes staring at you and no hole to crawl into, it is time to take a deep breath and reach into your heart for the most appropriate response. What you say will be remembered by your child, you can be sure.

- **Put Yourself in His Sneakers.** Even though you're telling yourself your child is ridiculous, try to imagine how he feels and why he would say this in front of people. Do you have more in common or a shared interest with one child over the other? If one of your children is quieter, does the squeaky wheel get more attention just because she's always squeaking? Is one child the achiever and demands more attention without you realizing it?

- **Validate Their Feelings.** "I can see how you would feel that way. You came out of the womb and it was as if you spoke a different language. We were very different, and it is more difficult for us to understand each other. But we try and we do it. Your brother came out of the womb speaking the same language I speak. So because it is easier for us to communicate, I can see that you would think it means I love him more. I don't. I love you both, but in different ways because you're different people."

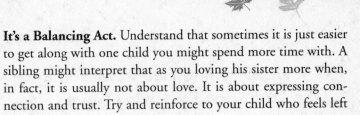

- **It's a Balancing Act.** Understand that sometimes it is just easier to get along with one child you might spend more time with. A sibling might interpret that as you loving his sister more when, in fact, it is usually not about love. It is about expressing connection and trust. Try and reinforce to your child who feels left out that you love him. Carve out special time and communicate your feelings. When you tell your child you love him, look him in the eye and say it from your heart. Balance time and energy you put into your relationship with each of your children.

> Getting to know your children takes time—
> sometimes a lifetime. In the process,
> they may or may not interpret your actions
> and attitude accurately.

# You Can't Always Get What You Want

Come on, you know that no one is riding up on a white horse or whisking you off to Paris at every spare moment—don't you? Or do you have some unrealistic expectations floating around in your head?

If you want a good relationship, you've got to know what to expect. Don't think your partner is going to go on long Saturday lunches and antiquing if his idea of a great weekend is catching up on paperwork. Sure, he'll be there for an occasional quaint getaway, but know that most weekends he'll be logging in computer time.

Save your sanity by getting real about your relationship and being clear about what you are able and unable to accept.

- **What Is Nonnegotiable?** What *must* you have? If you are clear, then you will narrow the field. If you *must* date someone who is the same religion, then *don't* go out with those who practice a different faith. If you *must* be with someone who likes children because you have two, then *don't* go out with someone who has no patience for kids.

- **Be Pleasable.** He doesn't want to feel as if he is constantly disappointing you. Instead he wants to please you. Talk about what you want, but be reasonable. Unrealistic expectations bring about disappointment and resentful feelings. You will turn into someone who is demanding. Is that who you want to be?

- **Negotiate What Is Not a Must.** Your ideal is Mr. Fix-It, but this guy doesn't know how to turn on a drill. If you love him, learn how to do it yourself or hire someone. Don't blame him for what he cannot or will not master.

People can only do what they can do—without compromising themselves. Learn to accept that special someone in your life or move on.

## Assistant Blurring the Lines

Your assistant is efficient and has proven herself to be smart, clear thinking, and helpful. Except you are getting the creepy feeling that she thinks she is you.

While she is very competent, you notice that the lines between the two of you are blurring. She finishes your sentences for you, answers people's questions that are directed at you, and makes decisions that affect you without consultation. You find that you are going to work with a pit of dis-ease in your stomach and have to do something.

- **Prepare Your Talk.** Focus in your own mind why this is a problem for you and what you need to have change in order to proceed. Breathe deeply and imagine what your work life would be like without this person. See if you can separate what works from what doesn't work. Be prepared to give her up if you need to.

- **Reinforce Her Positives.** In private, let her know what she does that is good and helpful, and emphasize that which is acceptable. Assure her that you like working with her and have come to depend on her good judgment in most things. Point to specifics.

- **Communicate Your Gripes.** Tell her what disturbs you about her work and what you need her to do differently. Ask her if she thinks she can work in this sort of setup. If she can't, assist her in finding a position where she will have more authority, can delegate, and can feel more in control.

Your assistant is there to assist you, not to be you.

# When May-December Relationships Get Older

Falling in love is great at any age. When you love someone who is significantly older than you, the older partner can slow down and may not be able to keep up with you or with the lifestyle you had years ago. This also happens with couples when one person is ill or has developed different interests.

You need to decide how you want to spend your time. What is important to each of you regarding selecting what you do together and what you do on your own? Forgoing events or activities may or may not work for your self-esteem or for the relationship. If you were avid tennis partners and he can no longer play, does it make sense for both of you to drop your rackets?

- **New Interests.** If you don't want to experience things without your mate, find ways to do things that satisfy your love of sharing things. Consider developing new interests together that you can both enjoy (photography, bird watching, etc.). Being in such different places in your lives does not mean you cannot enjoy each other.

- **Keep Your Interests Alive** . . . and find ways to integrate them into your couple life. If adventure travel was your thing and you still want to experience the world together, consider an occasional challenging trip on your own or with friends. Why not travel together to an exotic place via cruise ship, and you take the more adventurous side trip? If, however, you decide to give up something you enjoyed together, be sure you do it without blame or resentment. Life is about moving on, and at this point, you may decide to put that energy into developing a new interest either alone or together.

- **Are You Afraid?** Consider, frankly, what you feel is missing in your life and what you fear. Come to terms with whether your "couple pace" is shifting or you are facing your mate's mortality and the prospect of being alone or a caregiver.

- **Adjust.** Appreciate that the aging process is not only about loss but about shifting. When one half of a couple is not keeping up with his former pace, your relationship can get out of balance. It is important to discuss what your individual and collective expectations are so you can go forward together as a loving couple.

When your partner is no longer able to keep your former "couple pace," consider where in your life as a couple and as an individual you can still be challenged and satisfied.

## Time to Cook for the Family

Who's got time to cook? Most people don't have much time at all, it seems. Or do they?

Why are we running around with the kids and getting them fatty fast food for dinner in the backseat of the car while shuttling between soccer practice and ballet class? Why do many families live on takeout food loaded with MSG and at-home greasy pizza delivery? Or worse yet, why are we eating more and more processed convenience foods at home and stacking our freezers with the latest pop-in-the-microwave foods laden with sugar, trans fat, artificial food colorings, and preservatives?

You know this is no way to lead a healthy lifestyle, and your waistline might be telling you the same. So how do you find the time to cook nowadays? Save your sanity and the calories by committing to some home cooking no matter what your schedule says. According to Kathleen Daelemans, author of the *Cooking Thin* series, if you have time to watch television, surf the Net, cruise the clearance bins, or read even half of your junk mail, you have time to cook. It's all about your commitment to getting fit and using your time wisely. It's easier than you think, and there's no better way to bring the family together.

- **Get Over the Hate.** If you "hate" to cook, you won't. Figure out what it will take to turn your mindset around. What will it take for you to be willing to cook at home and for you to make your family's health your number one priority? Figure it out and teach your children to cook and eat well, which is one of the best gifts you can give them.

- **Create Culinary Triggers.** Every time the phone rings or the kids do homework, it's your cue to head into the kitchen to chop, slice, and dice. Focus on the evening meal. If you've got dinner in the bag, start work on kid's lunches for the next day (instead of cafeteria food) or for tomorrow's supper.

- **Be Busy When Idle.** When on hold, waiting in a doctor's office, or waiting for the kids at pickup time, whip out a cookbook or cooking magazine. Tab recipes you like. Choose five (look for short recipes with few ingredients), assign them each a day of the week. Create shopping lists from the ingredient lists.

- **Enroll the Kids.** Choose your sous chefs and give them their assignments (along with their modern-day toque, which is usually a baseball cap). After the age of five, everyone's capable of pitching in to help with dinner. Put someone in charge of picking the recipes, and another child in charge of shopping, table setting, and cleaning.

Start with one day a week that is home cooking night and build a healthy lifestyle for the whole family from there.

## Finding Time to Exercise

OK, we all know we need to exercise. But sometimes finding the time to get to the gym is not easy. When work, responsibilities, the kids, and just plain life gets in the way, taking that morning jog goes by the wayside and all other efforts to stay in shape are abandoned.

You can stay fit *and* fit it into your schedule. Try these:

- **Walk, Walk, Walk.** *Stop* driving your kids to the bus stop! Walking will not only be a great way to start your day but will also instill fitness into your kids' routines. Walk up those stairs instead of taking the elevator, park you car in the farthest parking spot when shopping, and walk the mall in foul weather. Instead of letting your pooch run around in the yard getting zapped by the electronic fence, grab its leash and go down the street, a woodsy trail, or the beach. Just walk!

- **Break Up Your Routine.** If you can't dedicate an hour to work out, wake up, stretch, and just work on your abs. When you can take a break, break out the hand weights and work on your upper body. Before dinner, go for a five-minute mini jog and then work on a few leg exercises while the water boils. A few yoga stretches at bedtime will ease tension in your muscles. Try ending with the "corpse" pose (lying flat on your back, totally relaxed) for the ultimate relaxation technique.

- **Find Your Optimum Times.** If you can't exercise every day, why try? Can your schedule allow for two mini workouts on

the weekdays and a full workout on one day of the weekend? If mornings are your best time to get it over and done with (even though it's hard to get motivated), lay your sneakers and workout gear next to the bed and put everything on when your feet touch the floor. That way you won't think too much and will be on your way to getting in shape bright and early. Maybe midday or evenings are a good time to sneak in a few crunches or deep knee bends.

- **Get Sporty.** Why not pick up your tennis racket, golf clubs, or bathing suit and head to the place where you can actually use these items? Mix social time with getting-in-shape time. Ever wanted to try in-line roller skating, horseback riding, or fencing? Now may be the time to get up and get going and try something new.

If you want to lead a healthy lifestyle, you will find the time to stay in shape.

## Beginning a New Job

Just hired for a new position? Transitioning careers? It takes courage and commitment to walk into a new work environment or start an entrepreneurial venture. With determination and focus, you can make it a success.

After the first days at your job, you will discover the office dynamics. It only takes time, an open mind, and keen observation skills to become familiar with the new workplace, tasks, people, personalities, culture of the organization, and the requirements of the job itself. You'll quickly find out who is grateful you are now there because they could not stand your predecessor, whose nose is out of joint because you got the job they coveted, and who needs to be coddled to get things done.

It also takes an honest assessment of your skill set. Are you experienced and familiar with the work to get the job done or do you need to ask some questions, seek out an on-site mentor, or study up where you are rusty? While you are feeling your way around or playing catch-up, you'll soon develop your own work habits for this place and settle into your new digs.

- **Approach and Be Approachable.** Greet people and introduce yourself since you are the new kid on the block. You may want to share information about yourself and your experience, previous work, and how you came to this organization. At the onset of your new career, offer personal facts (where you live, marital status, kids, and hobbies), if you care to, when you're in casual settings—at lunch or at after-work gatherings. Be available to someone who pops by your cubicle to say hello. Volunteer for

projects that get you into circulation, but don't lose sight of your job and your work purpose.

- **Observe How People Interact.** Do coworkers or business partners e-mail, instant message, walk into each other's space, or shout across the office? Know that there are different styles of interacting. As you settle into the space, settle into the way you best communicate.

- **Be Yourself.** You may work with or for people whose style is different from yours. Behave in a way that suits you and is consistent with who you are. Don't take on someone else's characteristic that demeans you.

- **Stay Clear of Office Gossip.** It can only backfire, and is not the best way to join an organization. You can always claim that as the new person you prefer to get all the facts before casting your vote.

When finding your way in a new job, always take the high road.

## Saying No to Your Children

You love your children. You want to gratify their every wish. And you can, so you do. Time passes. Your children begin to become acquisition monsters, demanding more and more, and appreciating what they have less and less. You feel angry and depressed and are "losing it" with them more and more often.

- **Say No.** Good parenting means *not gratifying every wish*. Follow your refusal to grant their request with a brief, to-the-point statement so they know why you are not obliging.

- **Get Your Children to Dream.** Talk about wishes and turn those into reality. Teach your children the joy of anticipation, the satisfaction of working toward a goal (saving those dimes, nickels, and quarters), and the sense of accomplishment when they finally get there. Help your children know the value of making their own lives what they want them to be.

Dreaming, longing, planning, looking forward to, and working hard for—these are the virtues and pleasures your children can grow up with.

## Losing Weight After Giving Birth

Why did pounds shed easily after the first baby but not after the second? Are you still wearing maternity clothes several weeks after you gave birth? Worse yet, are people asking, "When are you due?" . . . even when you're strolling with your newborn?

Your body and mood are not the same as before you got pregnant, and moods affect ability to lose weight. You may even be experiencing some depression. Many women feel this way (and don't know it), either because they are not *severely* depressed or their previous birthing experiences were so different.

Save your sanity and get your whole self back in shape.

- **Give it Time.** You've heard this one but it's true. It took nine months to put on the weight and it's going to take several months to take it off. If you are nursing, the pounds may linger due to hormonal changes and the need to intake more calories. If you eat healthfully and exercise, you can get back in shape.

- **Get Back in Emotional Shape.** It's not always about the weight. Consider your mental health. If you inadvertently blame the baby for the weight, you may be unknowingly keeping on pounds while having difficulty forming a strong motherly bond. Seek counseling if you are dealing with resentment, anger, or depression.

- **Accept Your Body.** Even if you lose the weight, your body will be slightly different. Hips might be wider, breasts might change shape, and your stomach muscles may be looser—even your feet

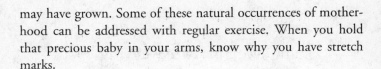

may have grown. Some of these natural occurrences of motherhood can be addressed with regular exercise. When you hold that precious baby in your arms, know why you have stretch marks.

You need to wait to take off the weight.

*Thursday*

*Partner*

## So Far Away

Long-distance relationships are not easy and require an enormous commitment from both people. With careers requiring people to move to different places from their significant others, and with Internet dating encouraging people from different parts of the country (and world) to begin romantic unions, how can you keep your sanity and your love intact?

There are many reasons why the relationship won't work. Although the cell phone comes in handy, you are often not in the same time zone, so you have to plan what time to have a phone conversation. But if you put your time and attention into connecting with this person in a variety of ways and allow yourself to be flexible and to trust, the miles in between really won't matter.

- **What's Your Tolerance Level?** Think about what you need in a relationship. If you need constant contact and immediate access, a long-distance relationship is probably not for you. If you are easily frustrated, impatient, and need immediate gratification, a long-distance relationship will be a tremendous challenge for both you and your partner.

- **Establish the Ground Rules.** Understand that your expectations and your partner's expectations may be different, so sort them out from the beginning. If you are away from each other, what is the understanding you have about dating other people or developing friendships and going out with other people? What is fair game and what do you care to know about? What is private?

- **Get a Routine Going.** Long-distance relationships present particular challenges for those who are not ready to sign on to a regular time when they will commit to talking with each other rather than catch-as-catch-can. If you know that every night you will be online with each other, talking via a Web camera or some kind of free Internet phone service, you can plan your day and look forward to having your time alone with your long-distance partner. Use some of the time you are talking to organize visits in person, and put the dates on your calendars so you can look forward to being together. Plan your life around those times.

Keeping up a relationship over the miles
takes energy and focus, but the rewards
may be worth the effort.

# Friday
*Friends*

## Reciprocity

Friendships and love relationships work best when the people involved feel that there is a back-and-forth—they offer what is needed and they receive what they need.

It is the classic give-and-take, and when it works, it is a charm. Sometimes, however, the back-and-forth is more weighted in favor of one person or the other. You may feel that you give and give and give, and are never on the receiving end. Or you take and take and take friendly advice, while your words of wisdom are never heeded or even considered.

In some relationships that may be OK but in others it just does not work. Are you waiting for reciprocal behavior in areas that the person is unable to give?

- **Are You Inviting?** Perhaps you wonder after you invite people to join you why you are not asked for social events. Is the face you present someone who is too busy, solely engaged in her own life, not interested, or unavailable?

- **What Are Your Expectations?** When you do something for someone, do you expect a return favor? How will you feel if one is not forthcoming? Do you feel the need to keep score with what you do for others and what they do for you? Can you give without expecting something in return?

- **Do You Need to Be Acknowledged?** Keep track in your own mind whether you do things needing to be acknowledged, and if you do, what do you need? Are the people you are doing some-

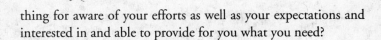

thing for aware of your efforts as well as your expectations and interested in and able to provide for you what you need?

If you are in a relationship that you feel is one-sided and your efforts are unacknowledged, and if it is important to you that the other person is aware of your perception, let them know.

*Well-Being, Midlife*

# Exercising Your Memory

You're over forty, are more forgetful these days, and can't recall things like you used to. You always take note of a great meal but can't remember what you ate at that scrumptious new restaurant last month. Or you tell someone on call waiting that you'll call right back but it is days later when you finally remember. Or how about leaving the tea kettle on the stove, and later you smell it melt to the burner because you forgot about it. Sound familiar?

Before you jump to conclusions and diagnose yourself with early Alzheimer's (which may run in your family) or consider yourself crazy or senile, why not try a mental workout along with that much-needed physical one? That way you can help to save your sanity along with your memory.

- **Name Recognition.** The old technique of pairing someone's name with a physical characteristic usually works with new introductions and helps you do some mental gymnastics as you are being creative (and often funny).

- **Visualize Numbers.** Be imaginative and have fun. If your friend lives at 12 Argyle Street, imagine one dozen argyle sweaters arranged on a shelf. If the apartment number is 2711, imagine twins stopping by the local 7-Eleven. By pairing a visual image with your numerical needs, you have a higher likelihood of recall and will feel better about your memory.

- **Play Mentally Challenging Games.** Scrabble, bridge, crossword puzzles, and playing a musical instrument (it is never too

late to learn how) all help exercise your mind. Also, try to recall phone numbers before you hit the automatic speed dial.

Whether or not you are predisposed to memory loss, you cannot lose by developing memory-sharpening skills.

*Well-Being, Family*

## Preventing Violence in the Home

Home should be a place of sanctuary and harmony. But when violent behavior of someone in the home erupts, it's like a black cloud coming over the roof, and this dark feeling is very scary to both adults and children.

If you are living with a person who has been and could again be violent, it is essential that you take into consideration your own safety and that of your children. It is important that you realize that domestic violence is not only harmful to emotional and physical well-being, but children usually feel personally responsible for what is happening between their parents. Your children could be crafting scenarios that allow them to believe that if they had done their homework sooner or had helped clean the kitchen, Daddy might not have said those nasty things or slapped Mommy. Children rarely, if ever, believe that the adult is the one who is supposed to control himself or herself. Somehow, they think, it is they who could have and should have been able to control the situation.

Help your and your children's world be safe and secure again.

- **It Doesn't Get Better.** No, it won't get better. You already know that. When the violence strikes next time, it will only be worse. Get security back in your family's life *now*! Do you need to get into counseling with or without the abuser, seek court action, get this person out of the house, obtain a restraining order, or leave altogether? Whatever your action to stop the violence, don't wait. *Do something now!*

- **Create an Exit Plan.** If you leave the abuser, get everything in order so when you go, you can leave safely and swiftly. Gather money and important papers (your and your children's birth certificates, bank cards, social security cards, passports, etc.) to take with you. Put all other items you can't lug along in a safe deposit box or with a very trusted person beforehand so you're assured everything is in a safe place. Tell a confidant of your plan and seek help from the many organizations out there for women and children. Know where area shelters are and a route to get there if needed.

If you are experiencing violence in the home, get yourself and your children to a safe place.

*Tuesday*
*Parent*

## Your Life as a Taxi Driver for Your Kids

As a mom you know you're responsible for bringing your children here and there, but do you have any idea how many miles you actually log while doing so? When they are young you are strapping kids in their car seats and maneuvering strollers in and out of hatchbacks while damaging your own back. As they grow, you're piling the entire girls' volleyball team into your mini-van or driving through streets you've never heard of to pick up your son's best buddies so they can surprise him at the bowling alley for his birthday party.

Are you driving through life practically asleep at the wheel and wondering who stole your identity? If you ever thought you would be calling the plumber, the school nurse, and the math tutor, and conducting your own business while having breakfast and lunch in your car, you would have rethought this whole arrangement. So how do you keep your sanity when you are five minutes late for pickup at school and your daughter gives you a long-faced pout, along with the classic eye roll and her unique exasperated exhalation, because "You're late"?

- **Car Time Is Talk Time.** Stay off the phone and eject your favorite CD. Use the time in the car to talk with the children about what has happened at school and what's new with their friends, and bring them up to date on what is happening in *your* life. Yes, you do have a life, and it is not outside of the realm of possibility to inform your children about it so that on some level they realize they are not the only concern in your life.

- **Do-overs.** If you get admonished with a long face when you pick up your child, lock the door and ask her if she would like to rethink that greeting before getting into the car. If you rise to the bait you will have a terrible ride home—another missed opportunity for conversation and connecting. Instead calmly say, "I know you are upset that I was late. Sorry about that. My lateness does not warrant your reaction, so how about rethinking it, rolling back the tape, and getting into the car with a 'Hi Mom, thanks for picking me up' and let's go from there." Or you may just want to make a joke (not at her expense). It is your choice to escalate, ignore, or deal directly with this attitude and behavior.

When the kids are in the car, engage in conversation, listen to music together, or play an old-fashioned game of capitals. And be sure you buy a chauffeur's cap for a really good laugh.

## Discovering Your In-Laws

Your in-laws are part of your existing family. The challenge is to discover who these people are and accept them.

The time is usually worth the investment because you will be connected to your spouse and his family for life. You can save your sanity by not judging them, but accepting that they are now part of your family.

- **What Makes Them Tick?** Treating each in-law as a close family member may or may not work. The only way to really know who they are and to develop a meaningful relationship is to know their background, their life experience, and their view of the world.

- **Change Your Glasses.** See the world from your in-laws' vantage point. Even if their way of doing something or relating to someone is totally foreign to you, and you don't understand their approach, don't give up.

- **Lay the Groundwork** . . . for mutual respect and consideration. Accept your in-laws for the people they are and not for who you want them to be.

- **Welcome Them.** Provide an environment where your in-laws can be themselves. Encourage and learn to be comfortable with their individuality and unique expression. By welcoming them

into your world, you're showing that the relationship you share has value and meaning.

Sometimes who we are is difficult for others;
we don't have to prove ourselves worthy.

# Thursday
*Single, Partner, Midlife*

## Be Ready to Find a New Partner

If you've gone through a devastating breakup or divorce, you might be telling yourself and your friends, "I don't want to get involved with anyone," "I'll never get married again," or "It's impossible to find true love."

Anything is better than feeling that heartache again. So you develop your life in other areas, which is a good thing. But, even though you've got friends, interests, and a good job, there's still emptiness. Let go of your fear of getting hurt again, your anger, and your attachment to your ex and give yourself the chance to meet someone new.

- **Get Over It.** Grieve for the loss. Let go of the dreams you had and future plans together. If you begin to date while you are still grieving, you will not be truly open to a new person. Any new love will just be a Band-Aid.

- **Grow and Keep Going.** If you don't grow, you may not be open to someone who is right for you. If you have a closed mind, you may miss a wonderful opportunity who sits right in front of you. Move ahead and evolve.

- **Do Your Work.** Is there something you keep repeating in relationships that is not working? Can your relationship skills improve? Think this through—dig deep. Then visualize yourself in a healthy relationship, with someone who appreciates you and vice versa. How do you treat each other, and what values do you

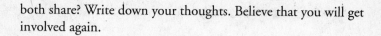

both share? Write down your thoughts. Believe that you will get involved again.

You will be ready to meet someone new when you have a good sense of yourself as a person who deserves to have a fulfilling relationship.

# Emotional Responses When Realizing Your Child Is Different

You appreciate that everyone is different. At the same time, you wonder what your life will be like now that your much anticipated child has arrived and seems to have developmental, physical, or emotional issues that you did not expect (although you may have feared).

Preserving your sanity as those around you talk about the possibilities or necessities for corrective surgeries, infant stimulation interventions, special programs, and more can throw you into a tailspin.

- **Your Emotional Roller Coaster.** Understand that discovering your child has extra needs will cause you to feel a variety of emotional responses. They will not come in any order, and once you feel one emotion you are not immune from it returning . . . in force. Do not judge these feelings. If you believe you cannot handle the responsibility, so be it for now. You may feel as if you were hit by a truck. In effect, you were. But you can recover from the injury with support, using your inner and outer resources (some of which you have yet to develop) and education.

- **Work Through Disappointment.** As you begin to adapt to your situation, you still may not like it. Your sadness may linger, you may feel angry or jealous. Allow those feelings to just be. Understand they are reasonable given the situation, and in time they will transform to feelings of pride, appreciation, and happi-

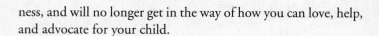

ness, and will no longer get in the way of how you can love, help, and advocate for your child.

- **Know Other Parents.** Most of your fears develop because you have limited experience with persons who have disabilities. Meet other parents and children in similar situations; many of your fears will be addressed in a positive way.

You have entered into a world that you likely did not want to be in, but you are here. Be open to the endless possibilities for growth and appreciation.

# Weekend

*Well-Being*

## Revitalization in a Pinch

As you go through your daily routine, do you suddenly lose your energy and feel the vitality sucked out of your system? You may feel tired, overwhelmed, overworked, or frustrated by something that is happening with your children.

So put aside the bills or the task at hand that is draining you and reach for some high-energy foods such as protein bars, nuts, or fruits (and be sure you are hydrated with water). There are a few things you can do to immediately feel better.

- **Breathe Deeply.** Focus your attention on your breath and breathe in and out, slowly and deliberately. This will slow you down, calm you, and help restore your balance.

- **Calming Exercises.** Take a moment and run your wrists under cold water. You can also tap the tip of your tongue to the roof of your mouth to help you calm your nerves and invigorate your hormones or gently tap your Adam's apple with two fingers to stimulate your thyroid.

- **Pamper Yourself.** Keep a facial spray (rosewater or lemon) in your car or in your purse to spritz some calming revitalization whenever you are about to melt or feel grimy. Soak your feet in a warm bath. Women who have cold feet feel the imbalance all over their bodies. Add some Epsom salts (or regular salt) to the water and close your eyes to imagine yourself walking into the surf of the sea. Keep an aromatherapy blend on hand and dab some onto your neck and behind your ears to lift your spirits.

*Week 8*

Soak two chamomile tea bags and put them on your eyes for a quick lift and revitalization.

- **Stay Away from Caffeine** . . . especially when you feel tired. Follow your body signals instead. Try an invigorating noncaffeinated herbal tea to avoid the burst of adrenaline that results from caffeine.

Take small but important steps to keep yourself in balance and revitalize.

*Midlife, Well-Being*

# Managing Menopause

You are in it. Sure enough, you are experiencing what you vaguely remember your mom went through when she was your age. One moment you are hot, tearing off your clothes and patting your face and neck with a cool cloth, and the next moment you need that sweater. And that goes on and on for days, months, even, for some, years.

Everything seems out of whack. Although you are drinking gallons of black cohosh tea and increasing your yoga practice, you still cannot believe you are at the age or stage of menopause. What on earth can you do to keep your sanity, when you feel as if you are losing your mind and everything familiar about your body is now changing to the "change" of life (understatement of the year)?

- **Accept Reality.** You are indeed changing and you feel as if you have no control over your own biological functions. You feel as if you're being held hostage in your own body! Acceptance is the most important part of the process.

- **Look to Role Models** . . . of women who have successfully weathered menopause and ask them how they did it. Drugs? Herbal remedies? Natural methods? Yoga and Tai Chi? Discover the combination that works best for you given what is going on in your life at this time.

- **You Will Get Through This.** Allow yourself to know that you will get through this best if you appreciate the enormous shifts

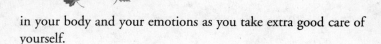

in your body and your emotions as you take extra good care of
yourself.

Menopause is about movement. Allow yourself to
adapt to the shifting that takes place.

*Tuesday*
*Parent, Partner*

# Kids Need Both Parents After Divorce

Often, after divorce, a woman is relieved to be away from her spouse. But it's healthy for the children to have a good relationship with both parents. Unless your ex was abusive or in some other way a threat to your children's safety, your kids deserve and need to have time with their other parent.

Divorces are usually stressful for children. The period after divorce should be a time for healing and creating a new image of what their family is and will be like. Kids need both parents to look up to and to help with this transition, and to be proud of them and listen to them. They need the different kind of love and appreciation that will come from their mother and their father. And the more you can encourage their connection with the other parent, the better they will fare.

- **Make the Effort.** Arrange for your children to meet frequently with their other parent, especially if you do not have joint custody. Having consistency in the relationship is important. Also, encourage contact with your former in-laws so your child has an extended family. Even if you don't like your ex-spouse or your in-laws, they are still family to your children, and relationships should be encouraged.

- **Don't Badmouth.** If the other parent is not making an effort to see the kids, is habitually late or undependable, you don't have to make excuses for them. Their unpredictable behavior will speak volumes to the kids, and they will know which parent they can depend on. Refrain from criticizing your ex-spouse but find words to explain situations to the kids. Instead of "He's always late and irresponsible," say, "Your dad cares about you but is not good with time. Why don't you stay busy until he gets here?"

- **Share Information** . . . about your children's academic, after-school, and social life so the burden is not on the children. However, you are under no obligation to share every single thing that happens in your children's lives. Try to find a happy medium that benefits everyone.

After a divorce, your children need to put together their version of family. Contact with both parents makes it easier for them to do this.

# Siblings Caregiving Their Parents

More often than not siblings step up to the plate to help each other care for their parents when they are ill or going through the normal aging process. There's so much to do that it's good to know who can tackle the paperwork and who can be more hands-on. The tricky part is dividing and conquering and making decisions as a team.

- **Keep the Focus.** What you all need at this time is to help your parents and adjust to the new reality. Even if you don't get along well and spending time together makes you nuts, when you share a common goal, you *can* put differences aside and focus on what needs to be done.

- **Work in Tandem.** Draw on each other's strengths and make decisions that affect your parents with your parents. If you don't advocate for your parents' care and well-being, nobody will, so find common ground when there are differences of opinion.

- **What's Fair and Equitable?** Consider what works for each of you and how much you are able to offer (time, expertise, and money). Talk with your sibs and divvy up responsibilities that demonstrate respect for each of your lives. If someone lives close by, it doesn't mean that she has to be the point person. Similarly, just because one of you has medical training does not preclude the rest from offering insights and suggestions.

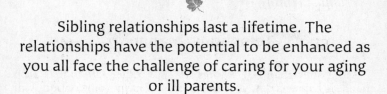

Sibling relationships last a lifetime. The relationships have the potential to be enhanced as you all face the challenge of caring for your aging or ill parents.

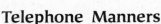

# Telephone Manners

Just when you are in the middle of a conversation with your friend, it happens. She is interrupted and has a conversation with her child or someone else while you are hanging on and listening.

Are you fed up with people who can't have a fluid conversation because they allow themselves to be constantly interrupted? Even after you mention it, your friend apologizes but somehow does not get the message because it happens over and over again. How do you maintain your sanity when facing such inconsiderate behavior?

- **What Bothers You?** Focus on how you feel and what this behavior means to you. Likely you believe that your friend's behavior signals a lack of consideration for your time and your friendship. Perhaps it indicates an inflated sense of self (a reflection of her self-importance?). Does she expect you to hang on while she talks, without regard for your time or your obligations (and a diminished sense of you)?

- **Call Her on Her Behavior.** If you haven't done so already, review in your mind's eye a few key points to emphasize. Tell her in person that you feel offended. Let her know you feel that this behavior results in you feeling cast aside and unimportant in her life, as well as giving you the impression that your life and what you need to do is not as valuable as hers.

- **Solution.** Instead of an apology, ask her what she will do the next time she is interrupted. If she does not offer a viable solution, offer one of your own (end your conversation, call back,

tell the other person she is busy and will get back to him in a few minutes), and try it the next time this happens.

When you are repeatedly put on hold
in your friend's life, it is time for you
to confront the situation.

## *Friday*
### Parent, Partner

## Sleepovers Not Just for Kids

Your daughter brings her boyfriend home and they want to sleep together. What do you do? Are you OK with having her "love interest" sleep in her room? Is there a difference to you if it is a serious or not-so-serious relationship?

It is quite difficult for many parents to think about their young adult child sleeping with a boyfriend or girlfriend in the parents' home. If you are not comfortable with your child's boyfriend or girlfriend sharing the same room, they need to respect your wishes. But remember that respect goes both ways. Your son or daughter has to respect your rules of the house, but you, too, need to respect their desire to be together and have privacy.

- **If You Say No.** If you are not comfortable with the sleeping-together arrangement, tell them *before* they come home. Full disclosure of your feelings prior to their visit will put everyone on the same page.

- **If You Say Yes** . . . then respect a closed door. What is going on behind that door is not your business. For this to work, there needs to be good judgment and respect exercised by all members of the family.

- **If You Ignore It.** Having the attitude, "I will not allow them to sleep in the same room, and I hope they don't ask" is not the greatest. It's better to discuss it beforehand so everyone's expectations are clear.

Come to terms with your feelings regarding your children's sexuality.

# Weekend
## Well-Being

## It's Decision-making Time

It's time to make an important decision. Should you get married, leave your job, purchase a new home, or dump someone from your life? Can you trust yourself to go about it in the healthiest way?

Whatever it is, you need your wits about you and should focus on keeping your sanity while considering what is before you.

- **Be in "Calm."** You'll need to relax as you decide what to do. Clear your mind. Don't think of the shoulds and shouldn'ts, but start with your gut instincts. Then do your research and homework. Get as much reliable information as you can. Know what your options and alternatives are.

- **Write Down Pros and Cons.** Keep notes and go back to them often. Write down the pluses and minuses in separate columns on the same page. Play out certain scenes in your mind's eye. What would your life be like if you did not work at this company? How might you thrive if you and your boyfriend were no longer together? What would you be missing? Be honest in your written assessment.

- **Let Intuition Be Your Guide.** Relax and "see" yourself doing what your sixth sense leads you toward. Listen to your inner voice and let it guide you. Without being critical or overly emotional, trust in your ability to select what will be a healthy choice for you.

Decision making can allow you to explore options
you may not have known were available to you if
you don't allow anxiety to be an obstacle.

*Well-Being, Friends, Family*

## Scary Doctor's Visits

For many women who have had a serious illness or who fear they are about to discover something is seriously amiss with their health, going to the doctor can be not only anxiety provoking but also downright scary.

The normal and predictable stress is bound to prevent you from hearing and processing everything that goes on in the office. If you do find out that you have a health concern, you may shut down after the initial shock and miss much of what is said as a follow-up.

- **Don't Go Alone.** Always take another person with you. Her job is to listen and take careful and complete notes about what is said and what is recommended. Names of medications or treatment options need to be spelled out, and anything that is confusing needs to be clarified. It is not at all 100 percent certain that you will get all the information if you bring one person with you, but the chances of getting clearer information is increased.

- **Bring Written Questions** . . . to ask the doctor, nurse-practitioner, or administrator depending on what you need to know and whose expertise you need to tap.

- **The Time Is Yours.** Remember *you* are the patient. Be prepared to ask the doctor to slow down and explain the issues in different ways until you genuinely "get it." If you feel you're being condescended to, rushed, or anything like that, be prepared to say so politely. Pay attention to the response the doctor gives you. If it does not feel right, leave and make an appointment with another doctor (no matter how highly recommended this one is). There's always another doctor who may be a better fit for you and more than competent.

- **You Are a Partner** . . . in your treatment and care. You need to feel comfortable and confident with your medical professionals. You the patient and your health care providers are a team. Strategize with them and seek to win your body back to health.

Before you are a patient, you are a person. After you become a patient, you remain a person.

# Tuesday
*Parent*

## Considering Divorce with Children

Are you contemplating divorce? Maybe you have been thinking about it for a long time but can't take the necessary steps because you have a family. This is not a snap decision. Make sure you've tried everything possible to restore and rebuild your marriage so guilt doesn't linger. Making efforts to save the marriage will never be wasted even if divorce is imminent.

Be available to your children to help them deal with the effects of the dissolution of their family and the building of a new one. You may no longer have to be married to this person, but you are connected for the long run because of the children.

It is important to note that if you are experiencing abuse in any form or there is a substance abuse problem that keeps getting worse, make sure you are safe and seek counseling. Keep your and your children's well-being above all.

- **Explore Your Alternatives.** Traditionally, couples litigated their divorce in court. But today many people end their marriage through mediation or a collaborative process. These alternatives may decrease courtroom time and focus on ending the marriage instead of dividing the family. Know your options and seek a professional who recognizes the importance of maintaining positive family relationships.

- **Get Good Financial Advice** . . . and set up workable contingency plans for your own and your children's future.

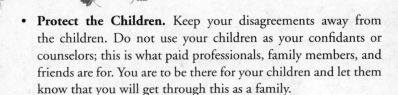

- **Protect the Children.** Keep your disagreements away from the children. Do not use your children as your confidants or counselors; this is what paid professionals, family members, and friends are for. You are to be there for your children and let them know that you will get through this as a family.

Do what you need to do to keep yourself whole during a divorce. Really focus on what's best for you and the children instead of what's going on with your soon-to-be ex-spouse.

# Gossip

Gossip damages the person who is being gossiped about and also reflects badly on the person who is gossiping. Comments shared by other people are often misconstrued, and the tale can grow out of proportion as it goes down the line, much like what happened when you played the telephone game as a child.

The bottom line is that gossip hurts. Save your sanity by keeping your focus on more important matters and getting away from negativity.

- **Go to the Source.** If you know something about someone and it can cause trouble, better to go to that person with your concern rather than spread information.

- **People Don't Like Gossip.** Assume that the person about whom you are speaking would prefer that you not share the news, unless he told you it was OK. Also assume that people don't want to hear about other people's business (and if they do, you don't have to be the messenger).

- **People Don't Like Gossipers.** If you talk about others, people will assume that you are also talking about them. Build people's trust by refraining from spreading gossip.

When you are inclined to gossip,
just hold your tongue.

# Recovering from an Emotional Affair

Emotional cheating is about forming meaningful attachments with a person other than your partner in ways that prevent your partner from having that deep emotional intimacy with you.

You know how damaging emotional cheating can be because it is all about connection. Feeling emotionally distant from your partner who doesn't appreciate you makes you more vulnerable to becoming emotionally attached to an idealized "friend," especially if this friend is someone who empathizes with your stress, "speaks the same language," and is always there with a supportive ear. He makes you feel terrific.

But when this "friend" gets in the way of your closeness with your partner, that is the time to deal directly with what's going on (or not going on) within each of you and between you.

- **Confess.** If you have given your heart to someone else and prevented your partner from sharing what is essential to who you are and what is important to you, you need to 'fess up that you went beyond the limits of trust. Change the dynamic of the "friend" relationship so you can once again focus on your partner. Avoid discussing such personal details of your life and save them for your partner.

- **What Do You Want with Your Partner?** Quietly sit and imagine in your mind's eye the relationship you want to have with your partner. See yourself telling your partner something you shared with your "friend." Also, try to discuss with your partner what you were looking for, getting, and missed in your relationship.

- **Work Things Out.** Recognize and be clear that you are still committed and attached to your partner and that you will discuss with him or her difficulties you have in your relationship and work on them together.

- **Get Close Again.** Find ways to share your feelings, goals, and dreams with your partner. Pay attention to your appearance; go out; find time to be intimate, erotic, whatever works for you to keep your love exciting and enticing.

Friendship, casual flirting, having fun with someone other than your partner is not necessarily a threat to your relationship. Becoming emotionally involved, sharing secrets that you would not share with your partner, and keeping yourself from being "known" can jeopardize your primary relationship.

# Vacationing with Your Family
# Without Others

There are many people who would do anything to have their parents or in-laws offer to take them on a vacation so that the whole family can be together. You, however, are not among them.

Even though you love your parents and in-laws, you really need time to just hang out and relax with your partner, if you have one, and your kids. Saving your sanity while keeping the lid on the well-being of your extended family is a challenge.

- **Focus on Your Vacation.** Visualize your time with your family and focus on the kind of experience you want to have. Is it a camping trip in the great outdoors? An opportunity to try every theme park in the state in the shortest amount of time? Traveling in a camper with your kids? Renting a house in the mountains and hanging around without any appointments, obligations, TV, or cell phones?

- **Make Yourself (and Your Family) Happy.** Tell yourself that you have the right to spend time with your family, and if your parents or in-laws are unhappy about that, you can deal with it. Living with a bit of guilt will not destroy you.

- **Open Up to Creative Solutions.** If you live far away from your folks and the only time they can see you and your children is this particular time, discuss viable alternatives. Split your time and spend some of it with them and part of it on your own, or create

another time when you can extend a holiday weekend and visit together.

- **Sometimes It's Just "No, Thank You."** If you live near your parents and they see you and your children frequently, then the issue is about having time together in a vacation atmosphere. If this does not work for you, thank them for their generosity and arrange to have some special time together closer to home.

Vacations are all about enjoying your time away from home, and you want to return having come close to reaching your goal.

## Relax to Create

You know you are creative, but brainstorms have not been coming to you lately. Rushing around at breakneck speed, you're wondering what happened to the creative juices. Are they all dried up?

With their challenging schedules and driving desire to fill each moment, it is common for many people to keep the clock running—and never turn it off. How do you keep your sanity while keeping your creativity alive?

- **Get Down Time.** For creativity to flourish, you need to take time off from work every day. That means turning off, tuning out, and recharging your battery by resting, relaxing, and leaving space in your head and in your life.

- **Be in a Restorative Place.** Creativity researchers refer to the magic trio of "bed, bath, and bus" as necessary for restoration of your creativity. When you are in any of those three environments, you are either sleeping, relaxing and letting your cares float away, or allowing yourself to be taken from one place to another. You are not doing anything, just being.

- **Find a Free Flow.** Creativity begins in a space that is free to grow, to associate, to "move." It needs to be nurtured in an environment that respects the process and cycle of work, rest, renewal.

If your creative juices are blocked, begin an alternate pattern of work and rest to give yourself time off to just be . . . your creativity will return.

# Fitting into Those Jeans

You may be just sick of looking at those jeans in your closet and getting up the gumption to try them on. Do they even fit anymore? Will your bottom look too big? Will they be too tight? Did you really put on weight since the last time you wore them? There goes your mood for the day.

Getting yourself in shape is not about forfeiting weekend pizza parties with family and friends or going on crash diets, but maintaining a healthy lifestyle. What to do to get into those jeans and keep your sanity?

- **Portion Your Portions** . . . and measure up. Take out your measuring cups and measuring spoons and grab a kitchen scale. Pay attention to everything you eat. Stick to recommended portion sizes and have portion control. Measure a serving of cereal, a serving of peanut butter, a serving of salad dressing, a serving of cheese. You will be amazed at the difference between what you think you're eating and what you are actually eating.

- **Don't Eat Like a Caveman.** A thirty-two-ounce steak for one? Maybe for Fred Flintstone, but not if you're trying to maintain a healthy body. Most recipes call for more protein than you need. Four ounces of lean protein per person is a healthy serving. When you're reading through recipes, adjust the quantity of protein accordingly. Don't cook more than you need, and when you eat out, ask the waiter to have the chef portion food for you and wrap up your leftovers.

- **Dress for Success.** Creamy dressings don't have to cost a dress size. Cut the calories from mayonnaise-based dressings by using equal amounts of low-cal mayo and nonfat buttermilk. Add honey mustard, finely minced garlic, and salt and pepper to taste for a super fast and savory, guilt-free, good-for-you dressing.

- **Feeding Your Starvation.** Once you figure out how much you're truly consuming daily, you're going to need to cut back on high-calorie foods. To combat the pangs of hunger that come when you reduce your daily caloric intake, build all-you-can-eat side dishes into every meal, such as garden salads, broth-y soups and microwave steamed veggies tossed with low-calorie dressing.

Visualize yourself looking good in those jeans when junk-food crave waves hit.

## When Grandma Becomes Mom

You lived through your unmarried daughter's pregnancy, and now you're raising her baby. Or your midlife career daughter decided to go it alone at the sperm bank and now, guess what? You're raising her baby.

First of all, kudos to you. You stepped up to the plate of unconditional love and made a choice to be there for this child. Instead of nanny care or full-time day care, you've undertaken a physically, emotionally, and mentally demanding full-time job. You were not meant to conceive at this age and you're not as well equipped to raise a child at this age as you were when you were a young mom. But you're managing and making the best of it.

- **Mourn the Loss of Freedom.** After years off from child rearing, you as a "grandma mom" will feel the loss of the life you previously had. There is less (or no) time to play tennis or golf or go bowling with the girls. You have enormous responsibilities. And even when you do have the time, you're pooped. Work through your mourning and get to the other side of gratitude for the gift of this new little person in your life.

- **Make Peace.** You have made a commitment to raising your grandchild. Deal with it as best as you can and accept your new role. Resisting will hurt you and your grandchild.

- **Why Yell? Laugh Instead.** When your daughter painted your prized rug (the one that cost more than your car) *and* the dog with permanent marker at the same time, you threw a fit. But

you're older now and oh so much wiser. Look at the humor in your precious one's mischievous behavior because, you know what? As you think back, your dog really did look funny with a yellow tail.

- **A Baby-sitter for the Baby-sitter.** Get out. I repeat, get out and do things you enjoy. Get your support system in place and go for lunch, a game of bridge, a massage, and to have your hair done. You'll need frequent breaks. Make a point to keep some of your old life interspersed with the new.

When Mom's at work or busy, Grandma's
in charge. But, when your daughter returns,
remember to let go of the reins
and do something for you.

# Get Out of the Blues When Working Alone

If you are writing a book, working from home, or undertaking a project on your own, it's easy to lose your motivation to get the job done. Your work space is void of another breathing body and the walls start to cave in. Before you procrastinate one more minute or, God forbid, reach for the clicker, or, even worse yet, another Twinkie, *stop* and save your sanity!

- **Get Out and Exercise.** Start your day with a walk, yoga class, or swim—some type of exercise that will get you out early and energize you for the day. If you can't get out every morning, an exercise tape or TV class will have to do. How about choosing one shot in a tropical location so you can virtually get a breath of fresh air? Come back to your home office or desk to start your day raring to go.

- **Get Out of the Kitchen.** Schedule your meals as if you were in a city office high-rise. Break for lunch at a predetermined time or reward yourself with a cup of tea after you finish a task or the chapter you are writing. Have healthy snacks on hand, like nuts, pumpkin seeds, and carrots, for the midmorning and midafternoon "hungries." Instead of giving in to the first stomach growl, tell yourself to go fifteen more minutes (surely you can wait that long) and delve into your work until then. Chances are you'll get absorbed by what you are doing and those pangs of hunger will wait until your next meal.

- **Get Out for a Meal.** When you do stop to eat, schedule a couple of lunches, dinners, or coffee/tea meetings a few times a week with business associates, someone you've been meaning to network with, or fellow writers for inspiration. This will get you out of that solo space while still in work mode so you're accomplishing something and not "eating" up time by making a meal. If you're unscheduled one week, take a break to eat out or bring a bag lunch to a park for a change of scenery.

- **Get Out of the Dishwasher.** Focus on your work and not on household chores. Do housework at the beginning or end of the day and don't waste productive work time. The only time domestic labor can come in handy is if you need some "thinking" space when you're really stuck for ideas. Sometimes vacuuming the rug is good menial work to do while pondering a problem or mulling over a thought. If you need to go this route, pick a chore that's weighing on you and can free up some brain power, such as folding a load of laundry. Don't get into cleaning several bathrooms or organizing the closet, which can eat up lots of time. Refrain from getting into the habit of mixing up your priorities, and keep work time for work.

When you work alone and feel lonely, a walk outside is the best remedy.

# When Your Partner
# Changes Your Life Plans

Before you married, did you talk endlessly with your partner about how it would be nice to move from the city and raise children in a less hectic environment, but after some time, your partner realized that the suburbs are just not for him or her? Or did you marry someone of a different faith who assured you that he would not interfere with your children's religious education, but now he's feeling differently? Perhaps you both agreed to work for three years, live frugally, save money, and then travel before having children, but he wants to forgo globetrotting and start a family now.

Managing your expectations and disappointment when someone you are committed to has a change of heart and "reneges" on your agreement is a significant challenge. Sometimes circumstances impact our choices, and the better part of valor requires that we change our plans. But it's not always easy to forget an unfilled promise and accept your partner's change of heart and mind. You might be angry and blame your partner for his about-face. But what you're really dealing with is feeling that you are not in control of your own life, loss of trust in your partner for not fulfilling a promise, and the possibility of your dreams being shattered.

Before resentment builds, remember that you are in a partnership and that problem solving is best when done together. Both of you have needs, and the healthiest thing to do for your relationship is to try to get your needs met. Realize that there may be a solution that is different from your (and his) ideal. Be open-minded and compromise.

- **Matter of Trust Versus Change of Heart.** If you think you were manipulated into a situation by being placated, "yessed" or hoodwinked, it will be difficult for you to release the disappointment and anger that you feel about losing your shared dream, and make it harder to accept the new situation. It will be even more difficult to develop trust. Seek out a counselor if you mistrust your partner.

- **Understand His Position.** However, if he is truly having a change of heart, trying to understand his point of view will help both of you tackle the issue at hand. Listen to your partner about what the real reasons are for his change. Try to be open to the life circumstances that have contributed to this new view. Try to accommodate any part of the old plan in a new way.

- **Plans Change.** One of the reasons you may have connected with this person was that you agreed to live your life together in a certain way, and now you wonder if that is possible. Things change. People change. Sometimes those changes impact us in ways that are difficult to accept or integrate. People make plans and God laughs. Sometimes we have to go with the flow.

- **Create a New Plan.** Work on releasing your attachment to the dream plan. Construct a new plan together that can work and satisfy the desire that drove the first dream. If you keep holding on to the anger and blame, you not only will hurt the relationship but potentially will poison others' views of your partner.

- **Release . . .** your partner from the responsibility of "making up" for letting you down.

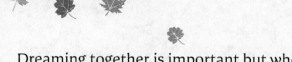

Dreaming together is important but when the
dream is no longer shared, letting go of part or all
of it allows you to create new
(and sometimes better) dreams.

# Friday
*Well-Being*

## Not Feeling Sexy

When you were younger, feeling, looking, being sexy was no big deal. It just seemed to happen and oozed from your every pore.

Today, being sexy is everywhere. Books and television shows are telling you not only that you *can* be sexy at your age—you *should* be! But you're not feeling particularly sexy these days. You may have had a marriage that didn't work out, carried the burden of supporting a family, cared for elderly family members, or were even ill yourself. In fact, you don't even have the urge to light candles and get in the mood and you're not all that unhappy about it. Are your sexy days over?

- **Is Sexy for You?** If the world around you applauds engaging in healthy, regular, safe, and—if possible—loving sexual activity and you still can't manage feeling that way, it's okay. If you're feeling good about who you are, you certainly don't *have* to feel the way the media want you to feel. That is, unless *you* want to.

- **Want to Be More Sexy?** Like and value yourself above all. Someone who is comfortable with her sensuality coveys a message of confidence. Think of the qualities others recognize in you that you often forget about. After you uncover your sex appeal, then you can hit the lingerie store.

- **Your Libido Comfort Level.** Be honest with yourself. If you really don't want to be sexually active at this point in life, accept it. If people are telling you, "You're too young to act like a person without a libido," consider that they're wrong!

Being and feeling sexy is one of the most personal expressions of who you are, and only *you* can assess what is right for you.

## Facing Risks

If you always thought of yourself as risk averse, it is time to rethink your definition of the label you have given yourself.

If you're cautious and conjure up the nerve to actually do something in the risky department (complete with sweaty palms), you might give yourself a pat on the back (as well you should) and then sit back on your laurels. But this might stifle you to go further. On the other hand, if you take a different approach and think of yourself as someone who *used to be* risk averse, you will find that you'll be more likely to try new things and have different experiences.

It is all in the way you think about yourself. Giving up that old label is part of the journey. So, when you are facing a new and challenging situation that will challenge your risk taking, know that you can preserve your sanity while stepping out of the comfort zone.

- **Pretend.** Visualize yourself doing whatever you are contemplating and see yourself doing it well. Feel the anxiety and allow it to be OK. Tell yourself that the benefit is worth the discomfort.

- **Take Small Steps.** Do whatever it is you are apprehensive about and notice your reaction. Take it in small increments. Go through the scary part not unlike walking along a trail on the edge of a mountain—you walk carefully, one foot in front of the other, looking in front of you, not down the edge of the slope.

- **Be Your Own Coach.** Tell yourself you are doing this thing—talk to yourself and give yourself positive feedback and support. This self-talk can and should sound like a coach or cheerleader,

encouraging you from within: "Good for me!" "I can do this." "I am able to do this thing that I was afraid of." "I will feel good when I know I have done this."

- **Celebrate.** Use this experience as evidence that you are no longer a risk-averse person but someone who *used to be* risk averse and is working on it.

You can change the label you have put on yourself by experiencing life through a different lens.

Parent, Family, Community, Friends

## Prepare to Move with the Kids

All kids have feelings about moving to a new place that may or may not be consistent with yours. They may not want to leave their friends, their school, their neighborhood, and they may feel as if they have not had a say in the decision (often they don't).

Keeping your sanity while you yourself adjust to the idea of moving *and* help your children get through the change takes planning and attention.

- **Do Your Research.** Find out as much as you can about the town you are moving to and gather information, such as chamber of commerce materials and relocation packets, about child-oriented activities and programs that reflect your children's interests.

- **Become Familiar with Your New Settings.** If you can, visit the place and see the house, the street, the neighborhood, the school, community center, and synagogue or church you will become affiliated with. Have the children take photos of their rooms and places in their new town to bring home and show their friends. If you cannot go in person, use online photos as much as possible to create a feeling of being there.

- **Throw a Party.** Plan a going-away party with the kids, neighbors, and their friends. Take lots of pictures and gather a list of e-mail and home addresses and phone numbers. At the party, circulate a journal and let everyone write a going-away message to your child. Have it on hand as soon as you arrive at the new house and whenever anyone has the homesick blues.

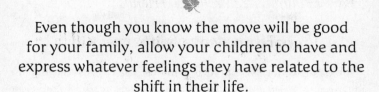

Even though you know the move will be good
for your family, allow your children to have and
express whatever feelings they have related to the
shift in their life.

*Tuesday*
*Well-Being*

# Firing a Professional

You know the situation. You have been there. Your attorney no longer seems to be able to truly be your advocate. Your conversations are punctuated with sighs that sound awfully like someone who is fed up or not on your team. Or you have seen a marriage counselor for a few months and wonder why you consistently leave the office feeling as if you are not at all heard and your position is not as legitimate as your partner's. Your hairdresser whom you have seen for years just doesn't get the cut right. Each time you talk to her, she tells you she knows best what looks good on you.

It is time to find someone who responds to what you need. Firing a professional who may have seen you through hard times can be intimidating.

- **Review History.** Have they been consistently responsive and just lately have fallen off?

- **Are You Realistic?** If you feel that you are not being treated well, that you are being railroaded on specific issues, or that you seem to get little first-rate attention, then it is likely time to address this relationship or move on.

- **Muster Courage to Speak Up.** Consider if it is worth talking with the professional about your disappointment and diminishing expectations regarding his responsiveness to you as a client. When you share your perceptions, do so in a measured and sensible way. State what your expectations were and your disappointment that they are not being addressed. Ask for time to discuss whether you will be working together in the future. Be very clear about the purpose of the conversation or meeting.

- **Pay Up.** If you do fire the person, pay your outstanding bill for services rendered. If the services provided (or not) were not up to par, talk about the bill and see if adjustments can be made. Don't stiff someone just because you are not satisfied.

Work with someone who hears and respects you and helps you accomplish your goals.

# When Is It Time to Retire?

Today people are deciding to retire at different times and for different reasons. If they can, many are opting to retire early in the forties to pursue other interests. You may feel energized by your job and want to stay as long as you are productive and challenged, or you may be one of the shall-I-retire? folks who keep delaying retirement because they may need to earn a living, or they just don't have the energy to move, until they become stale at their jobs, clinging to the only life they know.

When is retirement right for you? Making that decision at the right time can certainly save your sanity.

- **Reach Out and Explore.** Lots of research goes into this decision. If you are a person whose sense of self-worth primarily depends on your identity at work, begin to reach out to discover what kinds of experiences you can have in your retirement that will be fulfilling. It may take time, but it is up to you to become open to different possibilities.

- **Let People Know.** Talk openly about your idea to retire. What do your friends, family and fellow office buddies think? When you bounce the idea off them do they wholeheartedly support and encourage you? Or does their reaction have echoes of "This is premature" or "What are you going to do with yourself?" Sometimes people in your life see things objectively, but it's up to you to weed out their sincerity from their judgments.

- **Have an Exit Strategy.** Maybe retirement is best when a certain project is complete or when your daughter has twins. And after you retire, what will every day look like? Have a plan, even if it's not well hashed out yet. Don't forget to mark the event with some sort of "rite of passage." A meal with colleagues, visiting individually with your coworkers, or a "retirement" cake and coffee hour. Have some idea of what you might be doing after you retire and a way for people to remain in touch.

When you begin to feel uneasy about your work, which has been your anchor for so many years, recognize that as a sign of change and focus on opportunities you would like to explore.

# New Rules of Engagement and Intimacy

Many women say that they crave a successful, adult relationship that is intimate. Yet, when they are involved with someone, they behave in ways that brilliantly and perfectly undermine their desire.

What's going on? If this scenario sounds familiar to you, ask yourself if you believe that "the more one gives, the more one receives." Give to someone who appreciates you and whom you appreciate, love, and respect. If you do, chances are you can save your sanity by welcoming intimacy into your life.

- **Listen to Your Mate's Desire.** When you engage the people you love, emphatically, from your heart and soul, it is possible to listen to your mate's desire for a relationship (or anything, for that matter). Help your partner understand and feel unafraid in pursuing anything and everything with you.

- **Respect Boundaries** . . . of your loved one. Don't try to act as if you know better what someone else needs or wants. Listen and respond from a neutral, nonjudgmental position.

- **Open Your Ears, Eyes, and Heart** . . . to the other person's experiences, fears, hopes. Let this be "their" time, and establish the reality that there will be, later, a time for you to do the same.

Pay close attention to what your partner needs and wants as you develop intimacy together.

# When Fido Is Failing

That wagging tail, cute-as-can-be face, purr, hiss, neigh, or squeaky sound of the gerbil wheel is what you love to come home to every day. Your pet is there for you to enjoy no matter what mood you're in or what happened that day. In fact, you rely on your pet for unconditional love.

So when your pet is ill, you'll have lots of emotions. This will throw you off center as it touches your heart, as well as your pocketbook. If the care is costly, how much of your time, energy, and money are you willing and able to invest?

Saving your sanity while your pet is going through treatments will depend in large part on the support you have around you.

- **Find a Cocaregiver** . . . someone you trust who loves your pet. He can house-sit when you're away and be on backup when you are unable to go to the vet.

- **Take Care of Yourself, Too.** You are now a caregiver, so take care of yourself. Spend as much time as you can with your pet to give and get comfort. If you can, leave from time to time so you can get out. Realize that you and your pet will be OK. You may have to decide that you can no longer continue the animal's life. Get lots of support.

- **Be with Other Pet Lovers.** When your pet is the source of sadness, you need to get strength from others. Friends who appreciate the person-pet connection will be a great support.

Refrain from sharing with people who don't have an affinity for animals.

Your decisions about what you do for your pet are your business. Don't leave yourself vulnerable to others' judgments as you care for and love your pet.

## Be at the Ready

What do you love to do? Paint, garden, knit, or scrapbook? So why are you not in the middle of a masterpiece, planting bulbs for spring tulips, making a sweater, or commemorating your vacation?

When you discover what it is you like to do, be sure you have all the supplies available so you are not spending a lot of time looking for the "ingredients." Keep your easel, knitting bag, gardening tools, and glue and scissors at the ready and easily accessible. Then indulge yourself in pleasure when it's a good time and save your sanity with your passion.

- **Have a Beginning, Middle, and End.** It is important to differentiate your pleasure time from the rest of what you do. This is for your soul enhancement, and *you* are giving yourself permission to do it. So start when it's a good time and know that in an hour, or by dinnertime, you will stop for the day.

- **Do It with Intention and Focus.** Recognize that *right now* is a good time to do some weeding. Yes, you have some phone calls to make but you have not done anything special for yourself and you know you feel better after having been in the garden, even for a few minutes. Separate the rest of the day from what you are about to do right now.

- **Feel Accomplished.** When you finish, recognize not what you have yet to do (the rest of the garden) but what you did accomplish. Projects will be ongoing. Recognize and get the benefit of whatever you have done today.

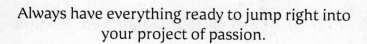

Always have everything ready to jump right into your project of passion.

# Addressing a Health Hole in Your Résumé

You deserve a medal. You have just gotten through one of the most grueling health challenges possible by withstanding a scary diagnosis and treatment protocol and all the emotional upheaval that goes along with them. Now it's time to put your life back on track and return to work.

With a new outfit, hairstyle, and attitude, you hit the job market. Save your sanity as you reenter the working world with confidence and determination.

- **It's Behind You.** When someone asks you about your résumé's holes, comment that you had a health matter that is in the past. Nobody can legally ask about the particulars of an illness. Sharing the information is your prerogative.

- **Move On** . . . and begin this job search as someone who has won her battle.

- **Know in Your Heart** . . . that you are up to the requirements of becoming part of the work force again.

As you put your illness behind you, integrate the lessons you learned from your illness and recovery and apply them as you pursue a new work situation.

*Tuesday*

*Single, Parent*

# Divorced Mom

After divorce, parenting is a new frontier. No one is there to back you up and hold the line with the kids on a day-to-day basis. On the flip side, you have more autonomy and now no longer have to pass every decision concerning the kids by your ex-spouse.

For these reasons, single parenting can be both empowering and exhausting. You have to stay balanced and confident in being a good parent and let some things go, while staying firm on other issues. When you feel the job is overwhelming for one person day in and day out, find ways to save your sanity.

- **Constructively Deal with Your Feelings.** Your children need you to be as "whole" and together as you can be for them. It is difficult enough for children to go through their parents' divorce without adding to that difficulty by using your children as your main support system. Your kids should not be your confidants or friends as you work out your own issues about your ex and your divorce. This is what good friends, support networks, counselors, clergy, and therapists are for.

- **Extended Family Members.** It is important that you not be sole nurturer for the kids. Children need to spend time with grandparents and other significant persons in their lives. It is essential that as many people as possible on both sides remain in the child's family to enhance opportunities for interactions, continuity, transmission of family traditions, morals, values, and legacy.

- **Good Terms with Your Ex.** At the minimum, maintain open communication with your children's father. Avoid negative comments about your ex but be realistic about what they can and can't expect from him. It is also burdensome, inappropriate, unkind, and unfair to expect a child to be the messenger between the two of you.

When you're a single mom, find the ways to stay strong and balanced through the parenting years and keep your children's best interests at heart.

## Road Rage

You may not normally define yourself as a person quick to anger, but that may change when you are behind the wheel. You may go from zero to sixty (and I am not referring to the speedometer) when someone steals "your" parking space or cuts you off. What is this about? Why would you allow yourself to continue to drive when you are incensed?

Without thinking, in a split second, you put your own safety and your passengers' safety at high risk. Using obscene language or gestures, sitting on your horn, riskily racing behind someone to "teach them a lesson," and "getting even" are common behaviors for angry drivers.

If you find you are easily provoked, think long and hard about getting behind the wheel. Angry drivers are known to take more risks on the road, and they get angrier faster and drive more aggressively, which, sadly, leads to more accidents.

- **Don't Take an "Angry Pill" and Drive.** When you are angry about *anything*, don't get behind the wheel. Take an extra few minutes before you get into your car to calm yourself or designate someone else to drive. If you are already in the car, make an effort to slow down instead of speeding up and pull off the road to collect yourself.

- **Find Soothing Diversions.** Always have a calming tape, CD, or radio station you like programmed in the car to find at a moment's notice. Listen to it and focus on the music or conver-

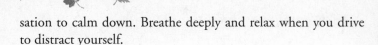

sation to calm down. Breathe deeply and relax when you drive to distract yourself.

- **Don't Take It Personally.** Think about the situation that angered you in a different, less negative way. Instead of believing that this driver is out to get you and you need to teach him or her a lesson, breathe and visualize the other driver driving far away from you, and don't look in their direction. Your anger will not help the situation.

You have nothing to prove while driving except that you can be a mature person in control of your car and your emotions.

# Thursday

*Family, Parent*

## If You Don't Like Your Child's Spouse

If you don't like your son-in-law or daughter-in-law, it can be very difficult to hide your feelings.

Even if this is not the person you would have chosen as a life partner for your child, save your sanity as you attempt to preserve your relationship with both your child and your child's spouse. Family accord is worth the effort.

- **Deal Directly.** Try to deal with your in-law directly and politely. Bypass your own child if there's an issue between the two of you. Do your best to be available to work it out and try not to put your son or daughter in the middle. Criticize your in-law to your child, and you risk your child choosing the spouse over you. Avoid creating a situation where your child has conflicting loyalties, and don't set up a win-lose situation in which you can lose.

- **Hear Without a Defensive Strategy.** Prepare yourself to hear what you may not want to hear without giving a defensive response. Sit and listen to what the in-law is upset about and share your thoughts on the problem. Begin this exchange with an open heart. Actually visualize your heart being open and receptive and protected. Do not accuse.

- **Intend to Get Along.** With your heart open and a noncritical mindset, feel deeply that you want to have the best relationship that is possible. Make your best, most sincere effort to reach out.

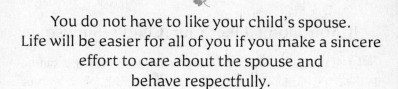

You do not have to like your child's spouse.
Life will be easier for all of you if you make a sincere
effort to care about the spouse and
behave respectfully.

*Friday*

*Partner*

# Get Back to "We"

When you cease to give what your relationship needs, it fails to flourish. It is during these times that people wonder, "What's wrong with him / her?"

It is normal for healthy relationships and marriages to go through phases. We need to be aware that we have the power to infuse humor, tenderness, vitality, interest, and joy into our relationships to make them more of what we want and need. When "life gets in the way," time pressures and stress from work, family obligations, and finances get the better of us, couples can lose sight of the importance of "we" as they focus only on "I." Remember, you're a couple . . . that means there are two of you.

- **Design a "We" Relationship.** Take what you like from your parents', family's, and friends' relationships and reject or revise what does not work for you. Just because your parents behaved a certain way is not enough of a reason for that behavior to be part of your relationship repertoire. Think creatively about new ways to relate to each other. Because your lives and your roles change, both as a couple and as individuals, revisit your "design" periodically.

- **Communicate Effectively.** Listen and learn to be descriptive instead of evaluative. Realize that communication needs will change over time. Talk about things other than your children, parents, or jobs.

- **Problem Solve Together.** If one of you has a problem with the other it becomes a problem for both of you. Find ways to work it out. Listen to your partner's approach.

- **Stay Connected.** Be aware of what is going on beneath the surface. Touch base with each other during the day, every day. Plan "alone" time as a couple. Put those dates on your calendar and *don't cancel.*

- **Don't Keep Score.** Your marriage is a team effort, not a team sport. Everyone needs encouragement. Scorekeepers do not belong in relationships.

Getting back to "we" is essential if you want
to reclaim a committed bond you once felt
for your partner.

# *Weekend*

*Well-Being*

## Always Connected

You may feel you are going crazy from all the noise in your head—actually, it's not *in* your head; it's all around you. It's your cell phone, office phone, home phone, and computer all buzzing, ringing, or vibrating at the same time. Four different sources of time eaters and noise makers that you feel compelled to check for messages. And to make things worse, those annoying lights and sounds won't go away until you do your duty.

- **Shut Down** . . . even for an hour. You could also simply turn everything off from five P.M. to eight P.M. (pick three hours of your own choosing). At the designated time, sit quietly at your desk or outdoors on a patio, or in the park, and check your messages, answering calls in whatever priority you like.

- **Take Control.** Try to minimize the modes of communication. Answering phone calls from several different phones and e-mails from several different addresses can be daunting. Why not leave a message on your home phone that says, "If you really want me to hear your message, leave it on my cell because I rarely check this line."

- **Be Silent.** Appreciate the quiet. Turn off the radio. Turn off the TV. Turn off the CD. Remove your iPod. Listen to the silence. You cannot imagine how intrusive all these sounds have become until you allow yourself to experience silence and feel in control of that silence. It's a beautiful thing. Try it!

## Disconnect to reconnect.

*Week 13*

# Teaching Kids Manners by Being Polite

In our rushed world, polite behavior is becoming the exception rather than the norm. According to a recent Associated Press–Ipsos Poll, people are ruder today than they were twenty-plus years ago. Parents are finding they have less and less time to teach basic character issues to their children, and manners are going by the wayside.

So how can we change this trend and get our kids back on track to being polite and respectful? The answer first lies in ourselves. As parents, adults, mentors, and guides, we need to model courteous behavior to others and to our children for lending a helping hand at home or for a job well done.

When they see you showing mutual respect to them as well as to others, your children will be more likely to behave respectfully and feel valued in the process.

- **Public Places Are Public.** Clean up and throw away cups and wrappers in movie theaters, toss newspapers in recycle bins at the train station, and pick up after your pet. And private conversations are just that—private. Find a quiet place to return cell phone calls and text messages and to discipline your children.

- **Respect Others.** Our seniors are a wealth of wisdom from a lifetime of experiences, and we are wise to honor their presence. Give help to the ill or distressed. Offer your seat (or the seat filled with your packages) to someone who looks like he or she could use it no matter what that person's age.

- **Learn Polite Listening.** Listen with attentiveness and avoid interrupting. Stop typing, take off headphones, turn off the TV, and put down the video game or PDA when talking or listening to someone. Interact and be present instead of tuning out.

- **Go Back to Kindergarten.** Mom, Dad and our teachers taught us the fundamentals that help us every day. Do you say, "Yes, please" and "No, thank you" or drop the courtesies? By saying hello when entering a room or meeting someone, and good-bye when leaving, you acknowledge others' presence and show that you value them. Holding a door for someone behind you and waiting in line at the movies instead of cutting in are the basics. Say thank you with a simple note. Let's acknowledge even the little things that people do.

Paying attention to our own courteous behavior
will become part of the legacy we give our children.

## Friendly Business

Some of the best friendships maintain themselves and deepen when friends go into business together. And some don't.

Before you put the "Open for Business" sign on the door, consider if your personalities are compatible for a business relationship. Also consider each person's areas of strengths and limitations, family and other life obligations, work ethic, business practices, and expectations. Many of the best friend-business partnerships have succeeded when each has a unique skill and their combined efforts make the perfect team.

Keep in mind that faults you overlook in friendship may be just the ones that can do you in as business partners. Someone who is chronically late will not be reliable to open the early morning doors of your new establishment. A short temper won't serve your business well if you are dealing with customer service issues. Not wanting to pitch in and get your hands dirty won't serve you well as you are building yourselves up. You want to be as sure as you can that both the friendship and the business flourish.

- **Get Clear on Who Does What.** Focus on each other's strengths and maximize abilities. Be honest about who is going to do what and why. Have realistic expectations for and about each other's contributions regarding creative input, work hours, finances, problem solving, decision making, etc. Write everything down and draw up a partnership agreement with a lawyer.

- **Keep the Friendship Going.** Plan to engage in some of the same friendship activities you always did before you started your business and develop new activities outside the office.

- **Leave the Scale at Home.** If you find you are carrying more weight than you feel is fair, instead of becoming resentful and calling in others to "take your side" or complain about your partner, discuss with her what is going on and how long this imbalance is expected to continue. As a general rule try to stay away from the scorekeeper's card.

Going into and maintaining a business with a friend is more complicated than the friendship itself. Pay attention to the needs of both.

## Shopaholic

You love to shop. No matter what is going on in your life, you feel better when you're in the mall or at a boutique. Just buying something new can lift your spirits.

That's a feeling lots of people share. But you may find yourself going on buying binges when you feel lonely, sad, depressed, or upset. After the binge you feel better, but soon afterward you feel guilty, ashamed, and anxious. You purchased more than you want or need, and you're embarrassed over your lack of control. How can you keep your sanity when you have these feelings that make you wonder if you are a shopaholic?

- **Trying to Fill a Void?** Pay attention to what you buy, when you buy, and whether you feel good during and after you buy. It is possible that you are trying to make up with purchases for some emptiness you feel inside. That just won't work.

- **Are You Denying?** Avoiding consequences of your purchases by not opening bills, hiding purchases from friends or family members, or lying about how you came to own these items can indicate a shopping problem.

- **Listen** . . . to what you _really_ need. Know that you can change your perception of what buying can do for you. This is really a self-esteem and anxiety issue, which you can explore. Tune in to what's going on inside.

If you believe you are a shopaholic, talk with someone who can help you deal with the feelings of emptiness in healthful and productive ways.

## Advocate, Don't Alienate

Your child needs some extra help at school—some support. And the school personnel are neither on top of it nor behind you. You know the answer to the question, "If you are not there for your child, who is?" And you are doing your best to be there.

At this point in your child's life, she is just too young to advocate for herself. It is up to you. Unless you do a good job securing the services she needs, your child's school experience is going to be less than optimal. "Working the system" requires patience, determination, a folder of *very* complete notes on who said what to whom and when, a dose of charm, and a lot of sanity.

- **You're the One.** You know your child better than anyone else. Present your child to the professionals with all her strengths, as well as the areas in which she needs support. Let them know how their involvement can have an overwhelmingly positive impact on your child.

- **Find at Least One Professional Ally.** Designate someone in the school system as your point person and keep in touch with him on a regular basis to monitor the progress of your request or the services required. Call or e-mail when you know it's best for him and give him reasonable time to respond. If the communication lags, keep on him. There is a fine line between being aware, involved, and persistent, and being perceived as a pest.

- **Lead with Empathy.** Understand that there's lots of red tape to deal with and that some cases fall through the cracks. You want to be sure your child's need does not, so make requests and avoid demands. Offer to help in any way you can to make the system work in your favor. Try this route instead of becoming adversarial.

You are your child's advocate and can work in concert with the school system to achieve your (and its) goals. Persistence is the key.

# Dating Again

Dating again after some time off—like a twenty-year marriage—is *not* like riding a bicycle. You can't just get back on and go; you have to learn it all over again because you're in a different stage of life.

When you were younger, there were no kids, ex-spouses, health concerns, work stressors, travel agendas, visitation schedules, home repairs, or aging parents to think about. How do you do this dating thing now when you have a body that has birthed three kids, crow's-feet, and sagging parts, not to mention a hectic life?

- **Work on Self-Image.** Do you feel good about you? Your physical appearance, accomplishments, the way you conduct your relationships? Can you work on a few things? Is it time to get healthy, move forward in your career, have more patience with your teens, and update your look so you're not stuck in the nineties?

- **Can You Calendar It In?** You're busy, it's true. Life is full. But Saturday nights can't be bustling. Dating takes some energy and focus, so free up some time. Should you join an interest group, go on blind dates, sign up for online dating or join a singles group? Start a dating plan of attack.

- **Work on the Law of Attraction.** What qualities does this person have to have? Date only someone with your must-have values. Instead of requiring a certain income bracket, what you really value is financial security and someone who doesn't overspend (unless, of course, it's to send you flowers). Make adjustments if your list does not attract the right people. Date those you might not have considered before.

Dating at midlife takes a bit of courage and willingness to look at yourself, make changes within, and be open to all possibilities.

*Weekend*

*Midlife, Single, Family*

## Writing an Ethical Will

You are midway through your life and have learned a lot. Hopefully you have a will. But have you considered writing an ethical will? Ethical wills convey your values. They can be an effective way to transmit your personal thoughts about what is important to you, what you have learned from life, and what you wish for when you are no longer here.

You can write about specific incidents that were never discussed or resolved, offer blessings, or express forgiveness to those whom you were unable to reach out to during your lifetime. Even if you are childless, this is a caring way to teach future generations in your family and community about what is meaningful to you.

- **Say What's in Your Heart.** Some people want their ethical wills to be private, only to be seen by individual family members in the form of a letter, audiotape or videotape, while others hope to have it read to the whole family or community. Your ethical will is your personal reflection, so communicate to whom you wish from your heart.

- **Say It with Depth.** Write about your feelings and things that are emotionally significant in your life. Writing about a difficult period of your life or a time when you were faced with a troubling decision gives your ethical will significance and transmits the benefits you received from having survived the trauma.

- **Say It for Others.** Your writing will also pass on life lessons you learned to the ones who come after you. It has the potential to

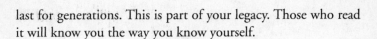

last for generations. This is part of your legacy. Those who read it will know you the way you know yourself.

Ethical wills can be healing both to the person writing and to the person reading.

## Roommates at Midlife

You've decided to move in with a friend to share expenses and companionship. Typically only young singles would do this, but today more and more midlife women are sharing households and giving each other support.

As two complete women, you certainly want to honor each other's individuality and respect each other's lives. Try not to be two hens competing for the same nest, but have ways to live comfortably together.

- **We All Need Our Personal Space.** Plan personal time when you're all alone in your place or have lunch out with another friend when there's too much togetherness. If her family comes over for dinner and you don't want to hear the "old stories" again, plan a night out at the movies. Find ways not to offend if you bow out by having the understanding that you both need time apart. A shared cup of tea works wonders before you close the door and escape with a good book.

- **Communicate, Listen and Learn.** When quirky habits get to be big irritants, discussing them in a nonconfrontational way as they arise can nip the problem in the bud. Remember to listen and learn how you can both be more considerate of each other. Try and let go of the "little" annoying habits that truly are little and focus on the real button pushers. We all know by now that you can't change someone, so accept what you can.

- **Use the Team Approach with Chores.** Sticking to a structured routine with household chores can become mundane. By pitching in and lending a hand even when it's not your territory, you show your roommate that you are a team player.

You can make a home at any age.

## Too Much TV

You are addicted to television. There are hours and hours of television to watch because you tape or TiVo all your favorite shows and you don't want to get behind.

It isn't all that hard to realize why you and your partner rarely talk about anything important anymore and your sex life is dwindling. Your sanity needs saving to get you out of the vicious cycle of watching TV, falling asleep, waking up, going to work, and coming home again to watch TV.

- **Non-TV Nights.** Put some limits on TV watching by going without your clicker one or two nights each week. Use that time to connect intellectually, emotionally, and physically.

- **Shake Things Up.** Do something different to turn your evening plan around. When you arrive home from work, have a romantic dinner and make love. Then, in your robes, make some tea and watch an hour of your TV shows together, cuddled on the couch.

- **Give the Taping a Rest.** Unless a program is a "must see," view shows only when scheduled on TV. This will cut down on your to-view list.

You need to manage TV so it does not interfere with your ability to spend quality time together to talk, relax, and have a meaningful sexual relationship.

*Friends, Family*

# Helping People Who Are Ungrateful

It is rare when helping someone is not a good thing. In fact, most of the time, people you help appreciate what you do for them, and you feel good about having the opportunity to be of assistance. There are so many people in your community and in the larger world who can use your help and who will benefit from what you can offer.

So if you find you are in a position of helping someone who is ungrateful and quite possibly undeserving, think twice about what you are doing. Have you given to this person before and felt drained and underappreciated? Have they had several opportunities to recognize your efforts but instead criticize anything you do for them?

- **Limit Your Assistance.** There are some situations when you are "obliged" to help (caring for parents, for instance) but even then, you can limit the way and kind of assistance you offer. We do not help in order to be appreciated, yet it is important to realize whether you are hanging in there waiting to be appreciated in a way that is not likely to happen. Perhaps this person is taking you for granted or taking advantage of you, your good nature, or your generosity. Recognize that you have choices regarding how and with whom to offer your help.

- **Give with No Return.** Try to understand why a person is unable to be responsive or receptive or grateful to you or for your effort. Lower your expectations, and before you do anything more for him, know that there will be nothing in return.

Place yourself wisely. There is only so much
of you to go around.

*Parent, Family, Friends, Community*

# Death of a Child

Having a child die is most parents' greatest fear. When it happens, you feel as if part of yourself has died and you will never be the same. Both are correct.

How you recover depends on many factors, including your attitude about life in general and your life in particular, your relationship with your child, the circumstances surrounding the death of your child, your belief system, your support system, and time.

- **How to Tell.** People in your life will want to console you and often want to know the details. But you may feel drained each time you go over the story. Certainly, sharing the particulars of what happened can be helpful, but consider, in a quiet moment, writing what happened and sending this recounting to your friends and family in the form of a letter. The result is that everyone has the same information and you can conserve your energy and spirit.

- **"Natural" Healing.** Surround yourself with fragrances and aromatherapy that can help you with the intense feelings of grief. Flower remedies, such as Rescue Remedy, honeysuckle, bleeding heart, and borage, can be helpful at times of intense grieving (and other times as well.) Often people take medication to ease their pain, and for some this is helpful. Very often, though, people can stay drugged for longer than necessary. Incorporate a natural approach.

- **Contact a Compassionate Friends Group** . . . near you or visit them online. Their mission is to connect and comfort those who are grieving, and they know how to console those dealing with the loss of a child (unique from all other losses). Other parents whose children have died can relate to you in ways that nobody else can.

- **In Remembrance.** Consider having a memorial service at some point as a tribute to your child. You may wish to establish a fund in his or her memory, or dedicate a park bench, swing set, books, or reading space in a library.

You can keep your children's spirit alive and with you as you think of them, talk about them, and remember the way they touched your life.

## Surviving Being Dumped

Being dumped is the pits. You think about the relationship backward and forward, analyzing interactions, conversations, sex, family life, and everything else. You feel you are a terrible person and blame the breakup on yourself. If you had only behaved differently, you would still have the relationship intact. You're left with terrible sadness and hopelessness.

But you can have hope, and you will prevail. First and foremost, take care of yourself; allow yourself the time to heal. And only be with people who support you at this time. As you go forward, to keep your sanity:

- **Put a Cap on It.** Take some time to get yourself together. Allow yourself to think about this person only during a specific time every day, say between seven and eight P.M. That means you cannot talk about it at other times and must force yourself to do other things when you are out of the focus-on-the-breakup zone. If you are thinking and obsessing when it's not the time, put it off till tomorrow.

- **Write from Your Heart.** Keep a journal of how you feel, what you think, and how you perceive both the future and the past.

- **Act "As If."** This approach works wonders. Act as if you are further along than you are. Focus on the knowledge that, given time, you'll be able to look back on your experience and take important lessons from it. Tell yourself that you will learn from

this experience and that your life will be changed for the better. Know in your heart that this is true.

- **Be Open.** Learn what you could have done differently and what your ex-partner could have done differently, so you can use that information to help you with future relationships. Tell yourself you are a good person to have a relationship with and get yourself back in the game of life when you are ready.

- **Don't Hide.** Time flies by and you have no idea where it goes. So get out there and be a part of life. Check in with your friends frequently. If they think you have been carrying this too far, listen to them and give yourself a timeline to stick to before you allow yourself to begin to feel better.

Trust that you will not only survive but thrive and that being dumped, although hurtful to your ego and your heart, will not destroy you.

# Step Through the Volunteer Door and Walk Back into the Work World

If you are a stay-at-home mom and thinking about getting back to your career or something new, consider volunteering. Think about what your past experience is and what you want to do going forward.

Your place of worship or town charities may or may not be the venue that places you back in the professional setting you yearn for. Seek out places where you can give your time and save your sanity by piquing your interests and helping you learn something new for the future.

- **Come to Terms.** Do you want to take a volunteer position similar to a job you left many years ago? If you believe that volunteering in a capacity that you had previously received a salary for seems insulting, think again. On the other hand, if you want to explore different work opportunities, realize that you may be low woman on the totem pole at your volunteer job, but starting on that learning curve is your first step to moving forward.

- **Gain a Renewed Familiarity** . . . with many facets of the work world that evolved while you were involved with raising your children. And you'll have the flexibility to call meetings and do work when it is convenient for you. Regain your confidence as you rise through the ranks and take on positions that use your skills and exhibit leadership.

- **Make New Contacts.** Establish relationships in a field you already knew or are beginning to know. One of these could help you in the future.

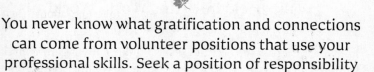

You never know what gratification and connections can come from volunteer positions that use your professional skills. Seek a position of responsibility that helps to remind you of your professional self!

## Hypochondria? It Makes Me Sick

For many people, focusing on, and complaining about, their health is a full-time job.

These are people for whom taking care of themselves—eating right, exercising, pampering, making scads of doctor's appointments—is all that matters. To them and to you. Or didn't you notice?

While these people (we call them hypochondriacs) are often intelligent and well read on medical issues, they can't fathom that a headache isn't the onset of a brain tumor, or that mild thirst isn't the beginning of debilitating diabetes. A strain in the chest while playing tennis? Heart attack, of course. Razor burn? Cancer, clearly.

Perhaps this behavior describes you. If so, ask yourself if your intense concern about your health is rooted in a recent illness, or an episode with a loved one. (Many relatives of a recently ill or deceased person become morbidly concerned with diagnosis, treatment, and cures.) If you have exaggerated health anxiety, you probably know that it is becoming increasingly difficult to function. Here's the road to a cure.

- **Accept Your Imbalance.** The feelings of distress you have are real and must be addressed. You can reduce your anxiety, but you must accept it fully in order to erase it.

- **Seek Counsel.** Cognitive-behavioral treatments (often with medication) seem to work well for most people who have hypochondria and are willing to engage a mental health professional to help them along their path.

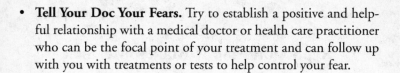

- **Tell Your Doc Your Fears.** Try to establish a positive and help-ful relationship with a medical doctor or health care practitioner who can be the focal point of your treatment and can follow up with you with treatments or tests to help control your fear.

If you are limiting your life by focusing on your illness, think about whether this is helping you in your quest to live a healthy life.

*Friends, Family, Partner, Work*

## Giving Criticism

Being criticized isn't much fun. But sometimes we are in the position of needing to give critical feedback to people who are important to us. How do we do it while maintaining our sense of self? And can we put ourselves in their shoes so we truly understand the impact of what we are saying?

- **Be Aware** . . . of how what you say will be received. This is as important as what you say (perhaps more important). If you are going to the trouble of criticizing someone, you owe it to yourself and to him or her that what you say will be heard in a positive way.

- **Be Kind, Generous, Respectful, and Fair.** If you are antagonistic, wait to say what you are going to say until you are not at risk for being rude, insulting, or insensitive. Share your own experiences if they are like the ones you are talking about. Admit that you, too, have had difficulty with this issue.

- **Be Specific and Avoid Generalities.** "I saw you bite Joey on the playground," not, "You are such a terrible child and a bully; nobody will ever want to play with you." Ask yourself how you would respond if you were criticized in a combative way.

- **Be Patient.** It takes time to change and it is difficult to hear criticism, especially from someone you respect. Once you have said what you need to say, leave it alone.

- **Be Alone.** Don't embarrass the person by criticizing him or her in front of other people. Discuss what you need to say in private. Unless you are witnessing something that must be stopped (abuse, acts of prejudice or injustice), confine your comments to a private place.

If you are criticizing someone, be thoughtful and concerned about how she or he will hear you.

# Fringe Benefits:
# Dating Someone with Children

If you happen to date someone with children, look closely at the relationship of the family that could someday be part of your own.

It is essential—and ultimately educational—to observe the relationship that exists between your possible future mate and your possible future stepchildren. Whatever your initial thoughts about this relationship may be, keep in mind that being a parent profoundly affects a person and his or her priorities. Notice how much time they spend together, what their interests are, and what's important to them. You will develop an intimate knowledge of these people to a far greater degree than in any other relationship you've entered.

- **Can You Really Love These Kids?** Ask yourself if you are someone who could ultimately accept someone else's children into your heart and your life. To love them means to accept them even when they're rude, self-focused, sloppy, and defiant. This is different from liking them, which is hard to do all of the time, because surely this type of behavior is not likable. If you don't think you can really love them, or if you find yourself forever leery of the proposition, don't attempt a relationship with anyone who has children.

- **Can You Live with Them?** While it is true that children, after going through the breakup of their parents' relationship, need more (not fewer) adults in their lives, it is equally true that they

need to be surrounded by open, loving adults who truly want them around.

- **Can You Be a Support?** Your mate will need a partnership in the wonderful, startling, and challenging role of parent. Are you up for the job?

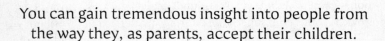

You can gain tremendous insight into people from the way they, as parents, accept their children.

## Long-Distance Grandparents

When families lived near each other, grandchildren would drop by their grandparents' homes after school or on the weekends, or stay overnight. Many intergenerational families lived under one roof, so when Grandma was around (which she usually was), she provided child care, supervision, and so much treasured wisdom.

Today many grandparents live far from their children and grandchildren. When they come for a visit, some grandparents roll up their sleeves and get right into the mix of things and some do not, expecting to spend only a few hours with the children instead of a few days. Many grandparents feel they do not have the stamina to keep up with their grandkids, while others will take the children on trips and have private, special time with them.

You may feel resentful that your parents or in-laws are neither spending every free moment with the children nor helping with your child care issues. It is essential that the generations communicate what they need and are willing and able to offer. If you believe that your parents' visit should be 24/7 with your children, then you need to give them an idea of what you have in mind and a chance to think about what works for them. Each of you has expectations, so see if they are anywhere near the other's.

- **Appreciate Any Time** . . . your parents or in-laws can spend with your children.

- **They're Only Human and a Bit Older.** Know what is possible and reasonable before you request that your parents participate

in taking care of your children. Going to the movies and dinner may work better than a theme park.

- **Getting to Know You, Again.** If they have not seen one another for a while, allow for some transition time so the children and the grandparents can get used to each other again.

- **Prepare the Children** . . . for what they can and cannot do with Grandma and Grandpa before they come to visit.

- **Invest in a Computer Camera.** If you can, hook up a camera to your parents' computer and your children's computer so they can have a more "face-to-face" interaction with one another between visits.

Give long-distance grandparents and the kids
bonding time so their relationship
can grow with every visit.

# Rejuvenate Naked with Your Lover

Why does the spark with your love slip away? It used to be so easy to get in the mood and feel sexy, romantic, and connected, but now it is a bit of a chore. Maybe it's because you are raising kids, multitasking, working, overscheduled, crazed, and otherwise trying to save your sanity in this hectic world.

It is time to change your attitude and put sensuality on the front instead of the back burner (if it is on any burner at all!). Believing that you can still have a sensuous bond (through mind, body, and emotional connection) with the person you love means you are halfway to making that connection happen in real time and real life.

- **Get Comfortable with Naked.** Stop turning off the lights and then getting undressed. Do you think your partner doesn't know what your body looks like? Despite your beautiful imperfections (which we all have), your partner still finds you desirable. Get comfortable with your own nakedness and then undress with confidence.

- **Do Naked Things Together.** Do things at home that put you in close proximity to each other when you are scantily clad or naked. Take a bath with some wonderful aromatic bath salts and just linger in the water together, touching each other and talking about whatever comes to your mind (that is *not* related to work, your kids, or your parents).

- **Sleep Naked.** Give yourselves a chance to lie next to each other and cuddle while feeling each other's skin. Explore or not. Just be aware of the way you feel in each other's arms and break out of the usual mold of those baggy PJs or ripped sleep shirts.

Admire your own and your partner's body and enjoy the chances to be together, skin to skin.

*Friends, Family, Partner, Work, Well-Being*

## To Err Is Human, To Repent Divine

This may come as a surprise to you, but you are not perfect.

We *all* make mistakes on occasion. If you're like every other human, you may make an unfortunate decision or a hurtful remark, perhaps unintentionally. You may put your foot in your mouth, do something that was not considerate, or snap at someone if you are having a bad day.

Whatever mistake you may make, big or small, immediately assume responsibility for it and try, earnestly, to understand the effects of what you did. Do whatever you can to make the situation right. Apologize, make restitution, offer assistance. If you follow any religious guidelines, you will probably try to make amends in a way that is comfortable for you morally—but do it, and quickly.

- **Don't Deny Your Act.** The biggest part of taking responsibility is acceptance. Once you accept that you did, in fact, make a mistake, you are one step closer to becoming a better, stronger person.

- **A Mistake Is Not an Obituary.** You are human, alive, and worthy. Rectify the mistake and live on!

- **Avoid Repeating the Mistake.** Find ways to act or react differently.

- **Do Many Acts of Kindness** . . . so you can focus on how you are going to offset the balance of what you did or said. This will make it easier for you to move ahead with your life.

Choose actions, deeds, and words that will make
you proud of yourself.

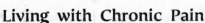

# Living with Chronic Pain

Are you living with chronic pain? You want to be present with the people you love but your constant aches often interfere with your ability to do just that.

Even though you have changed your life in many dramatic ways, listen to your body. You need to find ways to save your sanity while you live a quality life with chronic pain.

- **You Are Not Alone** . . . even though it feels that way. There are people in your life who can offer a helping hand so you can preserve your energy and avoid some of the more difficult activities.

- **Savor Your Good Days.** Appreciate when you feel well and when you don't. Try to stay away from despair on your off days. Know that there will be better times and that you will do what you can with the energy and purpose you have available to you.

- **Try a New Approach.** Engage others who successfully deal with alternative approaches or interventions such as acupuncture, Tai Chi, cognitive therapy, visualization.

- **Keep a Sense of Humor.** Be the first one to make a joke about your inability to do something that used to come so easily. If it takes a long time to get out of a chair and across a room, ask your child to time you to see if you can break yesterday's speed record. Attitude is everything in living your life the best way you can.

Focusing on the pain will deter you from focusing on what you can do and appreciate in your life.

# Pressure to Find the Perfect Mate

If you are invited to one more wedding of your peers, you will just scream! Of course you are thrilled for them and the fact that they found happiness. When, you wonder (and your mother continues to ask), will it be your turn?

Personally, I remember that pressure. I was "late to the altar," as they say. By the time I married, some of my friends were already into their second marriages! Keep your sanity by releasing the pressure on yours and everyone else's expectations of the day you walk down the aisle.

- **Be Your Gatekeeper.** Let "interested folks" know that you appreciate their concern and that you, too, think about meeting someone and having a house with a white picket fence. But you are not obsessed about it and you would appreciate their backing off.

- **Can't Force It.** Reinforce your belief that this is not something you can make happen. Love comes along when it's time. So prepare the way.

- **Continue On.** You're accomplished, like your job, do interesting things, and have good friends (even if they are all getting married). Continue to live your life and make it as meaningful and special as you can.

Other people's pressure is usually about them and their own fears. Stay far away from their "stuff."

# Coming to Terms with Your Child's Disability

When you discover that your child has a disability, you are in shock. You want to run to find the person who will tell you what you are waiting to hear; that the first news was really a mistake and your child is OK. But that doesn't happen.

You need to buckle your seat belt as you step onto an emotional roller coaster. As you begin to adapt to the fact that your child has a disability, you will understand that, yes, he or she *does* belong in your family. Your life journey shifts and you develop a pattern that will become your new normalcy.

- **Adapt with Time** . . . to life with a child who is different from the one you had fantasized about and expected.

- **Let Your New Parent Emerge.** Give yourself a chance to discover who you are as the parent of this child, and get to know this child as he or she is.

- **Be a Student.** Let this child teach you what you need to know about yourself.

When you find out your child has a disability, you may feel your life has ended. Give yourself the chance to begin anew with a child you have yet to know.

# Disciplining Someone Else's Child

This is a dilemma for mothers today. When you have a play date over who gets out of hand, do you discipline a child who is not yours? The matter might be compounded if it's your friend's child or a playmate that your child really likes. If someone else's child is upsetting your child, teaching him not-so-desirable behavior or language, or wrecking your house after you just cleaned up, what is the action you should take? And what is socially acceptable by your peers and the child's parents?

- **Focus on Your Children.** Bite your tongue and let go of behavior that is unacceptable to you unless your child is in jeopardy or can get hurt. You pick and choose your own battles with your kids, so bring this a step further with other kids. Holding back may be harder to do when your moral ethics are violated and you don't want you child exposed to behavior you don't condone. Use your best judgment, but a general rule is to try to refrain from disciplining someone else's children. And *never* put a hand on someone else's child. The best solution is to reinforce your rules to your kids. Talk to them after the play date, letting them know that their friend has different parents and a different set of rules.

- **On Your Turf, State the Rules.** If you need to say something because the behavior persists and is presenting a problem for the welfare of your own children, let the child know about your rules. This is easier to do when the play date is in your home. You can say, "This is the way we play and treat each other in our

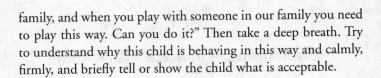

family, and when you play with someone in our family you need to play this way. Can you do it?" Then take a deep breath. Try to understand why this child is behaving in this way and calmly, firmly, and briefly tell or show the child what is acceptable.

- **Avoid Problem Places and Situations.** Get together outside your house for play dates or go over to the other child's house where you are operating under those rules. Also ask kids to come over right *before* you clean the house and not right *after*. If the problem persists or the behavior is repeated, question whether you want to foster this friendship for your child.

Don't assume your rules should apply to everyone else's children.

# Breaking Out of the Mom Mode

All moms have to face it. When your last child is around twelve or thirteen years old and cranky all the time, his stares no longer melt your heart the way they used to, you're in a transition. You're still Mom, but instead of being there for all your kids' needs, your primary role is probably taxi driver. You may start hearing a little voice inside you say, "Where do I go from here?"

Some women begin making steps to break out of the mom mode a little bit at a time in preparation for the empty nest, and some wait till their last child is out the door at eighteen. You may be afraid, tired, or just plain at a loss regarding how or what to develop at this point of your life, but it's a good time to start exploring and doing some research.

Not to worry, you will never stop being a mom. It's just that the role of mom no longer needs to be your primary way of defining yourself.

- **Get into Prep Mode.** Preparing to shed your mom persona a little bit at a time when your kids hit their teens is a good way to transition. But if you've waited until your kids are adults, it's never too late to make the switch.

- **Change Is Inevitable, Change Is Good.** Before you change, you need to believe it is possible to think about yourself in a new way, a way you never have before. You may have had opportunities pass you by because you were caring for your children. If this is the case, no wonder you still try to hang on to the mom mode; it is what you have known for all your adult life, and you

did it well. The problem is, that role is no longer doing you, your family, or your partner any good, because you need to grow, too. Open up to new possibilities.

- **Wave a Magic Wand.** If there were no restraints (age, financial, physical, geographic, etc.), what would you like to do with your life? Think about what you are good at and which skills as a mom you would like to transfer to another realm. Give yourself the opportunity to see yourself doing something different from being a mom. Allow all ideas to flow no matter how out of sight they seem. You have to get the ones out of sight before you can get your sights on the ones that are right.

- **Get into Explore Mode.** Give yourself permission to explore a range of ideas to see how you might begin getting information, training, experience, or whatever you need to become more aware of what is needed to accomplish something new.

Transitioning from mom to your next role where your talents and skills will be discovered and used requires a desire for adventure. Go for it.

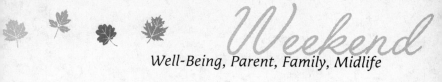

*Well-Being, Parent, Family, Midlife*

# Finding Your Passion as Your Children Grow Up

For many women, putting everyone else first is just the way life is. You may have stopped a career or pursued another one when you had children. Whatever you did, the child rearing years were part of "sequencing" your interests, passions, and careers to handle all that was going on in your life.

But as the kids go onto school, become teens, go off to college, and move on with their lives, you realize it may be the time to put yourself first for a change. At midlife you may feel restlessness, and maybe for the first time in your life, you can finally explore your passions. This is the time to consider the rest of your life and what you would love to do with it.

- **Rediscover.** Integrate as many of the things you once loved back into your life: sports, the arts, more time with spouse and friends, travel.

- **Explore.** If you're not sure what your passions are, take classes, read up, and try new things. You may find something you love or rule out something that isn't what you love to do.

- **Keep Up.** If you can't commit to a new career, dabble in your area of expertise through meaningful volunteer experiences. When the time comes, you will be able to dedicate yourself to projects that are deeper and more complex.

You will feel more prepared to let your children go and to continue to embrace the things you love as you discover new interests and passions.

## Preparing for Surgery

Discovering that you need to have surgery can be a sanity-saving challenge. Whether elective or mandatory, the idea of "going under the knife" (or laser) can be daunting. There are so many horror stories about hospitals and germs and, well, you can really make yourself crazy just anticipating the event.

Think about some ways to keep yourself focused on your good health.

- **Be Prepared.** One of the most difficult aspects of surgery is not knowing what to expect. Talk to a few people who have had the procedure to learn from their experiences. Ask pertinent questions. "How long will I be out of commission?" "What will the recovery process be like?" "What will I be able to do for myself and what will I need help with?" "Are there any particular foods that will inhibit or help healing?" Search for the hospitals and doctors who specialize in this surgery and find out how many of these procedures they have done. When you select your doctor, ask about the different variables that affect recovery.

- **If You Can, Time It Right.** Coordinate the surgery with the schedule that works best for your life and those who will be caring for you as you recover. If you have a choice, try not to schedule surgery during the first week of your children's school year or when your best friend and helpful neighbor is on vacation.

- **Be Fit** . . . and in the best physical shape you can be in before elective surgery. Any surgery is an assault on your body, and you need to have yourself in the best condition possible beforehand.

- **Before Surgery.** Visualize the doctors being rested, focused, and comfortable with performing your surgery. Bring whatever pictures, symbols, totems or good luck charms you feel will be useful. Listen to a calming tape or CD to relax your body and mind (*before* you are administered a relaxation drug) so that you see yourself coming through this successfully. "Talk" with your body.

A good before-surgery exercise is to visually embrace the parts of your body that are going to be cut and release them with love.

## Commuting

You sit in traffic or on the train and feel like you're wasting precious time. And the miles day in and day out are wearing on you and adding to your stress.

If moving closer to work is not an option, how do you save your sanity knowing that your commute may only seem worse with time?

- **Don't Add to the Stress.** Put down your cell phone, PDA, and laptop when it's over the top. It's good to start your day and get organized, but not if you're fielding all sorts of messages and it's driving you crazy (not to mention unsafe if you're behind the wheel and you're e-mailing or texting). Get some books on tape that you can comfortably listen to while traveling. If you're on the train or bus, how about putting some meditation music on your iPod and finding a few minutes to reflect at the start or end of the day.

- **The Road Less Traveled.** For a different perspective, change where and how you commute. If you are on the train, bus, or ferry daily, opt to drive in once a week, or carpool with some friends, sharing coffee, conversation, and tunes.

- **Rearrange Your Schedule.** Join a gym, tennis, or swim club and miss the morning commute. Or get in early, and walk in a park or by the water for your morning exercise. Schedule a match after work and miss the evening rush hour. Vary before- or after-

work activities so your commuting schedule shifts and you don't face the same mundane routine.

Make the most of your commuting time. That may mean using it to unwind or to finish something so when you get home you are free to relax.

# When Someone You Love Has Anorexia

If someone you love is starving themselves, it is important that you be a source of support.

Often, preteen and teenage girls and boys begin to show signs of anorexia, such as losing a lot of weight, to the point where they are extremely skinny. They fear getting fat and they become obsessed with their bodies. Their body image becomes distorted as they look in the mirror and see a fat person reflected back at them. They exercise more than normal, do not eat or eat very little (and often not in front of anyone else), will often become obsessed with food and take laxatives so they do not gain any weight. They will also cook for others but not eat with them or sit down for family gatherings around food.

- **Get Informed.** Do research and learn the causes, telltale signs, and heath risks.

- **Think About Your Attitude** . . . toward your body and those in your family and in society. Think about the value you place on appearance and weight and the messages you send about body image.

- **Don't Force Feed.** Observe this person without getting in their face and yelling or making every conversation about food. Avoid saying, "You must eat."

- **Offer Support.** Talk together and privately about what you observe and your unease. Be honest about your concerns and offer to be of help in finding an expert in eating disorders, particularly anorexia. If there is resistance, anger, or denial that anything is wrong, engage a doctor, school counselor, or therapist to help this person get the help they need. With the right support, you can help them battle their eating disorder.

Anorexia is a serious condition and does not go away on its own. Be a support to your loved one or find the help they'll need.

# Your Child's College Rejection

You haven't waited at the mailbox since your boyfriend went away to camp in 1975. But now you're on a first-name basis with the mailman and waiting to hear whether your child will be accepted to his first-choice college.

If the rejection comes, it can be a devastating blow to your teen's ego. Give your child time to process what happened while offering as much support as you can. Save your sanity and help your child to save his as you help him come to terms with what may be his first official rejection in life.

- **How Invested Are You?** First, think carefully and honestly about how you want your child to receive an acceptance and whether the rejection is viewed as a reflection on you. Is this rejection viewed as a "failure" of either your parenting skills or your child's intelligence? Keep in mind it is your kid who applied to college and not you. While you can feel for him and be disappointed on his behalf rather than at him, be careful that you don't feel rejected. This is not about you.

- **Your Actions May Dictate the Response.** Though it may be too late for this, your actions and attitudes are extremely important. If you have been putting pressure on your child to be top in the class and to attend a competitive college, then it's going to be harder to console your child and help him get through this.

- **Open His Eyes to Other Options.** Remind him that the college admission process is often based on the "making of a class," bal-

ancing the incoming class with students from different parts of the country or with different skills and talents. Share times when you were rejected in life. Encourage your child to be resilient and look at his second or third choice. It is up to you to reinforce other choices. If your child does not get into any schools, suggest some other life options for this year and let him know he can try again.

Your child's college rejection is not a rejection of you. Be there as steadfastly for your child as you can, and let him know he is a great kid and there are other choices.

# Romance, Anyone?

Most of us are deeply disturbed when romance dissipates. We know it happens to others, but we never thought it could happen to us.

Sexual intimacy wanes when people become involved with things other than their partners. Work projects and the kids take precedence over spending time to connect with your love. Do you give yourself the time and energy to feel attractive to your partner? Do you allow yourself the space to be playful and sexual? If not, get back on track.

It is important to realize your relationship may be in a readjustment stage and needs more attention to bring back the romance.

- **Touch.** Human touch is therapeutic and healing. It's no wonder that massage therapy is so popular today. Find ways to make skin-to-skin contact with your partner both in and out of the bedroom. Holding hands is a nice way to stay in "touch." Give your partner a foot rub or a head and neck massage after a tough day. Don't underestimate the power of cuddling.

- **Play.** Recess for grown-ups should be a requirement. But it's no fun to play alone. Arrange regular "play dates" with your partner and laugh. Don't just attend events or engage in a competitive sport together. Do whatever is fun for you and your partner—kayaking, antiquing, or eating cotton candy at a summer fair. Choose activities that make you both smile. Sometimes the simple things—building a sand castle on the beach or splashing each other while washing the car—bring out the most giggles. This sense of everyday playfulness will naturally spill over into your intimate life and make it more fun as well.

- **Be Spontaneous.** Unpredictability can make romantic sparks fly. Surprise your partner with something that gets them in the mood for love. And don't overlook the little things that make the romance last throughout the day. Leave an "I love you" note on the car dash or send a text message at lunch with an intimate thought that no one else can see.

- **Let Go of Anger.** Understand that unresolved anger and feelings of disappointment can get in the way of emotional or physical intimacy. Decide what you can release, and address what you have not been willing to examine. Get rid of the frown lines by confronting those issues with your significant other, get on the other side of anger, start enjoying life, and bring back romance.

Changes in your relationship need not signal an end to romance and sexual intimacy. Instead, make adjustments and create a new beginning of closeness and togetherness.

*Well-Being, Friends, Family*

## Making a Tough Decision

Sometime during your life you are faced with making tough decisions. You know, the kind you never want to make, that make you unsure which is the best way to go.

The doctors tell you there is something terribly "wrong" with your fetus . . . what to do? You receive a health diagnosis that requires serious measures and you need to decide among various options. Your loved one is on life support and you need to decide whether to consent to end his life. Tough issues and even tougher choices.

- **Allow Yourself Space.** Working within the parameters of the situation, give yourself as much time as you can to gather your thoughts and as much information as you can.

- **Ask for Guidance and Listen Closely.** Rally informed people about your concerns. Talk with a compassionate and sympathetic religious leader who can help you remain grounded. Discuss your situation and listen. If you ask trusted guides, you will hear an echo or theme or pattern in what they are saying. Decide if their advice is justified. If you are leaning toward one choice, you'll know whether they support you or whether there is judgment in their advice. If they differ from you, look into your heart to know if their opinion is a truth you might have overlooked.

- **Steer Clear of Second Guessing** . . . or wondering what it would have been like had you chosen another option. Reassure

yourself that given where you were at the time, with the information you had, you made the very best decision you could.

Know that limbo is a tough place to be, and that once you make a decision, you can go forward.

# When Your Parents
# Disappoint You as Grandparents

A friend of mine uses the phrase "parent reliability quotient" to describe how much or how little she can depend on her parents. You may be someone who relies on your parents for money, a place to live, and guidance as they do or don't bail you out of all types of situations. Sometimes you may invoke your own parent reliability quotient when it comes to your expectations and disappointment related to child care.

Bonds between parents and their adult children can be cemented or fractured around child care issues. Years ago, generations of one family lived nearby one another and grandparents often took care of grandchildren. They were often important contributors to their grandchildren's welfare. Today, with families living far from one another, it is difficult to have a reliable, organized arrangement for grandparental help with the children. And is that even a reasonable expectation?

With so many grandparents working and having their own active lives, how can adult children foster a closer grandparent-grandchild bond (and expect free baby-sitting in the process)?

- **It's Their Life.** It's hard to imagine, but understand that your parents have a life of their own to live and that being available to you and your children on a regular basis may not be possible. Discuss what will work so you can all plan and know what to expect.

- **Keep Them Posted.** If your parents have been out of the loop for a while and are not in regular touch, engage them into your life with specific and important information about your children—their interests, likes, dislikes, allergies, school subjects, teachers, friends, and after-school schedules. Hopefully, they'll get the hint and be more involved.

- **Come to Terms** . . . with your parents if they are not able to be available in the way you want and need. Let go of the expectation that they'll be interacting with your kids on a regular basis. Work with what you have.

- **Find Other Support.** Cultivate relationships with other friends, relatives, and neighbors so your children have a variety of people in their lives and so you have support and baby-sitters.

Grandparent involvement takes many forms and
can evolve over a lifetime.

# Logging in Frequent-Flyer Miles for Work

You wanted a job where you could see the world but it's wearing on you. This jet-set lifestyle is not changing anytime soon. Your goal is to avoid globetrotting burnout and start to really enjoy your travels again. Can you save your sanity and still see the world through fresh eyes?

- **Experience Hospitality.** If you're invited to someone's home, go. Meet their children and experience their food. It's a way for you to establish relationships in foreign lands that can last beyond the confines of your business.

- **Make Your Fashion Statement at Night.** It's not about your clothes unless you're in the fashion industry. On transportation, at meetings, and when touring, wear clothes and shoes that breathe and are comfortable. Dress up for evenings rather than risk being inappropriately dressed for day.

- **Open Your Eyes and Mind.** Even if you've visited this place a hundred times before, don't just lock yourself in your room and order room service. Get out and be with the people of this culture. Learn about this land, the history, and the customs. Give yourself a break from your work and plan a side trip or day excursion to someplace new.

You took the job because you love to travel, so embrace your rambling spirit and go beyond the confines of the job and explore your surroundings.

Partner, Well-Being

# Forgiving a Cheating Spouse

Marital infidelity means different things to different people. A one-night stand may cause the demise of one marriage while a long-term affair will serve as a wake-up call to another. It's all about forgiveness.

When you forgive someone, you are not agreeing that specific behavior is acceptable. The act of straying from one's wedding vows threatens the sanctity of marriage, trust, and commitment, and is not to be taken lightly. By forgiving, you are trying to move away from the anger to a place where you can work on your relationship. Only you can decide how long you are going to hold a grudge. Being attached to your negative feelings can cause you more problems than the transgression did in the first place.

Save your sanity by allowing yourself to be open and by examining the problems in your relationship.

- **It Takes Time.** Make sure the affair has ended and allow time to go by before you see dramatic change. Know that you may be suspicious for longer than you or your partner would like. If you are committed to work together, your marriage could become stronger and trust can be restored.

- **Accept Your Partner's Apology** . . . when you are ready to do so. This may be after you hear the details you need to hear. Process your feelings of betrayal, stupidity, anger, disappointment, and embarrassment.

- **If You Forgive, Others May Not.** Be careful about how you share information with your children, friends, and family. Re-

member, if you bash your significant other, you may damage his or her relationship with others forever. You may want to own up to your part of the problem to others. If your relationship survives, you'll want others to accept your partner . . . mistakes and all.

Forgiving a cheating spouse does not mean you forgive what he/she did.

Parent, Family

# When Your Child Tells You
# She Does Not Believe in God

Here you are, fully confident that you have raised your daughter to believe in God. You go to church or synagogue, mosque or temple, and celebrate religious holidays . . .

And then it happens. You are having dinner one night and your teenager tells you that she does not believe in God. If there was a God, says she, how could all of these terrible things happen in the world? How could good people suffer? As your heart sinks and you wonder what could possibly help her to find the faith that has helped you in your life, you feel your sanity waning.

- **You Can Only Own Your Own Beliefs.** Let your child know she is entitled to her beliefs. You have instilled your faith in your family and have done what you can. She may not feel a spiritual connection, but she may still follow your religious values. You cannot make her believe but can allow her to find her own belief system and comfort level.

- **Don't Challenge.** As she is exploring, don't challenge her or threaten her. Let her know that it is not uncommon for people to question the existence of a higher being when they see suffering in the world and in the lives of the people they love. This is especially true if she has experienced her own suffering and loss. You may want to encourage her to talk to your pastor, rabbi or other spiritual leader.

- **Share Your Doubts** . . . about the times you may have questioned the existence of God and how you dealt with your questions of faith. Affirm your conviction that you know that at different times in people's lives their belief systems change and that it is not only not surprising but to be expected.

When your children challenge the belief system they were raised with, embrace them and make it safe for them to question.

# Make a Smart Investment

You may be aware that today women live longer than men and have specific challenges for feeling financially secure. Nearly 90 percent of women, many of whom are single, will be responsible for their own financial world at some point in their lives (usually when they are in their elder years).

Don't wait around for someone to gallop along on a white horse or keep going to the bank of Mom and Dad to support you or to make your financial decisions. Invest in you. Do it by learning how to become financially self-sufficient. To feel financially secure you need to set some strategies and goals to provide for retirement, your or your children's educational expenses, medical emergencies, travel, or investing in a home.

Whether you are dealing with a lower-than-average paycheck, an ex who has not come through with the appropriate (or any) alimony or child support payments, or are financially responsible for your aging or ill parents, you need to know how to and what to invest in to feel comfortable financially.

- **Get Up to Speed.** Educate yourself about what is out there regarding ways to invest. Read one of the many guides or go online or attend a financial investing seminar to learn the basics about certificates of deposit, money market accounts, retirement accounts sponsored by your employer, and the many types of insurance products available. Ask around to discover the types of investment opportunities that attract some of the people you admire.

- **Spending Journal.** Keep a record of what you spend from your various sources (checkbook, credit cards, and cash) so you are aware of how much you spend and where your money goes. Visualize yourself managing your money carefully and wisely.

- **Make a Money Plan** . . . to appreciate what you spend and where you can cut expenses. You can only invest if you have an understanding about how much money you have and what your tendencies are with money. Are you a risk taker? Do you like things reliable, slow and steady? The kind of investments you make need to reflect the type of person you are.

Money does not make the world go round—but if you educate yourself, have patience, ask experts for advice, and are a smart investor, your world will go around more easily.

# The Value of Friends

Friends enhance life and help us live better. In fact, studies show that the absence of close friends or confidants is as detrimental to your health as smoking or carrying extra weight.

When you are with a true friend, you can be your authentic self. You can let your hair down and have fun. You can trust this person *not* to say what you have told her in confidence unless you specifically say it's OK. You're there for her and vice versa, to listen and *not* give advice or judge. This is a person you can ask for what you need or want. You can share your desires, thoughts, dreams, and mistakes. She accepts you unconditionally even though she may disagree with your choices.

How can you be a better friend? Believe it or not, the best thing you can do to be a friend to others is to like yourself. If you are feeling awful about yourself, other people are likely not going to find you terribly attractive. When you are content with who you are and not solely self-focused, you will have time, energy, and interest to cultivate meaningful friendships and attract positive relationships into your life.

- **Be There** . . . in the ways you can for the people who mean something to you. Select who is in that group. The group may be one or two people with whom you want to develop or maintain a close connection. Work on being a good listener, loyal, trustworthy, and a true supporter. Have your friends' interest at the forefront of your heart and mind.

- **Take the Time and Put It on Your Calendar.** When you are together, keep the distractions to a minimum. *Only* answer your

cell phone if it is *really* important. Time with friends goes by too fast. The fun, the focus, the feeling is what you want. Interrupting that flow minimizes the chances of that happening. You risk that your friend will feel she is not so important if you are answering your phone, text messaging someone else, or focusing on something other than your time together. Demonstrate the value and esteem for this person by your actions as well as your heart.

- **Don't Stand on Ceremony; Be Forgiving.** At some point, everyone in a friendship will have some type of disagreement or misunderstanding. A good friend, especially one who has been in your life a long time, who has helped you weather life's storms, with whom you have a shared history, is worth considering holding on to, but you need to be willing to let some things go. If your friend is usually a few minutes off schedule, don't expect punctuality. Be realistic. Try to work through the bigger clashes. Learn to agree to disagree. Don't ever keep score.

- **If You Say You're Going to Call, Do It!** Be sure you are as kind and considerate to your friends as you expect them to be to you. Listen and note what is important in their lives. Has someone close to them been in the hospital? Is their child waiting to hear about a college acceptance? What's new in the job market? Pay attention and follow up. If you have too much in your mind or on your schedule, write yourself a reminder note to check in with them.

- **If You Forget to Follow Up, 'Fess Up.** Don't make a thousand excuses about what has been going on in your life. Take responsibility for your inaction and then ask, "How is your mother? I

know she was ill. I am sorry I did not call for the last few days. How are you doing?"

Like yourself and others are likely to like you.
Know what you need to do to help
your friendships flourish.

# Seriously Ill and Telling Your Children

When you are seriously ill, it is important to let your children know what is happening in a language and level they can relate to and understand. Too often people shy away from telling children the truth about what is going on with their health. The kids, left out of the loop, sense something "bad" is happening and fantasize, worry, and become frightened because they do not have reliable information.

Often they are afraid to ask questions because they sense this is territory they are not supposed to enter. Children follow the lead of their parents. Depending on what is going on and what you know, you can include children in learning about your illness without scaring them. Children of different ages are able to process information at different levels.

- **Tell the Truth.** Describe your situation to them in the words they will understand so their reality is validated. If they ask you if you are scared, you can honestly tell them that sometimes you are and that it is OK to feel scared—but that you have good doctors and are going to take care of yourself to help as much as you can to get well. Be available to your children for any questions they have (even if you don't know the answers) and let them know you can work together to find the answers (use resources such as your doctors, nurses, mental health workers, books, and online sites for kids). Reassure your children that you love them, and that you have lots of feelings and expect they will too.

- **Be Realistic.** Be careful about what you say. Assuring children that you promise to beat the illness is different from telling them that you are going to fight as hard as you can to beat it.

- **Life Goes On.** Many children believe it is up to them to hold a vigil when their parent is ill and do not feel they deserve to have fun. Although your children may have increased responsibilities because of your illness, remind them that they are still children and you expect them to have fun, enjoy themselves, do their best job at school, and be with friends.

- **Support for Kids.** See if there is a support group for children of parents who have a similar illness to yours. Sometimes children need to talk to other kids in ways they will not share with their parents.

- **Be Together.** When you have good days or better times of the day, take the focus off your illness and do things with your children that you all enjoy. If you cannot go out in groups of people, walk in a quiet park. If you cannot watch your kids' games or recitals because of health risks that come along with being in crowds, ask someone to videotape the game or event and watch it together on your TV.

## Illness is scarier for kids when they don't know what is really going on.

*Family, Parent*

# Having a Good Relationship with Your Aging Parent

Your mom or dad is getting older and you want to improve your relationship. You know that time marches on, and if you keep putting off this one, you'll regret it.

Most positive relationships with aging parents are based on respect, appreciation for a life lived, and empathy for where they are now and what they are dealing with and facing. Decide what you are able to do to work on the relationship now, how you can be available, and how much of yourself you can share.

- **See Their Better Side.** Whenever you are together, try to point out at least one quality or attribute about your parent that you appreciate.

- **Bygones Are Bygones.** If you are waiting for an apology, give it up. Likely that will not be forthcoming, so decide how you will go forward accepting the past as an integral part of your life that you will have to deal with.

- **See Through Their Aging Eyes.** Understand what life is like for your parent *now*. Looking toward the end of life affects people differently. Do not impose or suppose. Have empathy for what they are dealing with.

- **Give Them the Time They Deserve.** Your parents have more time now and you have less. It's difficult to be available when they need you. Be open to discussions about whatever your aging parents need to discuss and respond as helpfully and as promptly as possible. Designate time during the weekend for an unrushed conversation over a cup of tea for sharing information and just listening. Know your own limits about time and respect them.

You'll not rewrite or reconstruct the relationship with your aging parents but you can improve on what you have.

## Be Real and Let Relationships Flourish

Do you allow yourself to be real? You cannot be in an intimate relationship with anyone without being yourself. If others don't know who you really are, they know your false self or the one you portray to the world.

If you can't be yourself, any intimacy will be a façade—even worse, a charade. Rather than presenting yourself as who you want to be, be who you are and keep moving forward as you save your sanity.

- **Be Yourself.** Be honest about where you came from and your roots. Acceptance of your past allows you to be comfortable with who you are today.

- **Live a Meaningful Life.** Live a life that reflects your true values. You can't live or behave in a manner that you find desirable or productive or conducive if you don't set some standards and live the life you want to.

- **No Judgments.** If you want to put your real self forward, you have to reciprocate to others and accept them for who they really are. No judgments. If the way you think of others impacts your ability to be close, open your heart.

Get to know yourself, let your true self come through, and share yourself as you are. When you accept yourself, you will be more likely to accept others as they are.

# Kids' Birthday Party Competition

When you were a kid you may remember some of the best times were at your birthday parties. There may have been a homemade cake or an ice cream cake or some three-layer beauty from the bakery. Since it was *your* birthday, you got the rose on your plate. Everyone played games and sang songs. Maybe, just maybe, there was a clown or a magician. Or you had pizza and a few girls slept over. That was really special.

Now you find that your children are invited to some of the most extravagant parties imaginable. And when it is their turn, they want to have something along the same lines. You not only feel it is inappropriate, expensive, and competitive, but you find that you need to explain why birthday parties in your family are not as extravagant as their friends' parties.

Among the things your children may be hearing is that the children who get the best parties are more highly prized by their parents than the children who have "ordinary" parties. Kids wonder what is "wrong" with them that their parents don't go out of their way to throw them a special party.

- **Explain Your Values** . . . and what you value about your children. Emphasize that your children are important to you. Let them know that their value is not measured by how many bouncy castles, live ponies, or professional circus clowns are at their party.

- **Involve Your Children in Planning** . . . within your parameters so they feel it is special for them. Ask them about some of the best parties they have been to and what made them special.

- **Stay Confident.** If your kids are comparing their lives to their friends' lives, chances are this will be a recurring theme (especially in their teens). Stay strong to the person you are, the children you are raising, and the values you keep. Your children might be impressed with what others have, but if you provide them with lots of love and a healthy home environment, more likely than not, they'll grow up to value the things that really matter.

We need to keep our children grounded by showing them that their value is not measured by showering them with extravagance.

*Friends*

# When Your Friend's Mr. Right
# Comes On to You

There are few things more uncomfortable than when your friend's Mr. Right comes on to you. You know, makes a pass.

You are shocked (or not) and immediately realize the inappropriateness. Do you ignore it, immediately call him on it, make a joke, or run and tell your friend? Keeping your sanity and your friendship are both at issue, so handle with care.

- **Don't Mislead.** When it happens, at that very moment and a bit afterward, gather your wits about you and keep yourself in check. Get the message across that you are *so* not interested and then disengage. Try not to joke or sweep it under the rug and please *don't* be flattered. If you don't act in some serious way, he just might come on stronger next time.

- **Mr. Right Is Wrong.** After the encounter, wait for (or create) an occasion when you are alone with your friend, to tell her that Mr. Right may not be so right for her after all. If she has been with him awhile, she probably already knows about his roving ways (or at least, deep down inside she does). You do not have to go into the fine points of what happened to get your message across.

- **She's Your Friend, Not Him.** If she continues to see this man and wants you to join them socially, consider wisely whether that works for you. If it doesn't, let her know that you are more

comfortable seeing her without him. Tell her that you value her friendship and ask for her understanding.

You owe it to yourself and to your friend to share your misgivings about someone she is with whom you know firsthand is not to be trusted.

# *Weekend*

*Friends, Family*

## What to Say When Someone Is Ill

For many of us, being supportive to a friend who is seriously ill can send us into a tailspin. Not just because we are sad about the friend's health, but because we don't know what to say. Fearful that we will do something inappropriate, we choose to say or do nothing.

The most important thing to remember is that your friend is the one in pain and your attention should be focused on what she needs. It may surprise you to learn that, most often, what she needs is simply someone to listen sympathetically, thereby sharing the burden of her suffering and helping to save her sanity.

- **Your Role** . . . is to make the person feel better by being present and listening. Just being with someone can be extremely healing. Knowing when to talk, if at all, and what to say is the key. Words of comfort are welcome, advice is not unless asked. If your ill friend wants you to share with others about her illness or things discussed, you may do so. Otherwise hold things in confidence.

- **Physical and Emotional Touch** . . . can bring great comfort. If it seems appropriate, give a hug, extend a hand, or touch her arm. Touching helps a person feel accepted.

- **Give Specific Help.** Rather than saying, "Call me if there is anything I can do for you," ask if she needs anything at the market. Bring over a hot pink nail polish and all the fixings for a manicure or pedicure, and then give it to her. Offer to water plants outdoors, bring in the mail, clean the house, drive her to an appointment, walk her dog, or deliver dinner for her family.

Instead of telling your sick friend you know
how she feels, listen sensitively and be
a source of comfort.

# Deciding Not to Have Children

Tick, tock, it's the biological clock alarm going off. But are you ready to have children, or are you seriously thinking that you may not want to have them at all?

When you consider the choice, think about what would satisfy you (and your mate, if one is in the picture) if you have a child. Having a child has a lot to do with economics, careers, relationships, self-awareness, and expectations. As you weigh the pluses and minuses, you may receive some intrusive or critical commentary from family, friends, and society at large about your choice. Clear your mind and make a decision that works for you.

- **To Be or Not to Be a Mom.** You have the right to live your life the best way you can. Not everyone is meant to be a parent. Only you know if parenthood is right for you. Once you make the decision to start a family, there's no turning back, so think it through thoroughly.

- **Let Go of Good and Bad.** Do you feel pressure to be good? Does being good mean that you should be a mother? Does the decision not to have children denote that you are selfish and self-absorbed? What messages do you get from family, friends, and society? Although many couples are opting to remain childless, there is still a societal expectation that most people will choose to become parents. Whether or not you decide to become a parent, respect the opinion of others that differ from yours. Know that this is your and your partner's decision.

- **Have Kids in Your Life.** If you're thinking of not having kids and you like them, there are plenty of opportunities to include and engage children in your life. Spend time with your nieces and nephews or surrogate nieces and nephews, be a "big sister," work with a foster child, or tutor a child through a charity organization.

Living a childless life does not mean you are selfish.

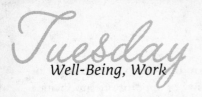

# Tuesday
*Well-Being, Work*

# Dealing with Frustration When Waiting for Others to Do Their Job

Few things are more frustrating than waiting for someone to come through . . . you know, do his job so you can move along. Say your car's sideswiped while you are in the market or you have severe water and smoke damage in your apartment because of a fire above you. You are left unable to drive your car or live in your house or apartment, and your whole life can be turned upside down.

These kinds of things are bad enough, but then you are in a position of having to deal with people who just are not doing their jobs (and their job is to help you.) You may have to see several adjusters, get various quotes for work, have different assessments, and why? Because of an act of nature or because someone else was careless or irresponsible. First you may get frustrated, then depressed, and then mad! But, there are ways to deal with this and keep your sanity intact.

- **Gather Your Wits.** Prepare for the long haul. No, you did not want this to happen, and yes, there are lots and lots of people along your red-tape trail. But, in the end, you will, hopefully, get to where you need to be.

- **Do Something for You.** Between calls or filling out forms, do something good for yourself. Read or watch something funny, put on hand cream and massage your arms for two minutes or call a friend.

- **Keep Good Notes** . . . about what happened, who you spoke to on which dates, and the gist of the conversation. Get everyone's name and position in the company. Whittle down the story to the bare essentials. It is amazing how little information is needed as you retell a story.

- **Control Your Anger.** Do not insult the person on the phone. She might hang up on you, and you will go back to the beginning of the line and have to listen to that awful canned music. When you are angry, take a shower with a sponge. When the sponge is totally saturated, throw it against the shower door and pick it up again and throw it as many times as you need. Nobody will get hurt and you will have expressed your anger.

There are ways to control and deal with your anger as you feel frustrated with the red tape of long-term problems that need to be solved.

## Mothers and Daughters-in-Law

If you have a daughter-in-law with whom you want to have a good relationship, get to know her. See her through your son's eyes, and you will be much more likely to move in the right direction.

Sometimes your relationship with your daughter-in-law may play right into your insecurities, and you are left with countless misunderstandings resulting in a thickness in the air that you can cut with a knife. You're afraid to say something and she's afraid to say something and you both don't know what to do. The key is to be open and accepting and refrain from offering your opinion or advice unless asked. Respect the couple's privacy and appreciate that you are not first in line for affection, secrets, or much else anymore. But you still have an important role.

- **Your Part in the Drama.** If you, as a mother, are used to being listened to all the time, running the show, never being challenged or confronted, then you certainly have a change to deal with. You may have made all your son's decisions and he was fine with that, but now he or she is not. Do you perceive your daughter-in-law as a threat, or bossy, or too independent or controlling? These terms are often used when describing in-law children and are often not meant as compliments. Turn the table and look at yourself from her point of view.

- **No Pushing.** If you never had a daughter, be careful about jumping at the chance to do things together. Don't assume your daughter-in-law wants to and is eager to have this relationship in the same way you do. Feel it out first. If you want to help out,

consult her first. Be careful about forcing anything on your kids. They are now making their own life together . . . with their own taste and decisions.

- **If You Can't Get Gold, Go for Silver.** You are no longer the number one person your son turns to for advice or to whom he speaks in confidence—your daughter-in-law is now that person. You will need to mourn the "loss" of your child as well as your top-seeded position in your son's life. Get comfortable with second place. You are still in the game.

- **Get to Like Her.** You will alienate your child and your daughter-in-law if you let it be known that you don't like his choice of partner. This makes for a strained relationship at best. If there is a split, your child will likely blame you, and you might not have access to your grandchildren. It gets messy and it need not. It will be easier for you if you avoid making waves and determine to enjoy her.

The most loving gift you can give your adult child is to fully welcome and accept his spouse into your heart as one of your own.

# Thursday

*Partner*

## Breaking Up Because of a Deal Breaker

You are breaking off a relationship with someone because you just cannot stand something about this person.

Annoyances like smoking, drinking, swearing, poor eating habits, hot temperedness, entitlement issues, or prejudices really bother you. This person isn't "all bad," and you sometimes wonder if you are making the right decision. Others may comment that you are being too picky or you'll lose a great person. You hear, "No one is perfect"; that you should "lighten up." And by the way, they never forget to remind you that you aren't so easy to live with, either.

Saving your sanity when you are single and wonder if you will ever meet someone else is a challenge.

- **What Is the Guilt About?** Check in with yourself that you are making this decision for the right reasons. By putting your health and well-being high on the list of what is important in your life, you are taking care of yourself. When you know that not having this person in your life will benefit you more than having him or her in your life, it's time to move on.

- **Forget Trying to Change Someone.** I hope you know by now that you can't change someone. It is not your job to do that anyway. If you can't work with the issues and accept this person flaws and all, it is unfair to you and to them to keep going. Both of you will be miserable.

- **Listen to Your Heart.** Maybe you cannot be the one to take responsibility for breaking up a relationship because you may

feel that your issues are not important. Or you feel you should be strong and able to accommodate anything. Perhaps you were raised by someone who hung in there in a relationship that was abusive or in some way mirrors yours. You feel that if you break this off you will somehow be going against the family credo, disappoint your parents, or be a quitter. Think instead about *you* and how you can love yourself. Does that image include this person?

When you know the right thing to do regarding ending a relationship, do it and attempt to understand the source of your guilt rather than stay in the relationship because of guilt.

*Friday*
*Family*

# Better Sibling Relationships

Good adult sibling relationships are first and foremost about communication. We all have our lives to live, and it's sometimes difficult to maintain close bonds when family members live far apart, have different lifestyles and busy schedules. Whether your sister lives across the country or across town, keeping in contact via telephone, e-mail, and in-person visits is the best way to maintain the connection. Being in touch on a regular basis will help your relationship thrive. There is less of a need to play catch-up.

But no matter how often you talk or have family get-togethers, there still might be "stuff" lingering from years back or family dynamics that get in the way of maintaining stronger ties. It may be time to take a closer look at your relationship with your siblings and see if better awareness can improve your connection.

- **Your Sibling Model.** Look at your parents' relationships with their siblings and other sibling relationships that may have affected you. If your father had a falling out with his brother and did not speak to him for fifteen years, how has that affected your relationship with your brothers and sisters (to say nothing about your cousins)? Maybe it's time to challenge what you were raised with, do things differently, take another approach, or define and design a better model.

- **Appreciate Your Sib.** Does your adult sibling relationship reflect the kind of people you are now? Does it capture your relationship at this moment in your lives? Recognizing your "little" sister or "big" brother as individuals, who have their own lives,

desires, interests, and values that may or may not mirror yours, allows for respect and better relationships.

- **We're Adults Now.** We all grow older, but some of us don't grow up and our view of our sibling may not change. Just as your mother still talks to you as if you are twelve years old, you may be treating your brothers and sisters as you did when you were kids. Bring your relationships with your sibling into the present.

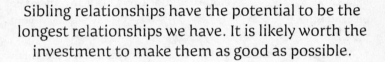

Sibling relationships have the potential to be the longest relationships we have. It is likely worth the investment to make them as good as possible.

# Don't Stop, Keep Exercising

You've started an exercise routine and feel good. But getting to the gym is harder and harder to do.

Studies show that as little as a 5 percent reduction in body weight can help reduce some of the risk factors associated with obesity and can help improve some of the symptoms linked to diabetes and high cholesterol. So stay motivated, don't procrastinate, and keep on exercising.

- **Work in Workouts.** Make exercise nonnegotiable. Do it for yourself; do it for your family. Lead by example. One of the greatest gifts you can give your family is to instill in them good eating and exercise habits.

- **Link Exercise to Your True Passions.** Think out of the box. If you support a charity, chances are it sponsors a fun walk or run every year. Sign up and train for an event. If you loved ice-skating as a child, you'll probably enjoy it as an adult. If you've always wanted to learn how to scuba dive, sign up for lessons and go early and swim a few laps before each class.

- **Take Ten Fun Facts.** Think you can't accomplish much in ten minutes? Think again. Park your car an extra ten minutes away from work and you can burn forty-three calories before you clock in. Add another forty-three calories lost for the trip back to your car. Do that five days a week for a year and you can kiss up to six pounds bye-bye. Walk up the stairwells with a friend for ten minutes during your lunch hour and ten minutes back down

and you'll burn up to one hundred twenty-five calories a trip. Five days of stair walking a week for a year, and you just may lose up to nine pounds. Every time you answer the phone, let it trigger a brisk walk or at least pacing. Ten five-minute standing-up phone calls a day, and you'll burn one hundred calories.

- **Excellence Matters.** Halfhearted efforts yield halfhearted results. Each and every time you exercise, leave the world behind, focus on your performance, and work to your true potential. Strive for perfect posture and good form. Get maximum results for every minute you've set aside to nurture your good health. Focus. You're worth it. You deserve it.

Just as you brush your teeth for good dental care, make exercising part of your everyday routine for good body and emotional care.

# Monday

*Single*

## Buying Your Own Home as a Single Woman

Married women are not the only ones who need to invest in their futures. In fact, everyone, single or married, is wise to think about how their lives will be enriched by creating a home for themselves.

Think about why it doesn't make sense for a woman to wait for a guy to come along to make a great home. Whether you live in a home of your own for one year or ten years, purchasing your own home or apartment may help you to feel grounded and secure. And if you do change your living arrangements somewhere down the line, you might be able to hold on to that property as an investment for the future.

Your own home means you can decorate it in the way you like and have it truly reflect you, your taste, your energy. For some single women, renting apartments keeps them focused on being in a temporary "limbo" state. They focus on waiting to begin their lives when a man comes along rather than appreciating what their life is worth now. Somehow, owning your own place can help you feel as if you are "grown up" and a "real" adult. When women own their own home, they describe feeling more settled and "at home."

- **Is It Possible to Buy?** Think about what it would take to purchase a condominium or house and see if this is possible. Weigh the positives and negatives. Renting means you can call the landlord when the pipes burst, while owning means that year after year you'll be building equity in your property. Go online or call

a reputable bank or broker who can qualify you for a mortgage that you can afford.

- **Visualize Yourself in Your Own Home.** Picture it decorated in the style you like, in a neighborhood where you will feel safe, with neighbors you can relate to.

- **Women *Can* Buy Their Own Nest.** When someone else's negative comments related to your purchasing a home come into your mind, focus on the top five reasons you believe you will benefit from living in your own home.

Your home can be a reflection of what
is important to you.

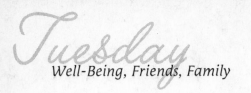

*Tuesday*

*Well-Being, Friends, Family*

## Recovering After Surgery

This is not the time to be Ms. Independent. Healing is more about allowing your body to rest and restore than it is about proving to the world how tough you are. Making your recovery a priority is the only way to get back into everyday life as soon as possible.

- **Get Help and Accept Help.** Having a competent, comforting person whose touch is reassuring and who also knows how to read your vital signs will allow you to do what you need to do— take care of yourself and heal.

- **Music Heals.** Listening to music during your immediate recovery period is therapeutic. Gentle instrumental (string) music in particular is thought to have a particularly soothing effect on cardiac recovery.

- **Limit Visitors** . . . the number and who comes. Some people are very healing and will not drain you. Others come and you need to take care of them. Not good for you. You will have enough visitors with the nurses, doctors, interns, residents, food service people, chaplains, cleaners to keep you going for a long time. Also, after surgery, you need to be able to nod off at your leisure. If you feel the need to stay awake because Uncle Jack drove two hours to see you, you will not get the healing rest you need. Having said all that, if someone makes you laugh, invite them over. After all is said and done, laughter is the best medicine.

Surgery takes strength. Preserve yours
and recover well.

# Workaholic Children

You have a strong work ethic. Your parents had it. You have a need for approval, and people tend to reward you for your dedication. It is a legacy you want to pass down to your children.

So why are you so shocked when your child runs for office at school while juggling a full course schedule with no lunch break, and signs up for a variety of outreach programs and after-school activities? Why is she more like a little adult than a child, cannot relax, and is so competitive with her peers?

It is time to save your sanity while you help your child save hers by realizing the benefit of letting her be a child and enjoy life.

- **Take Responsibility.** Parents who are workaholics present a dichotomy for their children. Children appreciate the value of hard work but see a parent who is distant or more concerned about what is going on in her work world than the rest of her world. Tell your child that you are sorry and will take the necessary steps to become more available (and then do it!).

- **Don't Let Them Miss Out.** Model for them that you can enjoy time off, take care of yourself, relax, and engage in activities that are non-work related on your own and with your family. Let your children know that fun experiences and time with loved ones is essential for developing as a whole person.

- **Live with Humor.** Whenever life gets too serious, sprinkle giggles and laughs along the way and lighten the load for your kids.

Consider what is truly important in your life, share this with your child, and insist that your child take time off to play.

# Generational Differences at Work

When you work with someone from another generation you may need to open your mind to what her experience is in the world of work.

You may be someone who challenges authority, balances your work and personal life, takes risks, has technological know-how, loves to multitask, and values change, while demanding meaningful and interesting work. And next to you, working on the same project, is someone from another generation who is more practical, respects authority, works 24/7 (even on the weekends), and would never challenge the rules of the office.

Keeping your sanity when working with someone from another generation who comes to the table with different expectations and experience can be challenging.

- **Revel in Your Differences.** Recognize the background and generational influences of yourself and your workmate. Rather than condemning her or her characteristics, see the value in her attributes and different point of view.

- **Focus on Your Strengths.** Find ways to emphasize the areas in which you can work together despite your differences. Someone's experience and familiarity with a company's history can help give perspective, while someone else's technical savvy can help you think in new ways.

- **Share and Learn.** Listen to each other's perspectives and notice each person's expertise, to gain the most from an intergenerational workplace experience.

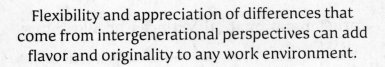

Flexibility and appreciation of differences that come from intergenerational perspectives can add flavor and originality to any work environment.

# Caring for a Partner with a Chronic Illness

You vowed to stay together in sickness and in health. But, in fact, you did not *really* think you'd be caring for your significant other who is managing a chronic illness at this point of your life.

Much of your pattern and rhythm as a couple will be reflected in the way you deal with each other and this particular health challenge. Save your sanity, your dignity, and your marriage by caring for your partner with compassion.

- **Be an Adult.** You may be asking "why me" and feel disappointed, angry, tired, or restless. It's normal to feel this way. Try to maintain self-control and respect instead of taking out your frustrations on your partner. Seek couples therapy if either of you blames the other or you are both having difficulty adjusting.

- **Get into Your Role or Get Help.** What is needed to help deal with this change in your life? Do you have to get a job? Will care need to be provided when you are out of the house? Who is in charge of making dietary decisions? Try not to become a mother but instead be a supporting player.

- **Do Couple Things** . . . ones that allow you to be conscious of the illness but not totally focus on it. If your spouse tires easily at the end of the day, and evenings out are no longer viable, meet friends on a weekend afternoon for a movie or lunch. If you are music buffs, attend uncrowded concert rehearsals instead of the evening event.

Although your partner is living with a chronic illness, there are ways to preserve and deepen your bond as you find unique ways to "marry" your new roles with the challenges you both face.

# Getting Through Sorrow

As you go through feelings of mourning and grief, it is essential that you do whatever is necessary to accept that you have suffered a profound loss. Permit yourself to experience the pain, and if you can, while in the process, try to focus on positive memories of and experiences with the person who is no longer in your life. Develop and maintain your own rituals that can serve as a structure to help negotiate the loss, particularly during times of celebration.

- **Process and Keep Moving Forward.** Work on getting closure with your feelings. Whether the relationship you had with that person was a good one or not, try to close the chapter on your feelings of grief. If you're angry, sad, depressed, feel abandoned or dumped, try to work through it with counseling and the support of loved ones.

- **Create a Ritual.** If you're blue on your mother's birthday and you are estranged, take out your childhood album and revisit the pictures with joy of once sharing a better time. If you are sad on your anniversary, but it evokes unrest because of a divorce or unhappy marriage, why not book an annual massage to help you get through the day.

- **Journal.** When sorrow overcomes you, write down what you feel. Hopefully you will find comfort in releasing your feelings on paper so you can enjoy life around you.

- **Engage** . . . in good works to help cope with feelings of loss.

Sorrow is highly personal. No one can tell you what you should feel. Your relationship determines how you feel and how you move on.

# That Ticking Clock

Fed up with references to your biological clock? "You're not getting any younger." "Why don't you find someone, settle down, and have babies?" "When am I going to see my grandchildren?" Tick, tock, tick, tock, tick, tock.

I don't blame you for getting angry at all. But when you sit down and really think about it, there just doesn't seem to be someone on the horizon who will be a good choice for your mate, let alone someone to coparent with. Stop the ticking clock and save your sanity.

- **Want to Be Mom?** Get honest with yourself. This is not the time to please others. Is being a mother important? There's always the option of not having children because the desire is just not there.

- **Mom Options.** There are lots of ways to become a mother. As you get older, consider some of the options available to you to have a child—your own or someone else's. There are a lot of kids out there waiting for loving parents.

- **Stay True to Your Beliefs.** Your decisions about parenthood are nobody's but yours. Single parenthood or not? You decide what to do.

Whatever you decide, understand that raising a child is no easy task. If you choose to do it on your own, line up the best support you can for you and for your child.

# The Waiting Game: How To Handle the ER Before a Doctor Handles You

A visit to the emergency room is often a distressing experience—whether you are the patient or the caregiver to someone who has been injured or is ill. You need a lot of patience to be a patient in the ER.

If a visit becomes lengthy, or if every single form or document isn't in its proper order, your sanity can be roughly tested. Begin with a simple goal to be prepared, and your visit can be effective and less of a sanity buster.

- **Always Carry Personal Identification.** Bring your medical insurance card, medical history, and a log of the prescription drugs you currently use to the ER. It's a good idea to also bring a list of the phone numbers of friends and family who will need to be contacted.

- **Write Down Facts.** After waiting six hours to be seen by a doctor, you may have forgotten important facts such as time of injury, what you did immediately, how you felt. While you're waiting, write down what you can recall about what happened to you and why you are there.

- **Think of Questions** . . . you will need to ask the staff when you are finally seen. If you are cold, ask for a heated blanket or booties and ask if it is OK to drink hot liquids.

- **Save Your Energy.** Try not to become too engaged with everyone else in the waiting room, as this may drain your much-needed reserve of energy. It is tempting to strike up a conversation when you're facing four-year-old copies of magazines or battered children's books, but keep yourself focused on what you can do to keep yourself calm and comfortable. Visualize yourself being treated well and visualize your healing just around the corner.

When you are in the ER keep yourself as calm as possible by reviewing what happened, taking notes, and visualizing yourself being treated well and becoming well.

# Your Unforgiving Child

Unless we address it at some point in our lives, the unpopular and sometimes hurtful decisions we make as parents can haunt us into the future.

If your children have a difficult time forgiving you for something you did in your life or a decision you made that they didn't agree with, how can your relationship go forward? Moreover, how can you meet their high expectations or conditions they constantly throw out to you while you save your sanity?

- **What's Reasonable?** They may try to guilt you into doing what they feel you owe them or what they want from you. Only you can decide whether their expectations are equitable and whether you will ever be able to make up for the pain your children feel you caused them. You cannot make up for what happened but can only go forward. At some point, it is up to your children to deal with their past in the healthiest way possible.

- **Doable or Not?** Listen, and separate what your adult child wants and needs from you and what you can give. "I want you to be with your grandchild as much as you can." Does that mean every day? Every week? Does it mean you don't take a vacation so you can spend more time with your grandchild? Is this about her feeling cut off from her own grandparents when you left her father? Assess what's going on and what is possible.

- **Blame Does Not Equal Guilt.** Just because someone blames you does not mean you need to be guilt-ridden. Tell your child what responsibility you are willing to accept and what you are no longer willing to carry because it never applied or no longer applies. This needs to be said with empathy and understanding. And remember, it takes time to heal.

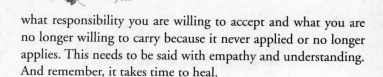

You cannot make up for the past with your children. You can, however, factor it in and keep it in your heart as you plan your future together.

# Thursday

## Separating Work Friendships from the Rest of Your Life

Everyone needs a break from work. Hopefully you are one of the lucky women in the world who enjoys her work and wants to do a good job. Hopefully, too, you have colleagues with whom you feel comfortable and supported and whom you look forward to seeing each day. How good are you at separating work from the rest of your life?

When you leave for the weekend, don't bring it home with you. Being friendly with people at work and not outside it can help you keep your life separate. But if you have created friendships in the workplace that spill over to weekend time, how can you make sure that you are able to keep work and the rest of your life separate to save your sanity?

- **Don't Mix.** If you hang out with the people from work on the weekends, be clear about not talking about work. If you do, monitor your conversations. Cultivate other aspects of your lives and relationships (go bike riding, hiking, take in a museum, go to a movie) as you consciously avoid referencing work. You need to have down time to turn off your work and recharge your batteries.

- **Make Boundaries.** Tell people at work that you are unavailable on the weekends and then make that statement a reality.

- **Break Away.** Initially plan a weekend with at least one day (and hopefully two) away from any work-related interactions (via

computers, PDAs, cell phones). Move toward the goal of leaving your PDA unattended and ignoring your work cell calls unless there is a crisis or emergency.

Nonwork friendships can develop out of the office; don't bring the office to them.

# Friday

*Friends, Family*

## When Someone Disrespects Your House

Letting a friend stay at your home while you're off somewhere else is a nice gesture. The friend gets to enjoy your town and save on hotel charges while your plants are watered, the mail is taken in, and someone is watching over your "stuff." Unless she isn't!

Coming home to a dirty house that you left spotless is not the best way to reenter your life. Coming home to sticky floors, beer and soda bottles around, dirty bathrooms, and soiled sheets can not only contribute to your loss of sanity but also leave you feeling personally violated.

- **Take Inventory and Regroup.** Look around the house and note what has changed. Then sit down and think about what you want to do and how you want to begin dealing with this mess and the disappointment. Gather your wits, breathe deeply, and focus on the fact that you will be able to deal with this either by phone, in person, or in a letter.

- **State the Problem.** After you have calmed down, call the person and begin positively. "You know I love you. I've known you for years. I simply can't believe that you would leave my home in the condition you left it. In case you were unaware, this is what I came home to." Tell her each problem you encountered that's on your list.

- **Respond to Her Response.** If you can't believe you are hearing, "But we tried to clean it up," try this. "You may have tried and I know it can be difficult to keep up a house. The point is that you

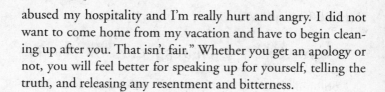

abused my hospitality and I'm really hurt and angry. I did not want to come home from my vacation and have to begin cleaning up after you. That isn't fair." Whether you get an apology or not, you will feel better for speaking up for yourself, telling the truth, and releasing any resentment and bitterness.

When someone takes advantage of you, it is imperative that you tell her how you feel so you are not harboring ill feelings.

*Community, Well-Being*

## Giving Back

Community service expands your world and can be done at any point in your life. Even if you are in the throes of building your career, raising your children, or taking care of your parents, there is something you can do to serve outside the parameters of your life. Why? Because, believe it or not, the old adage of "What goes around comes around" rings true. Only by giving can you be touched in ways beyond your imagination.

Sometimes you'll be able to give more time and less money or more money and less time, but there will be always something you can do for someone or some cause. Think about the places, organizations, and people you know that can use a bit of help. Find something you believe in and offer what you can.

- **Give What You Enjoy Doing.** If you are a good cook, prepare an extra meal for a mother in your child's class who had surgery. Or sign up at the local soup kitchen and drop off your famous lasagna. If you have good writing skills but are busy with the kids, why not edit an online newsletter for a great organization after bedtime. Whatever your interest—animals, the environment, children, homelessness, education, poverty, or finding a cure for an illness—you can always help out in some way.

- **Be Realistic with Your Time.** If you cannot commit to a regular "volunteer" job, offer what you can and look toward the day when you will be able to give more of what they need. Giving back is about giving to the cause while fulfilling something in

you. If you're overextended, volunteering will seem like a chore and will lack spirit.

- **Imagine** . . . as you hum the Lennon tune, about your immediate neighborhood and world you would like to live in. Align the issues you care about with your available time and resources and construct the best opportunity to offer yourself and your talents, no matter how big or small, to make the world a better place.

The world will only become a better place
if you help it along.

# Monday

*Friendship*

## Keeping a Friend's Memory Alive for the Children

As sad as it is to lose a beloved friend or family member, it is essential that we remember him and keep his memory alive—for us as well as for his children, grandchildren, and the community in which he lived.

Sharing stories about the person is healing. Sadly, though, with so much sorrow around the time of the death, some of these stories are not heard by the people who need to hear them and remember them the most—his children. As a friend or someone who knew him well, you can give a major gift to the surviving children (especially if they are young) by keeping in touch with the family.

It is difficult enough to lose a parent, but to lose the parent's community of friends makes it worse. As difficult as it is, consider yourself an extension of the parent and, without being intrusive, be present during celebratory as well as challenging times. Offer the children tidbits about their parent's life so they can feel as if he is still with them in some way.

- **Remember the Children's Birthdays.** Keep a connection with the children by sending a card or, better yet, giving a call. Having the treasured friendship of their mother or father's friends and community will keep the children feeling as if they have an extended family and that their parent's life mattered to other people, not just them. When a friend who is a parent dies, you have a golden opportunity to keep their parent's memory alive. Why not also call when it's the birthday of the deceased parent

and let the children know you are thinking of their mom or dad too?

- **Record Memories.** Open a file in your computer or keep a notebook and jot random thoughts or stories or comments that you remember about this person that, over time, you will share with his children and others. It is very important to children, especially as they grow up, to hear from their parent's friends; what they were like, what was important to them, and things about them that they don't have access to because as they matured, their parent, sadly, didn't.

- **Share Your Stories.** Sometimes children worry when they cannot recall their parent's face or smell or touch, and they worry that they will not have access to the parent if they cannot remember him. As a lifelong friend, remember their mother or father and share stories about them with the children. It is so important for them to feel a sense of legacy and continuity.

- **Be a Link to Their Parent's Thoughts.** Keep a memory book with specific quotes about what their parent said so over time you can give the children actual memories with as many of the parent's own words as possible.

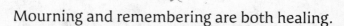

Mourning and remembering are both healing.

# *Tuesday*
*Parent, Work*

## When a Parent Loses a Job

You (or your partner) got fired, laid off, or permanently terminated at work. It's bad enough telling each other, but now you have to tell the kids.

It's not the actual news that will upset them, but how your children will perceive their world changing as a result of your job loss. Will you have to cut back on expenses, postpone their tennis lessons, or move? What will your children anticipate that might conjure up fear and anger because you lost your job?

Depending on their age and how you handle explaining the news, kids will react in different degrees. To minimize the repercussions, be honest and open about what is likely to happen. Hopefully, they'll come around and actually pitch in to help in some way if they are included in the discussions and their feelings are acknowledged.

- **Gently Explain What's Going On.** Minimize fears as realistically as possible and answer their questions. "This is temporary and I am doing the following things to get another job," or "I might not find something right away but I'm looking. In the meantime, let's all try to live conservatively."

- **Be Careful About Making Promises.** "I am sure we will not have to move." Or, "Another job is just around the corner, so let's still plan a ski vacation this winter."

- **Have Family Meetings.** Review the changes everyone is making and new changes that are expected. Offer to hear ideas of how

the children can contribute. Help them become part of the family solution. "We can't go to Disney World this year but can go to grandma's lake house or camping. Which would you like?"

- **Appear to Be Able to Cope** . . . even though it is difficult.

> You are your family's rock, so stay steady when times get rough and you'll all see this through.

# Wednesday

*Well-Being, Friends, Family*

## Confronting a Sexual Abuser

If you are in the throes of working through the horrors of having been sexually abused as a child or an adult, you will probably ask yourself whether it makes sense to confront the person who abused you. As you work with someone such as a mental health professional to come to terms with what happened, the combination of fear and rage may make this thought difficult to process.

As you learn to express the anger you have felt for so long, confronting the offender may or may not seem viable. How, for instance, do you deal with this if the person is part of your family and nobody knows? Or what if the person is now dead?

Confrontation is not easy. The person may never admit that the abuse took place or that he was the perpetrator. You may never get an apology or an acknowledgment. Here are ways to preserve your sanity while approaching the intense feelings that can result from sexual abuse.

- **Stop Self-Destructing.** Take the opportunity to express your anger in ways that will not damage your sense of yourself any further. You may be able to confront in person, but if you think it will be too traumatic, there are other ways to work through this. Write in a journal, work out at a gym, role play with a therapist, and scream and punch pillows when you are alone in your house. These outlets for anger can help to begin to let off some of what is boiling within you.

- **Write a Letter.** Sit quietly in a place where you feel safe and write a letter to the sexual abuser, enumerating all the thoughts

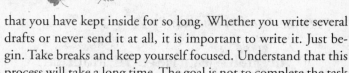

that you have kept inside for so long. Whether you write several drafts or never send it at all, it is important to write it. Just begin. Take breaks and keep yourself focused. Understand that this process will take a long time. The goal is not to complete the task in one sitting.

- **Talk Out Loud.** Focus on an empty chair and visualize the abuser sitting in it. If this doesn't work, associate to something that puts you in mental contact with the person. Although you're alone in the room, you're the one who needs to hear yourself talk directly to that person. Tell him what happened, how you felt, how this terrible experience has influenced you and your life, your relationships, and your outlook on the world. If you care to, place a tape recorder in the room because you may want to hear what you said, and likely you will not remember much of your "conversation."

- **Heal over Your Lifetime.** You'll be healing from sexual abuse throughout your life. Confronting the abuser either in person, by mail, or by talking to an empty chair may help you to feel some closure.

Confrontation is not for the abuser. It is for you.

## Thursday
*Partner, Family, Friends*

# Interfaith Marriage in Practice

You are one-half of an interfaith couple. The challenge for you is overcoming what you had been taught about "the other" and appreciating your spouse's family's religion, traditions, ancestral background, and beliefs even though they are foreign to you.

Keep your sanity as you reaffirm your commitment to each other and demonstrate respect and appreciation for each other and where you came from.

- **Learn All You Can.** Attend worship services, be involved in traditional celebrations, and read books. Know about your partner's faith and the depth and importance of his or her commitment to the religion.

- **Have Patience.** You partner's family may resist being open to your faith.

- **Draw a Line** . . . and know your boundaries you expect each other's families to respect. Negative or insulting comments may be born of ignorance but are unacceptable.

- **Adjust How You Worship and Celebrate.** People change and their spirituality evolves. Review and reassess holiday practices. Know whether you can support each other in your separate religious and spiritual beliefs.

Loving someone of a different faith requires
both an open mind and an open heart. Remember,
they are who they are in part because
of their religious teachings.

# When You Don't Care to Share

Sometimes people put their foot in their mouth. They may say something that makes you feel uncomfortable or may hint about something personal you are not ready to discuss. "Hey, when are you guys going to get pregnant?" Or, "I notice you aren't drinking, what's up?" Or, "I like your old hairstyle better."

They may be overstepping boundaries that they just don't recognize are there. Once again, you have a choice. Just because someone asks you a question, makes a comment, or tries to engage you in some way, you are not compelled to respond. Take a moment and breathe. Think about whether you want to engage with this person seriously, or maybe making a joke will be the best way out.

If you act as if you did not hear him, walk away, or just play it down, and then later realize that his words are still affecting you, what can help to save your sanity?

- **Why Are You Affected?** Pay attention to the hurt or distress and try to understand why you are upset. Is it because the person was intruding into your life? Is it because it is something you are embarrassed about? Is it because you feel others believe they have easy access to what happens to you and you feel you are powerless to change that perception?

- **Privacy Is a Right.** Know that you are entitled to a private life and you are under no obligation to share details of it with anyone. Because someone wants information is not enough of a reason for you to share it unless you want to.

- **Let It Go.** Understand that some people really do not pay attention to the possible effects of their personal inquiries and feel they are entitled to ask or say whatever they want (either because of their position in the family or a real or perceived sense of familiarity.)

- **Give the Benefit of the Doubt.** Consider calling or writing to the person and let him know that his remarks made you uncomfortable and that you found them insensitive and meddling. Hopefully, he'll think before behaving similarly with someone else.

Respect your own life, and others will learn to deal with you respectfully.

# Healthy Self-Image

We are the masters of our own self-image. Whether you define yourself, let others define you, or a little of both is essential as you come to terms with who and what you believe yourself to be. If you want to have a healthy self-image, recognizing and knowing your values is the first step. Do a "self-value" scan. Ask yourself: What is truly important to you? How do others see you? More importantly, how do you see yourself as a person?

Only when you define your values can you start living by them. You will naturally feel good about your choices in life, work, and relationships.

- **Focus on Your Strengths.** Look at your accomplishments rather than outstanding obligations. Put value on things that you might be overlooking. Are you a good listener? Then you're probably a great friend. Do you like to get people together? Then you're likely a good networker, too. Appreciate your uniqueness and don't underestimate your own potential.

- **Trust Your Inner Voice.** Have you made decisions based on someone else's advice you knew you shouldn't have taken in the first place? When faced with a choice, reflect on past experiences when you alone have made the right decision. Knowing when to listen to your inner voice (your "gut") is something that takes time to cultivate. Start exercising your intuition with small decisions and see if you get more positive results.

- **Choose Who You Spend Time With.** *Do not* spend time with people who do not respect or see your value. *Do* spend time with people who care about you and whom you care about.

- **Decide for Yourself Who You Are.** *Do not* accept other people's opinions of who you should be. Determine what is important to incorporate into your life and discard what is not serving you. Be honest with yourself, and do not do or be something you are not.

Talk positively to yourself using the language
of a kind and supportive person. Visualize this
person and hear her voice as you begin
to make your own choices.

*Partner, Parent, Family*

# Marriage Survival While Raising a Child Who Has Extra Needs

Dealing with the challenges that are raised by having a child with a disability difference can serve to strengthen a relationship that is already strong or can tear at the fabric of a weak one.

Everyone (the individual parent and the couple) needs time off to escape and be away. It's important to save your sanity and have fun, develop interests together and separately, and realize that your child is a whole child who happens to have a disability.

- **Know Your Responsibilities.** You are both a parent and a mate. Pay closer attention to each other as a couple. Those who raise children who have extra needs must take care of themselves and each other, nurturing their relationship apart from their children.

- **You'll Contribute Differently.** As with many parents, what you give to your child may be different from what your spouse gives. You may enjoy more playtime with your child while your partner may be better dealing with caregivers and teachers. Pay attention to the positive aspects of your life and your relationship, determining ways to acknowledge each other's effort and value that you put into your child.

- **Guilt Doesn't Help** . . . and does nothing to enhance your time together. Give yourselves specific opportunities to share your feelings and concerns. That way you can maximize enjoyment during your free time together. Having a child who has a disabil-

ity difference doesn't mean you can't get away. Find good child care and make special times away a priority.

Find the balance between making time for parenting and doing things as a couple that have nothing to do with your child.

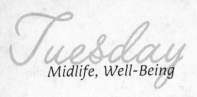

*Tuesday*
Midlife, Well-Being

# Dealing with Hot Flashes

You may know the feeling of sitting somewhere, perfectly content and comfortable, when suddenly you feel as if your entire body is on fire. You sweat through your new silk blouse and feel as if you need to tear off your clothes. Just when you begin to cool down, another one hits. Welcome to menopause!

- **Breathe Through Your Personal Heat Wave.** Before you hit the medicine cabinet, try keeping your sanity and your "cool" by paying attention to your breath. As soon as you feel the hot flash coming on, take long deep "belly breaths" (breathe in so your belly rises and falls—shallow chest breathing just does not do the trick). Slow your breath, focusing on keeping it long and gentle rather than on the fact that you are feeling old and out of control. Yes, it is all about the breath. Relax your body, one area at a time (relax your feet, then your legs, then your hips, and progress, mentally, up to the top of your head) affirming that this change will allow you to focus on renewal.

- **Keep Exercising.** The hot flashes may reduce in intensity as your physical condition improves through exercise.

- **Visualize Coolness.** Imagine bathing in a cool lake or in a chilly ocean with the waves cooling you down on a hot summer day. Mental imagery helps your body focus on feeling cool as you deal with the physical symptoms of the hot flash.

Hot flashes come at any time, so deal with them by focusing on slowing your breath and relaxing your body. Imagine a cool place.

# Standing Alone on Ceremony

If you are a person who is waiting for everyone to behave exactly as is written in your etiquette book, more likely than not you'll be disappointed a lot of the time. No one has read the book that's in your head, and furthermore, not everyone cares to the same extent that you do.

There is no question that there are correct and incorrect ways to behave and conduct your life. Some may agree with you and rise to your expectations. Others may feel that no matter what they do it will never be enough, so why try to do anything? Their defeatist attitude will surely frustrate you because they don't want to play your game. Anyway, it's time to stop playing games in which no one wins.

- **Take the Initiative.** If you are waiting for a call back to make plans, rather than stew and miss the chance to go on with your life, take the initiative to follow up. If you want to chew out the person for being inconsiderate and rude, go ahead—or give her the information she needs to know if she is going to join you. This is a way to direct your own life rather than blame others for missed opportunities.

- **Make the Effort.** Rather than waiting till people find out news about you from the grapevine, inform whomever you want about your news so that you can go forward with the business of living your life. The attitude that "It is up to them to reach out to me" will keep you waiting and alone.

- **Look in the Mirror.** Whatever you expect of others, you can probably do for yourself. So instead of looking to someone to make your life easier, think again. You are the person who can make things happen for you.

If you insist on standing on ceremony,
you'll likely stand alone.

# When Your Teenage Daughter Is Pregnant

The words you dread hearing from your unmarried teenage daughter are "I'm pregnant." When you hear this, do you roll back the clock? Take your daughter in your arms and hold her and try to make it all OK? Yell at her for going with that boy to begin with?

The feelings you have when you hear that your daughter is pregnant include shock, disappointment, anger, betrayal, sadness, and confusion. It may take you a long time to figure out not only how you feel but what to do. Your fears focus on your child and her future. Will she have an abortion? Will she give up the child if she chooses to have it? Will she keep the baby and raise it on her own? How will she support herself, return to school, raise her child? How will you fit into her life? Will she and her child be living with you? Will you be the baby-sitter or the nanny or the primary caregiver? How will this alter your relationship with your daughter? How do you keep your sanity as your dreams die and you find yourself still being a mother to a daughter whose life situation is both such a surprise and a disappointment?

- **Flow with Your Emotions.** Allow yourself to experience whichever emotions you have in response to your daughter's news and the known and unknown changes in both your lives.

- **Find Gratitude** . . . that your daughter came to you to share her situation and looks to you for support.

- **It's Not Your Fault.** Even though you believe you did everything wrong and that it was definitely your fault that your daughter became pregnant, stop blaming yourself.

- **What's Your New Role?** Reevaluate what you think your role is in the life of your daughter and her child (if she decides to keep the baby). Consider ways that you will help her learn to care for her child or make the decision to terminate the pregnancy.

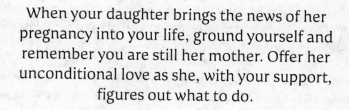

When your daughter brings the news of her pregnancy into your life, ground yourself and remember you are still her mother. Offer her unconditional love as she, with your support, figures out what to do.

# Friday
### Friends, Family

## When Someone You Love Is Experiencing Loss During the Holidays

When someone experiences a loss, such as divorce, the death of someone because of an illness or accident, or the end of an important relationship, the holidays are extremely difficult. Your loved one is grieving, and nothing you can do or say can change the circumstances. The person just has to deal with the process of loss and go through it in his own time and way.

- **Be There.** All you can really do is be there for the loved one, especially around festive times, which stir up memories. Be there to spend time, to listen, and to comfort. Just accept that other holidays may be more joyful, but this one simply will not be.

- **You Can't Make Someone Smile.** It is a mistake to force cheeriness on someone. Yes, it can be difficult to have someone around who is sad, but it's important to let him shed a few tears even at a "happy" occasion. Honor the grieving process.

- **Don't Personalize.** If your dad doesn't want to join you for the annual New Year's day brunch, give him his space. He may just be feeling lonely and is missing your deceased mom who loved to ring in the New Year this way even if she died some time ago. Or if your sister seems detached, angry, or a bit jealous when your kids open their presents, realize she might be feeling pangs of loneliness and despair because her last relationship ended along with her dreams of starting a family. Don't get offended or feel slighted. Console instead of muddying the waters with your feelings.

"Being there" for those who are grieving means honoring what they need.

# Weekend
*Well-Being*

## Gratitude in the Face of Illness

It may sound like it's too much effort, but being grateful when facing difficult health issues seems to really help in healing and in keeping a positive attitude.

A woman who had two heart attacks in one month and who underwent a quintuple bypass is one of the most grateful women I have ever met. One of the things she does is her daily gratitude walk, paying attention to her body and being grateful for it. Much can be learned from her practice.

- **Give Thanks to Your Body.** Treat it well. Walk every day. If you cannot walk, do a personal "body scan," paying attention to each part of your body. Beginning with the top of your head. Focus on the shape of your head and face and how the real you can shine through. Continue to "visit" your body in this fashion and realize that not only do you not have to take your health for granted but you can make a particular effort to acknowledge that you have a body that functions.

- **Be Grateful for Your Mind.** Take a moment to acknowledge that despite your illness, your mind is able to imagine, dream, and conceptualize. If you do have Alzheimer's or some degenerative neurological disorder, be grateful for the fact that you live in a time when it can be treated with medication or therapy.

- **Appreciate the Healthy Parts.** Be grateful for your eyes and that you can see or that you can hear. Revel in the fact that you have your natural voice and that your arms function. If you have

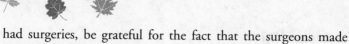

had surgeries, be grateful for the fact that the surgeons made your body their priority.

- **Say Thank You That You Are Alive.** If you had major surgery, be grateful that you survived. If your illness is affecting some of your body while other parts function, be grateful that good medication and medical services are available to you and that you still can live a joyful life.

Whatever shape your body is in, become aware and feel grateful for it.

# Monday

*Parent, Family*

## You and Your Stepchildren

Family life in general is hectic today with everyone going in different directions and so many things to do. Add to the mix stepchildren and a new husband, and you've got a whole lot going on.

If the goal of a family is to develop unity and keep the stress levels to a minimum, how do stepfamilies do it? And how do the kids factor in, especially when they may not even want to be in a stepfamily relationship? You can help to navigate the drama and create a family identity that will reflect all of the members of the family. Even though this takes time, there are things to consider as you try to maintain your own balance.

- **Feel Secure** . . . in your position of new wife and stepmother as you learn who your stepchildren are and what interests them. Be aware of the way you talk to and about them and the foundations you are building.

- **Attaching Takes Time.** Be OK about kids taking time to get close to you. They may feel guilty or disloyal to their biological parent if they attach to you as their stepparent. They may really want to know if you will be around for a while and not leave.

- **Open the Doors of Communication.** Develop a way to talk with the other parent so your stepchild is not in the position of go-between, teller of secrets, or spy. Without passing judgment on either them or their parent, allow the kids to talk about their parents with you without feeling guilty.

- **One-on-One Time with Stepkids.** Find something enjoyable, fun, unique about each child and let them know you admire and appreciate them. They need to learn that they are OK as they are and that you really notice them.

Taking time to know your stepchildren is a great investment that will teach you a lot about yourself as well as them.

*Midlife, Family, Partner, Community*

## You're Retired, Now What?

Now that you've retired from a job that tied you down to a routine and specific schedule, how do you fill up your time? You were dreaming about this day for years, and now your new sense of freedom is kind of scary.

How can each day fulfill you, and how can you stay active and feel alive as you save your sanity?

- **Get Out of the Starting Gate.** Some people retire "well" and have developed themselves outside the office. If you are of the other camp, you're not alone. Understand that you eagerly anticipated this change, but now you're dealing with fear of the unknown. Get out there and develop your interests, talents, and skills in other areas than how you used them at work. Give a new hobby, sport, organization, volunteer position, or social gathering a try.

- **Can You Contribute?** If you find that you don't have a good sense of yourself without work, think of becoming part of a community, perhaps mentoring someone learning in your field, and contribute that way.

- **Redefine Work.** If you want to keep your hand in the work world, consider working part-time. Be aware that the significance of retiring and keeping active is reducing stress. If you take on a part-time job that fills you with stress, you are not doing yourself or those you serve any good. If creating stress is your thing, then think about what you are looking for at this time of

your life. What do you need to function healthfully in a challenging and stimulating environment?

Retire from your job and work at creating a rewarding life.

# Firing Someone Because of Company Downsizing

You may be in the position of firing someone because of company decisions that have nothing to do with the quality of the employee's work but rather because of the nature of the business at the time. Showing someone the door is never easy.

- **Prepare Yourself and Stay Focused.** Realize that in your interaction with this person, you represent the company, and you need to be sensitive to the human side of this experience. Although you are aware of it, that may not seem obvious to the person being fired. Talk to him directly in a private setting before he finds out from office gossip or reads an e-mail about the company's new turn of events.

- **Assure Him of the Quality of His Work.** Even though the company is downsizing, most people take a firing personally. Assure the employee that letting him go is not reflective of the quality of his work. Give him specific examples of work that was especially well done or mention a unique quality about his professionalism. Allow time to review what contributions this person has made to the business or team and what his strengths are. Stressing positive qualities will allow him to retain confidence in his abilities and help him find a comparable or better job.

- **Be Supportive.** Offer to be supportive and provide references or any connections you may know for a new job search.

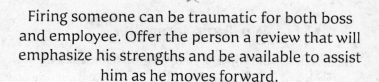

Firing someone can be traumatic for both boss and employee. Offer the person a review that will emphasize his strengths and be available to assist him as he moves forward.

*Partner, Family, Friends*

## No-Fault Infertility

It's month ten and you're still not pregnant. You're dealing with the difficult and disappointing issue of infertility, and your mental and emotional well-being is intertwined. You're drowning in a sea of emotions as you feel anxious, depressed and confused, not to mention disrupted in your life.

How can you and your partner save your sanity when you're dealing with emotional overload and the side effects of infertility drugs, and no longer having a carefree and unscheduled sexual life?

- **No Pointing Fingers.** Take the fault out of infertility and come to terms with what you are dealing with. Stay clear of blaming yourself or your partner for the choices made, such as deciding to go forward in your careers without paying attention to the difficulties of getting pregnant when you're older.

- **Prepare Your Body and Mind.** Give yourselves the chance to relax and employ coping strategies to minimize anxiety, confusion, and depression. Use techniques such as guided imagery, progressive relaxation (relaxing one body part at a time), self-hypnosis, and deep breathing.

- **Invest but Be Realistic.** Keep optimism within reach but know that the odds of becoming pregnant in the early stages of treatment are low. Weigh the financial and emotional costs of pursuing several attempts or dealing with the news of multiple fetuses. Be open to other options such as adoption or surrogacy.

*Week 26*

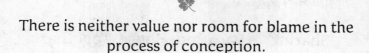

There is neither value nor room for blame in the
process of conception.

*Friends, Family*

# Sharing a Vacation House Together

"Wouldn't it be great to rent a house on the Cape this summer?" Your friends want you to vacation with them *and* share the same place. The more the merrier, as the saying goes, doesn't always apply to "together" vacations unless you have some ground rules in place.

Before you panic, save your sanity by being clear on who does what before you sign that lease and by preparing yourself in advance for a group experience.

- **Be Clean and Tidy.** Regardless of the housekeeping habits of the others in the house, keep your space neat. If you tend to let things go on vacation, this is not the time to be Oscar Madison. Nor should you be Felix Unger. If you are uncomfortable with the arrangement of the furniture or accessories, it is not your prerogative to redecorate. You can do this in your mind's eye but not in reality unless everyone agrees on the new placement of a table or chair. Just be reasonably neat and clean up the kitchen when you cook. In the bathroom, keep your stuff contained in a toiletries kit and wipe out the sink. Put your gear in its place so it's easily accessible and organized. Pitch in with exiting cleanup.

- **Everyone Needs Privacy.** Give each other space. If someone is involved in a private conversation, excuse yourself, take a walk, or read a book in another part of the house. Do not share information you have overheard. Try to keep to your own routine of exercise, quiet time, or whatever you do to keep your balance.

- **Cooking Creatively.** If you're cooking together, know if people in the family are vegetarians *before* you prepare your famous chicken salad. Also find out preferences, allergies, and no-no's. Some people are allergic to garlic and others can't stand the smell of it, so opt for balsamic vinaigrette instead of your knockout ten-clove salad dressing. Cook easy, no-nonsense meals or just grill the meat or boil the lobsters and add great prepared salads and side dishes.

When you share space, you don't have to share every aspect of your life.

# How to Avoid Catching Stress

Do you ever wonder if stress is contagious? Do you sometimes try to devise a method for moving away from a loved one who is stressed out just so you won't "catch" what he has? Fighting stress, our own and that of others, is a daunting and endless task, and we are wise if we find ways to succeed in the battle.

Who among us hasn't had a day when you feel terrific, optimistic, bright, and then, after only a few minutes with someone who is stressed, you are drowning in their pool of distress. *Not good.* First your outlook changes for the worse, so you not only share the gloom but you are in no position to help the other person. Second, your physical, mental, and emotional reserve is automatically put into use and soon depleted. Women often think their job is to be responsive to the emotional needs of those they care about (and they are usually correct and usually very efficient), and so they are often the recipients of someone else's stress.

- **Do Not Take on Their Problems.** You can offer sincere help and support without taking on their baggage as your own. Understand that your job is not to make people happier or less stressed, but rather to help them take care of their stress and problems in a way that makes them stronger and calmer. You can stress yourself out by feeling the failure if you're not able to "heal" them. This is not your job or your responsibility. Set limits on what you can do if you are asked to help in ways that are unreasonable.

- **You Can't Solve Their Problems.** Only they are the ones who can truly make changes in their lives; your role is as guide and

support. Ask what you can do to help. If you are not given any immediate answer, don't assume that you know just what to do and stitch together a I-know-how-to-help-you-feel-better quilt. It may be better to leave them alone, take a bike ride, watch a funny movie, prepare or send out for a gourmet meal. In short, ride out the moping with a coping script that helps you both.

- **Remove Yourself** . . . from the stressor periodically so you can rejuvenate. You are not abandoning this person. Think of it as helping yourself so that you can help both of you in the long run and the short run.

- **Communicate.** Inform the stressed-out person how you are reacting to the stress. This is very often a shock to the stressor.

Protect yourself without losing your ability to empathize with someone you care about.

*Monday*
Work

# Take This Job and Love It

To take on a new job, especially in a new field, even when you initiate the change, can be very stressful.

You may be unable to sleep as you ponder all the many unknowns of your new job. Then your mind can wander into many uncharted, dark corners, and you'll wonder if you are good enough for the job or if you've made a mistake leaving something safe for something challenging. If you are an older woman, you may also wonder if you'll be able to keep up with your younger colleagues.

- **Be Calm.** If you are tossing and turning for more than twenty minutes in bed, get up and drink some calming tea, such as chamomile. Find other ways to put calm in your life so fear doesn't get the better of you.

- **Be Inspired.** Read something about someone who has survived significant challenges in life. See how she got through. Recognize how people use their great personal resources and draw on their strength. There are so many books by and about people with incredible courage.

- **Be Objective.** Try to look at your life, and your situation, as objectively as possible, as you did the person in the biography you read. Analyze your options, your emotions, your strengths, as if you were a character in a narrative. This can not only be stimulating, but it can provide the means to take care of the problem from the strongest perspective.

When you doubt yourself and are about to accept a personal challenge, look for inspiration to others who have survived their own significant challenges.

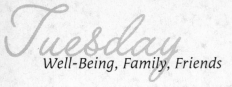

# How Much Is That Doggie in Your Memory?

As most pets have a shorter lifespan than their owners (save a parrot or two), it is inevitable that you may experience pet loss and the grieving and mourning that accompany it.

Those people who don't feel a close connection to animals find it difficult to understand the attachment and companionship you have enjoyed. They simply don't get that pets have unique personalities and insinuate themselves into a household—and a heart. Because pets love unconditionally, they are always present for us and are loving companions in their own right. Consequently, the passing of such a companion is an enormous emotional experience. Everyone grieves differently, even within the same household, as the family pet served different functions for each person who feels its loss.

- **It's OK to Grieve.** Despite what others tell you, you must allow yourself to grieve and give yourself time and space to mourn. Be patient. Understand that there will be times of intense sadness that may overcome you when you see someone with a pet. It may also be difficult when you go through a routine you once shared with your pet, such as taking your daily walk together, so try to avoid those places for a while. When you feel you can go there again, take a friend. Remember that grief will pass and life will be pleasant again. Don't be afraid to lean on friends.

- **Memorialize Your Pet.** Pay close attention to what your pet meant to you and recognize its place in your life. You may want

to put an album of pictures together or frame a special photo that captures the personality of your pet. Dedicate a bench in a garden in your pet's honor or donate to an animal shelter or an animal-therapy program.

- **Ready for a New Pet?** If you are considering getting another pet but you aren't quite ready yet, consider volunteering at an animal shelter so you can get your animal fix, while at the same time giving something to the animals who aren't lucky enough to have a loving home.

If you have opened your heart to the unconditional love of a pet, give yourself the time to heal from this profound loss.

# In a Relationship with a Workaholic

Some people can't seem to relax. They believe they will not be able to slow down. They think taking it easy means they are not doing anything worthwhile. If they are not busy, they feel that they are not being productive. And if they are not accomplishing something, working, or obtaining some goal, they do not feel worthy, and certainly don't feel worthy of relaxing. And on and on the cycle continues.

Is this someone you know and love? Is your significant other always at the office or always bogged down with paperwork at home? Does your partner become preoccupied with a project or disinterested in social and leisure time?

How do you save your sanity when the person you're in a relationship with doesn't relax or spend enough time with you but clearly loves you?

- **Don't Equate Time with Love.** Working too much is your partner's issue and it is not about how much you are loved. If you know you are cared for, don't take the late hours personally. If, however, you think your partner is busy as a way to avoid you or push you away, then you need to consider whether this relationship is the right one for you.

- **Communicate Your Needs.** For whatever reason, your partner has the need to work . . . a lot. Maybe there's a need to fill some void. Maybe there was someone, somewhere in your partner's life who equated busy with productive. But you have needs, too. If you enjoy leisure time together, you must discuss appropriate

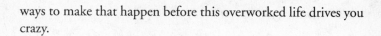

ways to make that happen before this overworked life drives you crazy.

- **Negotiate Couple Time.** If your partner wants to work half a day on Saturday, then Saturday afternoons and Sundays may be your sacred days together. If bringing work home at night is part of the deal, why not meet at the gym before the computer is turned on? How about scheduling a few ski weekends (as opposed to committing to a condo rental for the whole season) and making sure there's online service for the laptop.

- **Stay Busy.** How many items do you have on your list that you just can't get to because life is too busy? And what about that book that you have been trying to write for years? Let some of your partner's productive energy energize you and propel you to accomplish some of your own goals. Lucky you, that you have time to indulge in a bubble bath with your favorite novel. The time you have to do your own things may be a gift, so use this gift wisely instead of wasting time complaining.

- **Enlist Your Women Friends.** Come on, you know you want to see the latest chick flick. Call up your women friends and have some fun. Seek out friendships with women who also have busy mates, and don't bash your partners when you get together. Instead, find comfort in one another's similar circumstances and company when you feel the need to get out.

If your partner loves to work, you can't change that. Instead, work with the extra time you have on your hands to do things for you.

*Thursday*
Community

# Disability Differences

Hearing loss, learning or developmental disabilities, visual impairment, and spinal cord injuries are among the multitude of disability differences that set some of us apart from the "norm." But what is "normal," and how do we form our attitudes about who or what is "different"?

By examining your attitudes and being open to establishing a new perspective, you can free yourself, your family, and your children from a restricted and often stereotypic view of the world and begin to look at people who are different from you with compassion. Remember that your attitude about people who have a disability may have a vast impact on how they feel about themselves and how they are viewed by others. By exploring ways in which you can alter your attitude, you will be taking a stand for what is right and showing others love, care, and support.

- **Your Belief System.** It is normal to have a range of feelings when you think about or encounter someone who has a disability. Most of what we believe about people who have disability differences comes from stories, peer pressure, and other's perceptions. Rethink your point of view and add in doses of empathy.

- **Don't Let Them Get Away with It.** Prejudicial jokes and comments are unacceptable. Refusing to go along with the joke is not enough. Be vocal and don't become a bystander.

- **Become Educated and Educate.** Learn about the challenges of those who have disabilities and share what you learn with others.

Model to others exemplary behavior and spread the word about what is and is not OK.

Your attitude about disability difference was likely formed in ways you are unaware of. Be bold and open to changing your attitude and your thoughts.

# Friday
*Friends, Family*

## Remember Loved Ones on the Holidays

The holidays usually make us think of those who are no longer with us or of relationships that are no longer the way we would like them to be. Our loss is more keenly felt as we evoke memories of the past with the person who is absent. The loss is further accentuated because we miss them at our joyous occasions.

Pay attention to who *is* present while consciously bringing to mind stories or traditions that were unique to the people who are not there. This can be emotionally moving as well as a wonderful opportunity to recall with joy the gifts you have received from the special people in your lifetime. By allowing yourself to be open to how your grief transforms you, the chances are greater that you will be more able to appreciate the holiday spirit.

- **Quietly Reflect on the Loved One's Life.** How are you like him, what fond memories can you recall, what stories about the deceased loved one can you pass down to your children? Visit the cemetery or create a memorial space where you can have time to just "be." Show pictures from family trips, wear your aunt's heirloom pin and tell others about the day she gave it to you, or pass around your mom's scrapbook.

- **Create a Remembrance Ceremony.** Make a candle centerpiece where each candle represents someone who has died. As you light each candle, share a memory about each person. This does not have to be maudlin. It can be a joyous memory, a funny story, something that makes you smile and keeps their memory

alive. Try to incorporate new traditions that will give you and
your family a fresh outlook and hope for the future.

- **Continue a Tradition the Loved One Started.** Bake Grandma's
  favorite pie, attend a community church service as your deceased
  mom did, serve at a soup kitchen before dining as a family as
  your father did.

By dealing with your feelings of loss in anticipation
of and during the holidays, you prepare yourself to
celebrate the life of the person and appreciate the
gifts he gave you.

# Not Taking Things for Granted

Usually it takes an illness, your own or that of someone you love, to remind you how incredible it is to take anything in life for granted.

With your busy life, you can chain yourself to a computer or seal yourself in your car as you rush to and from appointments, without paying attention to the view as you drive by. You may also make it a point to consciously avoid making eye contact with people so you can keep in your own bubble. Although time alone to refresh and restore yourself is essential, becoming too focused on your own life and self without being conscious of the natural world around you can impede your ability to keep your sanity intact.

Whatever stage you are in your life, make it a point to consciously appreciate all you take for granted—whether it is something in nature or the qualities of a person.

- **Music, Music, Music.** Listen to great jazz, classical or another style of music that you love or that you know little about. Really listen to it as if hearing it for the first time. Encourage yourself to get into the mood, the intention of the composer and the musicians, and just allow the music to wash over you.

- **Follow the Sun.** Find out where the sun sets and go to a place to watch it—from the yard, the top of a building, someplace at the edge of town. Make it a special event and do nothing but focus on the sun itself, getting ready to drop into the sea, behind a building, or near a distant mountain. Think about the power

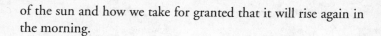

of the sun and how we take for granted that it will rise again in the morning.

- **Unconditional Love.** Take time to enjoy an animal in your life who gives you unconditional love. Appreciate your mom and dad, who did the best they knew how to do. They proved their love for you by raising you and even surviving the teen years. Show them you care about them as they age, as well as other important people in your life.

Taking life for granted prevents you from appreciating life in the day-to-day.

# Monday
### Work, Partner, Parent

## Working Long Hours, Married, and Raising a Family

Raising a family is hard work. Raising a family with both parents working strenuous long hours is lots of hard work. If you are part of a couple that works very long hours and are trying to raise a young family, take extra good care of yourself. Why? Because study after study reports that you experience the lowest quality of life among working couples, as opposed to working couples, who do not work long hours, who have the highest quality of life. Oh no! What to do?

Couples who work less stressful hours have gratification from various aspects of their lives, and they also come to rely on the predictability in their lives. They know what time they will leave work, what time they will arrive home, and they can manage day care options much more easily. Although tired, they are not "spent" by the drain of working very long hours.

So, I repeat, take extra good care of yourself and see what you can do about trimming some of those hours off your workday.

- **Sleep as Much as You Can.** Getting to bed on the earlier side each night will help you to get your rest. Take catnaps during the day if you can to avoid fatigue. If you commute on a bus or train, wear your headset and try to catch some shuteye while listening to some relaxing music or inspirational or religious music or passages.

- **Organize Your "Home Work"** . . . in such a way that you will be able to do it as efficiently as possible while still having some time to "play" with your partner and your family.

- **Call on Family and Friends.** Accept help from family, neighbors, and friends. Join a baby-sitting pool so you can get out as a couple. Plan your time so you can all help each other and feel less alone while doing what needs to be done.

- **Get Energized.** Whenever you have a break, move your body in ways that protect your back and ease your neck. Walk slowly, stretch, breathe, and renew your body in small installments throughout the day. When you eat, be sure you are feeding yourself nutritious food that will help you to keep your energy where it should be.

Stretch the time you have to include
taking care of you.

*Midlife, Family*

## A Healthy Sandwich

You've heard the term and now you really understand what it means to be in the sandwich generation. You are the inside of the sandwich because you are between two generations—your parents and your children.

Do what you can to maintain your sanity and be the healthiest sandwich you can be.

- **Don't Spread Yourself Too Thin.** Take time for yourself when you are involved with caregiving and get help so you can maintain your energy level.

- **You'll Need Help in the Kitchen.** If you also have a job, understand that many things on your list just will not get done. Give yourself a pass and engage as many other people to help you as you can.

- **It's a Good Sandwich.** Enjoy the individual moments of levity and understand that much of what you are dealing with can be accomplished if you keep a positive attitude.

If you feel afraid or inadequate, focus on the love you have for these people and you will be able to accomplish your task.

# When Your Young Adult Child Has a Drinking Problem

Many parents don't pay attention to the warning signs when their kids drink. Drinking is so much a part of life and "partying" with teens that many moms and dads don't intervene to help their children get the help they need. Sure it is difficult when your child is away at college or living on his own while working, but the problem is real and must be addressed.

- **Put to Rest Your Drinking Tales.** Stay clear of glamorizing or joking about your own drinking days. This gives your kids approval and reinforces that this is normal behavior for their age.

- **Role Model.** Look carefully at your own drinking patterns and habits. If you drink alcohol irresponsibly, what are you presenting to your kids?

- **Let Them Know the Facts.** Neither hide the truth nor overreact. Yes, many kids at college drink too much and lose control of their ability to make reasonable decisions and take care of themselves. In fact, most car accidents and date rape incidents happen when there is alcohol. Remember that many college students die from alcohol poisoning, which occurs most often from drinking games.

- **Open Up Lines of Communication.** Talk with your child and express your concerns not only about their ability to take care

of themselves but also about putting other young people at risk (e.g., when they are at the wheel). Even if you are far away, you can talk and be available to listen.

## Excessive drinking needs to be discussed openly and seriously with your young adult child.

## Emotional Abuse

Emotional abuse is insidious, and for many women, it goes undetected or ignored. Perhaps you have been in relationships where you are insulted, demeaned, blamed, undermined, or trashed for a long time. If you've heard yourself say and perhaps believe that "This is the way my husband is," "My daughter doesn't mean anything by it," or "It's the way my boss handles his stress" maybe you are being abused . . . emotionally.

Over time, women who have experienced emotional abuse lose their self-esteem, their confidence, and their ability to care for themselves. When you are the target of an emotional abuser, you may be holding anger within yourself that ultimately comes out, directed at you or other people in your life. You wonder why when you are with this person you feel "less than," intimidated, frightened, incapable, depressed, and stuck, instead of good about yourself.

If you find you are in a situation in which someone is repeatedly abusing you verbally or nonverbally, wants to harm you by making you feel diminished, or is trying to control or gain power over you, your sanity may be at risk.

- **Everyone Deserves Respect.** Remind yourself that nobody has the right to treat you disrespectfully. Observe people who speak kindly to each other. Imagine yourself in such a relationship with this person or without this person. Whether you have experienced this or not, believe that problems can be addressed without insulting, demeaning, or devaluing another person in the process.

- **Don't Blame Yourself.** When you hear that you are to blame for whatever is causing the verbal or emotional barrage, tell yourself that you cannot "make" anyone do or say anything. We are each responsible for our own behavior, words, and actions. Put the responsibility squarely on the shoulders of the person who is abusing you.

- **Connect with Others.** Rather than feel isolated, feel yourself connected with the life around you. Walk outdoors and be with people who lift your spirit. Remind yourself and let others remind you of all the things you do that you are good at, enjoy, and appreciate.

- **Say No.** Practice saying, "Enough"; "Stop"; "I will not allow this to go on." When you really believe these words, say them firmly to the abuser.

- **No More.** When things are calm, talk to the person, write a letter, compose an e-mail, or send a voice tape, informing the person that you are no longer going to accept behavior that you specifically describe. Share with the abuser what you will do when that behavior happens again. Assure the abuser of your commitment to the relationship (if it's one worth keeping) as you reaffirm your stand as someone who will no longer participate when this behavior repeats.

Once you stop abusive behavior you will begin to feel freer to explore ways to care for yourself because you have taken your own side.

## Love Ya but in Small Doses

Is there someone in your life you can't live without but can't live with—your mother, sister, or old friend? Why? There may just be a basic personality clash. Your sister may be a bit of a control freak and you want to keep your sanity while figuring out ways to maintain your bond. Cutting off the relationship is not an option, but there are plenty of good reasons not to do those long family dinners!

- **Stay in Neutral Zones.** Do things that are time limited. Two-hour dinners are terrific, and there are other people around for good behavior so the conversation can't get too out of hand. (You can always change the subject when the next course is served!). That time limit thing? It's really important. All of us can handle two hours, but after three hours things tend to deteriorate. If you must spend longer time, add an event—like a concert or a movie. And please, no coffee and dessert after! Put your diet into effect and go home!

- **You Can't Redesign Their Personality** . . . so why try? It is not worth your time and nothing good will come out of it. Focus on the good parts and stay clear of the danger zones. It is only a couple of hours, and unless you are both truly committed to working on your relationship, you will likely feel unsatisfied with both your effort and your result.

Some relationships, even if they are family, work better in small doses.

# Weekend
### *Well-Being*

## Manage Your Mood with Movement

Some days you can feel your mood drop. When you can't get outdoors, feel overwhelmed with too many things, or can't focus on any one thing, your upbeat outlook may wane.

Instead of reaching for a drink or comfort food, move your body. Depending on how you feel and what you need, moving will help release the "happy hormones" that will contribute to saving your sanity as you improve your mood.

- **Move Your Energy.** First stand still with feet planted on the floor, yet relaxed. Close your eyes and feel yourself in space. Open your eyes and begin to swing your arms, first in small circles and then in increasingly larger circles. Stop and feel the way the energy flows in your arms to your fingertips. Tell yourself you are a storehouse of energy that is yet untapped.

- **Reach for the Sky.** Gently move your body and feel yourself lifting off of one foot and then the other. Reach up to the sky with one arm and then the other and lift and stretch. Tell yourself the sky is the limit.

- **Open Up and Discover.** Swing your arms from side to side, gently reaching and stretching in all directions. Tell yourself there are places you have yet to explore, and that you have not yet reached your potential.

### Simple movement can help you to manage how you feel.

*Parent, Family*

## Your Grown-up Child Is Far Away

Your "baby" lives across the continent, and you are proud of her ability to be on her own working in a brand-new city, and of her adventurous spirit. But she knows no one there. Is she *really* up to taking care of herself, and what happens when she gets lonely or wants a home-cooked meal?

This is different from when she went to college. Then you had a sense of security that she would be looked after, had access to healthy food, and was protected because she was in a locked dorm with one hundred other students. This may have been a false sense of security, but nonetheless you felt it. Keeping your sanity when your son or daughter is beginning life oh so far away is another story.

- **Pray Daily for Your Child's Safety.** This is important. Visualizing your child being safe and guarded by a higher being allows you to do something positive for your child, every day, from afar. Rather than filling yourself and the air around your child with negative, worrisome thoughts, you can focus on positive images, which will help both your child and you.

- **Take Your Cues** . . . from your child about how often and when to visit, e-mail, and call. You want her to determine how much is the right amount, and this might be a work in progress. Take notice of how much is too much and how much is not enough so she knows you are always there for her.

- **Visit.** If you can, stay at a hotel nearby so your child can have privacy, go to work, and see you in the evening. If she is able to take some time off while you are there, do something fun together. Your mission is not to make her feel guilty for moving far away. Encourage her to bring friends to dinner so you can meet who is in her life. Get maps of the city and explore so you can keep busy during the day, so that you're not a worry to her.

When your kids are far away, you can still be connected . . . just not in the way you were.

## Playing Real Games in Court

You have to go to court for a traffic violation, small claims action, or sexual harassment suit, or because you're in a custody battle with your ex-spouse. No matter what the issue, big or small, dealing with the judicial system can be intimidating and a bit scary.

It's also very stressful. This is the time to mediate, journal, take warm baths, and do yoga. To save your sanity, learn how to maneuver in the court system, and when you are not in court, do anything that relieves your anxiety.

- **Find an Advocate.** Does your attorney really believe in your position? Does he or she talk to you on your level, really understand your case, and want the best outcome for you? Most importantly, do you have respect for this person who may very well have great influence on your life? If you get the feeling that your lawyer is judging you or is not in sync with you, find someone who is. Even if you have to change attorneys midstream, the right advocate will keep your best interests at the forefront. And make sure you have your own support team in court—your mom, sister, or friend.

- **Visualize People in Their Underwear.** Did you ever do this as a kid when you were nervous about speaking in front of people? Well, under that polished professional attire and behind those icy stares from people in the courtroom, they're all wearing underwear just like you. No one is better than anyone else. So say what you need to say because it's the truth and because you have to stand up for your rights and your dignity.

- **There's Nothing Warm and Fuzzy About It.** Our judicial system is not based on empathy, but on serving justice. That said, you and the court may differ on what justice is. If you led this action with the truth and an open heart and did what you needed to do to prepare your case well, the decision rests with a jury or judge and it's out of your control. This is the stark reality. Learn acceptance and work on letting go of resistance . . . and move on.

Surviving a court case takes courage, strength, and a solid support system. Be good to yourself during this time and don't add any more stress; court is stressful enough.

# Don't Dump Your Partner Just Because You're in the Dumps

Is your relationship unfulfilling? Have you been down this road before with past loves and wonder why you're once again traveling the same path? Are you contemplating dumping your partner because this isn't the relationship you envisioned?

You may be inclined to blame the person you love, but why don't you try something different this time? Rather than pointing the finger, look to see what *you* can do to shift the balance. Often we blame and criticize our partner for not giving us what we have stopped giving to them and to the relationship. If you feel ignored, are you no longer reaching out? Are you less grateful or appreciative or supportive of your partner? What does your behavior reveal about your feelings for the other person?

- **Rewind for a Moment.** When you wonder what has happened in your relationship, spend some time reviewing good memories of your time with this person. You both may be going through a bad patch and may feel distant toward each other. Create moments in your mind to connect with the relationship so you do not create more distance.

- **Reach Out.** Without demanding anything, just be present and do something thoughtful for your partner. Focus on pleasant memories and positive qualities of the other person and why you chose to be with this person in the first place.

- **Share Your Thoughts.** Remember something good or funny or interesting that happened to you, and how you thought of your mate during the interaction or event.

- **Compliment and Demonstrate Appreciation.** Recognizing your partner's contribution to your family, well-being, and life can make you feel closer as a couple and contribute to feeling less lonely.

First look at yourself instead of your partner when trying to improve your relationship.

## Keeping Score

Because humans are not perfect and everyone makes mistakes, relationships are challenging. Nobody gets it right all the time. It is up to you to decide how much you are willing to give the person you are with the benefit of the doubt.

Every relationship is different, and what we tolerate in one we might not tolerate in another. Why? Because we are dealing with personalities, agreements, commitments, histories, benefits, and losses, and for each of our relationships we need to acknowledge the differences. A wise person knows that if you keep score you are likely to come out the loser.

- **Look at People's Strengths.** Pay attention to the nature of your best friend who is compassionate, caring, and a great listener but who cannot get it together to initiate a telephone call. Do you cancel her out of your life? Can you be fine with being the one to make the calls and leave it at that? Or are you going to use her inability to call you against her and cancel out the rest of her positive attributes?

- **Ask Not What Others Can Do for You.** Focus on what you can comfortably do for your mate, friends, and family without feeling as if you are being taken for granted or taken advantage of. When the line is crossed and you feel uneasy, you can reconsider the imbalance and either pull back to a comfortable level or discuss your situation with the other person.

- **Nothing is Equal.** People offer one another their personal gifts, which are not always equal but can still be equitable.

If you want to keep score, go to a baseball game; don't try to build a relationship.

## Love and War

One of the most uncomfortable, and untenable situations is being caught in a fight between friends. So many people have witnessed savage and consistent arguments between couples, both in public places and in private settings.

What is the correct thing to do? Do you silently endure the damage? Do you step in and try to resolve the conflict? Do you take sides if a question is hurled your way? Do you get up and leave, making your position known via a slamming door?

- **Can You Help?** First things first; decide if you can be helpful in the situation. If you think you can, ask how you can do anything constructive and do only that. Then see if you can remove yourself from the situation.

- **Do *not* Take Sides.** You are not a fireman who can put out fires. Don't offer an opinion on either the tone of the argument or the subject at hand. Sticking up for one or the other will only put you in an awkward place. You may also lose the trust and alienate the party you are not siding with at the moment. This is a no-win situation. Instead, back off and let your friends know that you are not interested in being the middleman in their drama.

- **Give Them Privacy.** Give your friends the adequate space to discuss—or harangue—privately. Go for a walk; go to the restroom. You can even set a time limit and let them know you'll be back in half an hour—or never if they can't get their act together.

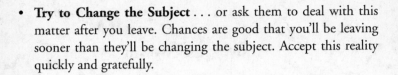

- **Try to Change the Subject** . . . or ask them to deal with this matter after you leave. Chances are good that you'll be leaving sooner than they'll be changing the subject. Accept this reality quickly and gratefully.

Sometimes only *you* can be fair in love and war.

## Time Yourself Out

Are you overdue for time off for good behavior? (For *any* behavior, come to think of it.)

Vacations are supposed to be time away to restore and rejuvenate, but it is becoming harder and harder to accomplish this if you insist on being away with a cell phone, a PDA, and a laptop. Whenever you do manage to get away, be sure to take some real time to take care of yourself. Begin by losing the schedule you follow when you are at home or at work. Create a vacation schedule that is packed with only those things you really want to do that will relax and refresh you.

- **Travel and Relax.** Take time on the plane or train to read for pleasure, listen to music, or just enjoy the view of the clouds. Bring an eyeshade to relax and *do not* work on your laptop. Make it your goal to arrive at your destination relaxed and ready to explore.

- **Set a Different Pace** . . . preferably a slower one. If you plan two days at a spa during a busy tour, take the time to study the types of offerings and carefully select and plan time between your sessions. Don't book every moment of a vacation. Let happy accidents and spontaneous, sensual events happen for you.

- **Tune In to the Natural World** . . . and tune out your links to the electronic world. Turn off cell phones, laptops, and beepers, and instead connect with the people you are with. Connect

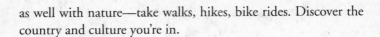

as well with nature—take walks, hikes, bike rides. Discover the country and culture you're in.

Time off allows you to return with a new and refreshed point of view. Nobody is so important and no task is so big that you cannot take some time for yourself to restore.

# When Your Child Decides to Be Childless

You have spent much of your life looking toward the time when you will be a grandparent and want to see the joy of watching your child parent his or her own children. It's important to you that future generations carry on your values as well as your genetic code, and that you leave a legacy. It's overwhelming for you to think that your "line" stops with your child.

Understand that your child needs to make this life choice, not you. It is not appropriate to pressure your adult child into becoming a parent because of your need to become a grandparent. If your son or daughter cares to engage you, listen to the true reasons he or she has decided to remain childless.

- **Look at Things as They Are.** To support your child, you may have to let go of visions of sharing grandparent experiences and stories with your friends and family. Also, release the notion that your son or daughter will only be complete as a parent.

- **It's Not About Good or Bad.** Come to terms with the fact that not having grandchildren is not a reflection on your being a good or bad parent. Neither choice reflects good or bad, generous or selfish. Challenge yourself to adapt to the situation so you do not make your child feel guilty about the decision to remain childless.

- **Enjoy Time with Your Child.** Talk about things other than children with your child. Find areas in common to explore and develop together.

- **Be Around Kids.** Share your gifts, wisdom, and love with other children who don't have grandparents or whose grandparents are not around. Engage in volunteer work with children who need mentors and tutors. Give your time as a "baby rocker" in hospitals for babies who are infected with HIV.

Parents and their adult children can have other areas to share aside from children. Find those areas and engage in them lovingly.

# Bullying at Work

Whether this is your first job or tenth or if you've been at this firm for a long time or short, you are now facing a bully at work.

Unfortunately, bullying in the workplace is increasing and may actually be an accepted practice in your office. It is difficult to enforce and even more difficult to challenge someone of authority who is yielding power to get the job done. You may even fear getting the ax if the bully is your boss. Bullies at work often seek personal or professional gain by ostracizing their victim from other employees. Your life at work can be made a living hell while your health, attitude, and ability to rise through the ranks can suffer.

Since you can't control someone's negative behavior directed at you, you instead can:

- **Use Healthy Coping Strategies.** Take a break, journal when you get home, get support from friends. Exercise and create time for your own interests to get your mind and body in shape to deal with the work situation. Bullying can affect many of the body's functions, such as blood pressure, cardiovascular issues, muscular problems, fatigue, and digestive disorders. And be careful about abusing alcohol or other substances. They can lead to problems with your job performance, which may exacerbate the problem.

- **When You Leave the Office, Leave.** Watch that your irritability does not spill over to your personal and social life, contributing to conflict with friends and family. This will only increase your

feelings of isolation. Stay connected to your family and people you care about and who care about you.

- **Change Your Language.** Stop saying, "Work is killing me," "I cannot stomach it," "He's breaking my back," and "I cannot stand it." Instead, say, "I need a strong heart to deal with this" or "Work is a challenge that I can deal with better when I am healthy and strong."

- **Consider Standing Up for You.** Attempt to work it out with the person or enlist the help of a manager or someone in human resources. Companies have a moral (if not legal) obligation to intervene and stop employee abuse. Sometimes, however, people who speak up for themselves and challenge the bully become further ostracized, are transferred, or are given bad work reports. Weigh the risks of speaking up or staying silent. Is being verbally abused worth it?

- **It's Not Your Fault.** Even if you make a mistake on an assignment, bullying is not OK. Yelling and verbal abuse is unacceptable and potentially harmful to your health and the health of your company, as well as society at large. Bullying is not an indicator that someone is a tough manager—it only means he is a bully.

- **Don't Play the Game.** Resist resorting to the same level of behavior. If you must enter the duel, retain your dignity; be creative and incisive with your response.

- **Dodge Insults.** Repeat to yourself that this person is not worth listening to and act as if he is not there. Imagine the words flying

by you, missing you as if arrows aimed at you are way off target. Tell yourself nothing can pierce you. Ignore as much as you can, and when the barrage is over, ask if the person was talking to you. Suggest if he has something to say, perhaps he could try again in a way you would hear.

Bullies get what they want through intimidation.
Resisting their actions by keeping yourself
strong and healthy prevents them
from achieving their goal.

# Couple Identity

You have your own individual identity, which has been developing since you were a child. From the time you began dating your partner, you have developed another identity, your couple identity.

A challenge in marriage is finding the balance between these two identities. As a couple, you grow simultaneously, and often complementarily (and sometimes in opposition to) with your individual identity. You need to be aware of how you think of yourself in relation to each other. At times, the strength of your couple identity may interfere with you being your true self. How does it enhance or inhibit the best or worst of you?

- **Define Your Couplehood.** Take a few moments and consider how you describe yourself and your spouse. Think about how you as a couple and you as individuals have changed since you have been married. In which ways do you and your spouse complement each other? What are your strengths and what are your partner's strengths? When you think of yourself as a couple, how is your marriage like and unlike what you had hoped it to be? Do you depend on your spouse to help you achieve and maintain your goals? How? Who are you as a couple?

- **Retain, Regain, or Forgo.** What do you still do that you used to do before you were married? What do each of you no longer do, and why did you stop? What would you like to do again? Think of what is good about your life and what is missing. See if there is a way to include whatever it is that you benefit from doing. I have seen many women in their sixties pick up a paintbrush for the first time since their early twenties and return to this form of expression with a peaceful passion.

- **A Strong Personal Identity** . . . will strengthen the marriage. Keep fulfilling your own needs while giving to the marriage. Encourage your partner to work on a strong sense of self. If participating in a book group, joining a bowling team, or attending a once-a-year spiritual retreat has been part of your life, think about how doing things just for you benefits your marriage.

Maintaining the balance of you, me,
and us requires attention. All the parts
are constantly evolving.

# Keeping Good Memories When Relationships Change

One of the most difficult as well as potentially rewarding aspects of life is coming to terms with change. People change, so relationships change. Life is not written according to a script.

You intended to stay married for a lifetime and now you are divorced. Your once open and carefree, uncensored conversations with your son are now circumscribed and guarded. Your images of playing at the beach with your grandchildren are clouded because you have a strained relationship with their mother.

Keep your sanity while protecting your memories of times that were pleasant and emotionally rewarding and fulfilling. Because you are going through a tough patch, you need not erase or deprive yourself of the good times you had and the feelings of joy that you felt. It is up to you to preserve them.

- **You Own Your Memories.** Even if the people in your life are not in your life the way you want them to be, nothing can take away from the wonderful memories or times that you shared when things were going well.

- **Remember with Fondness** . . . the surprise anniversary party your son hosted for your friends even if you and he are presently estranged. Recalling good memories is potentially good for your health. Staying entrenched in stress is potentially detrimental to your health.

When relationships change, remembering good times will ease your anger, disappointment, or loss.

# Holding Secrets

Everyone, at one time or another, has told someone a secret or has been asked to keep a secret.

When you're told a secret, you are being valued as a friend. You are perceived to be trustworthy, loyal, and safe. When you hold a secret, you have a responsibility to honor someone's privacy. A really good friend resists the urge to tell.

Some secrets may be fun to share, while others offer too much information. What if a friend tells you about a serious illness or that she is quitting her job? Others may confide their infidelity, unethical business practices, abuse as a child, or unhealthy addiction. When your sister tells you, on the QT, that she's pregnant, what do you do when your mom comments that darling sis needs to drop a few pounds?

- **Don't Wait.** If you don't want to keep a secret, let the teller know right away. Give them a reason for your discomfort so they don't take it as a personal rebuff.

- **Your Mission Is Not to Tell.** You may be persuaded to divulge the secret. First, relax. You don't need to reveal anything you don't want to. Talk normally, give a simple response, and resist becoming angry or defensive. "I make it a habit of not talking about people's private issues because I don't like it when people talk about mine." Beware responding too curtly. "I'm not at liberty to talk about anything," may actually speak volumes, running the risk of letting the cat out of the bag.

- **Don't Tell Even If the Secret's Out.** It is never your prerogative to share someone's confidence with a third party. Only the teller can share that information.

- **Harmful Information Is Not a Secret.** This is one time when you don't have to keep a secret. If the information is illegal, perilous, or harmful to another or the teller himself, assume a more active role. Confide in someone else who can help or go to the appropriate authority. Strongly consider doing something even if it means jeopardizing the friendship. Helping your friend to avoid a destructive path will be more beneficial in the long run.

No matter how juicy, how tempting, or how interesting, you must remember that the secret is *not* yours. You are its guard.

# *Weekend*

## If You Can't Be with Your Family for the Holidays

This year you cannot be with your family for the holidays, and it's getting you down. You'll miss your aunt's famous sweet potato soufflé and your favorite uncle's war stories.

Be with your family in spirit and contribute to those around you this holiday season, and you'll make it through. Saving your sanity as you anticipate a holiday on your own takes some planning.

- **Send a Note.** Think about the people who mean so much to you whom you won't be with in person. Take the time to write a note (not an e-mail). Let them know how much you care about them, how and why you value their being a part of your life, and how important they are to you.

- **Schedule Your Next Visit.** Plan to travel and see your family at some point in the future. Line up a special activity to do with or for each family member so that you can totally absorb the experience of being with them.

- **Give to Others.** Why be alone when you can lend a helping hand? Buy or prepare a holiday meal for a family that cannot afford it or volunteer to serve meals at a local shelter. Visit a local nursing home and talk with or read to an elderly person who would appreciate the company.

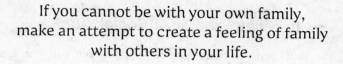

If you cannot be with your own family,
make an attempt to create a feeling of family
with others in your life.

# Single and in a Social Rut

You really want to meet people, but going out with the same crew each weekend is getting old. You're tired of the bar scene, and all that partying gets you nowhere.

How can you get off the merry-go-round and get a new perspective? Keep your sanity by branching out and developing new connections that give you a whole different view of life and how to live it.

- **Sign Up.** What have you wanted to do? Cooking class, bike riding, a wine-tasting class? Do things you have never done or have not done in a very long time.

- **Give Yourself a Chance** . . . and the nerve to meet people who are different from you. Open your mind to know those in other areas of town, in different income brackets, involved in new interests, or from other ethnicities or cultures.

- **Commit to Attendance.** It may be forced at first, but once you find the things you enjoy and the people you like, going to a meeting, class, or get-together will become enjoyable. It just takes that first step—so commit to attend something that gets you out there, once a month.

You're in a rut and can pull yourself out.

# Older Mom

OK, so you have accepted that you'll be the oldest mom at "Mommy & Me" classes and have the gray hairs to prove it. But as a midlife woman who has decided to become a new mother, have you come to terms with whether you can keep it together and do what is required to be a mom? You may ask yourself if you are capable of putting a child's needs ahead of your own. Are you concerned with how your life will change and how you will take care of yourself?

To date, much of your life has focused on yourself. You have spent much of your energy responding to your own needs, not having to be concerned about a child. Can you be responsive to the needs of anyone else, let alone someone so vulnerable and dependable? And what happens to those after-work parties, massages, and traveling to exotic places?

- **Allow Shifts** . . . within yourself to take place. You may not have wanted to have a child earlier in your life. Or you may have been trying for a very long time and now find you are going to be a mother. Many things about being a mom are out of your control, but allowing yourself to learn from the experience is not one of them.

- **Settle into Motherhood.** Ambivalence is part of coming to terms with any resentment that the child is "interfering" with your life. Even though you may have strived for perfection in your work and accomplished significant things in life, being a mother may slow your pace for a while. Learn your new maternal rhythm and revel in being the best mother you can be. Focus

*Week 31*

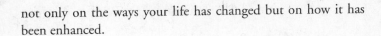

not only on the ways your life has changed but on how it has been enhanced.

- **"Be" with Your Baby.** Teach yourself to live in the moment and be present with your child. Tickle those toes, sing and play. Savor each precious moment you are together.

- **"Be" with Yourself.** Save some time just for you and schedule that massage. Rest, exercise, eat healthfully to be strong and energetic for your child. Get as much help as you can muster.

- **Focus on Your Unique Qualities** . . . that you can give to your child, and transform your limitations into strengths. An older mom generally has more patience, more life experience and more money.

The qualities that make a good mother are not necessarily limited by age.

## It's a Family Affair

Joining the family business, rather than carving a career elsewhere, may or may not be something you have been longing to do. If you have been groomed since the cradle to follow in your parents' footsteps, then working in your family's company has always been at the forefront. Just like the British royals, doing something else was never an option.

Hopefully, you've been put on the letterhead because you want to be there. If this really isn't your idea, question whether this job is something you're doing out of duty or loyalty, or whether you can find your own satisfying niche to save your sanity when the inevitable differences of opinion between family members arise.

- **Keep Your Identity.** Get out of old familiar and not-so-healthy roles you developed growing up in the family. Hold your personal power and know you are to be treated as an adult. Defer to your family mentors, but don't get steamrolled by the leader of the clan. Hold your own.

- **Value You.** You have something valuable to contribute to this business. Show respect to other family members who have put in the long hours. But expect recognition for a job well done.

- **Avoid Family Rivalry.** Pay attention to your sibling relationships and recognize if you or other family members treat one another in ways that were forged in childhood. If so, treat your family as adult peers and colleagues and set an example. Kindly confront those who exhibit less than professionalism standards.

Being a part of a family business could be the most rewarding job you'll ever have; just get off to a great start by setting unassuming boundaries and knowing your value.

## Coming Back after an Affair

Affairs usually signify that there are unresolved issues in the relationship. Affairs are about betrayal.

When you have an affair you take part of yourself away from your spouse. You lie about where you are going, where you have been, and you make up excuses why you cannot be together or sleep together or share yourself. There is a whole part of your life that you cannot talk about.

The real key is how you can begin to have an honest relationship after you have been in a dishonest one. Trust and expectations are shattered. It takes time, energy, and a fair amount of risk taking to rebuild a new foundation for the marriage. Start one step at a time to attempt to get your marriage on track.

- **Examine What Happened.** First consider the reasons that you had an affair (sexual frustration; inquisitiveness; payback; boredom; need for recognition, acceptance, or appreciation) and try to assess whether these issues can be addressed within the marriage without the third party involved.

- **Save the Marriage or Not?** Can you make a serious commitment to your spouse to try to work out your differences honestly, renegotiate your marriage agreement, and rethink the way you want to be married? This takes strong will, determination, and an open heart.

- **Can You Take the Consequences?** Are you willing to accept your spouse's emotional and behavioral responses to your affair,

such as intense anger, disappointment, accusations, and rejection? Can you take responsibility for "leaving" the relationship and the problems you have with it?

- **Change Your Ways.** Agree to become more trustworthy, open, and honest. Understand that you may never be forgiven.

If you take responsibility for what led up to the affair and commit to examining yourself and your marriage, you may have a stronger and more committed marriage in the end.

## Insert Foot Into Mouth

Ever been in the position of saying something and then, afterward, realizing (either because someone comments or you have an epiphany) that you said the wrong thing? You feel awful. It may have been said in innocence or without thinking, but nonetheless it was said.

It's difficult to make a comeback after you blurt out something that's inappropriate. Kidding someone about not having a drink at a party without appreciating that he may have begun dealing with a drinking problem, or sharing the news that someone is pregnant when she wanted to keep it a secret is embarrassing. How do you recover from these awkward moments?

- **Let Experience Be Your Guide.** It may take only one comment such as "When are you due?" and realizing that her three-month-old is in the stroller to learn to think before you speak. Sometimes we don't think what we say is going to be inappropriate or put someone in an uncomfortable position, and yet we keep at it. Joking about it can really add to the level of discomfort. Learn from experience so you know that in a similar situation in the future you will act differently. And that may be enough.

- **Apologize.** But it also may be useful, after you are aware of what you did, to calmly approach the person either by letter, e-mail, phone, or in person and let her know you are sorry you pushed her at a time when it was inappropriate. You hope you did not cause any grief and if you did, you ask her to forgive you. Tell her that you learned from the experience and will, in the future,

contain your enthusiasm for commenting about something you
are not sure of.

**Sharpen your awareness of what can offend people,
and steer clear of these topics.**

# Deciding to Be an Organ Donor

If you are in relatively good physical shape, regardless of age, you can donate your tissues and organs to help those who would otherwise not have the opportunity to live their lives to the fullest, or at all. Such selfless giving is a truly generous act, because you are giving the possibility of life to people who you do not know. It is up to you to reflect on and come to a decision about what you want to do with your body, and it is also up to you to make sure that your family understands your desire.

- Even if you have a signed donor card on your driver's license, discuss your decision with your family, since they may be the ones to intervene by signing a consent form to permit your organs to be donated.

- You can give back to your community in many ways—when you are alive and when you are dead. Think seriously about what the gift of life would mean to you if you, your child, parent, or sibling was in a situation where they were waiting for an organ that could save their lives or provide a quality of life they would otherwise never have.

Each of us can consider contributing to the well-being of those we do not know in ways that can change their lives forever. You have the gift of life should you choose to use it.

# Monday

*Partner, Parent*

## Loving Your Spouse and Your Children

Having a strong, dynamic, vital love relationship with your spouse is a wonderful gift to give your children. The love you feel for your spouse and the love you feel for your children are different kinds of love. And you have plenty for each.

There need not be a competition. Don't get hung up with whether you love your spouse more or less than your children. It is futile to ponder whether you would save one or the other if you were in a sinking boat. What *is* important is not to pit your spouse and your children against each other and to make one feel "less loved" than the other.

- **Remember What's Important to Both.** Take interest in what your spouse values and be aware of what he finds important. Concentrate on your kids' schoolwork, friends, and other activities. Focus on the person who needs you the most at the time, without disregard for your other family members.

- **Carve Out Time for Each.** At night, create bedtime rituals for your children, such as reading out loud, talking about the day, or cuddling. Reserve the rest of the evening for your spouse. Children need structure and parents need private time.

- **Demonstrate Your Love for Both.** Little things matter. Everyone needs a hug, a kiss and hearing "I love you." Everyone!

The love between spouses is a different kind of love and not comparable to the love between parents and their children. You can love both at the same time.

## Adapting Your Pace to an Elderly Person

Your elderly parent, relative, or friend is not at the same level of stimulation or activity as you. Often a simple meal and a visit provide a much-needed change of scenery for someone who doesn't get out much. Or simply taking someone on a walk along the beach takes little effort on your part and can make their whole week.

Giving someone a little attention and diversion while recognizing that you have to slow the pace in his presence just might be a sanity-saving tactic for the both of you.

- **Take Your Time.** Watch carefully what you see when you slow down. If you are used to moving fast, keep a constant check on your speed. Learning to take the time to really "be" with someone will create more balance.

- **Be in the Moment.** You may be particularly saddened to see deterioration of the person at your side or wonder what your own aging will be like. When you feel this way, bring the attention to the present moment. Focus attention on the breath, sounds, and sensations in your body.

- **Know That Your Kindness Will Be Felt.** Elderly people often do not have the energy or are not in the frame of mind to show their appreciation for your efforts. Learn to give without being praised and know that you are making a difference, even if they don't show it.

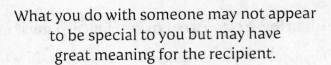

What you do with someone may not appear
to be special to you but may have
great meaning for the recipient.

# Do You Have to Love Your In-Laws?

Let's face it, not everyone has a great relationship with in-laws. You just cannot enter the realm of who they wanted their child to marry, and no matter how hard you try, they cannot appreciate any of your many fabulous attributes. So what to do?

They are still your spouse's parents and the grandparents of your children. Even if you don't like your in-laws very much and they react toward you as if you are an outsider, can you appreciate that they have enhanced your life because they raised your spouse? Even if you have been decent, respectful, and hospitable and they still won't accept you, understand that it is not up to you to change them or their perception of you.

- **Get-Together Survival.** Before you interact with them, engage the support of your spouse and tell him what you need to help you navigate the time together. Decide what is tolerable and what isn't and plan events that are doable for all involved. Leaving you alone with your mother-in-law while he watches the game with his dad isn't going to work.

- **Keep Your Sense of Self Intact.** It just happens that in some families, you will not please everyone. There is no rule that says they have to like you or you have to like them. So you might as well just be yourself. There is, however, a rule of conduct that says you have the right not to be insulted, disrespected, or diminished, nor do you have the right to do this to others.

- **Focus on Your Marriage.** Accept that you married their child or brother (although it may seem as if you married all of them) and put your energy into the relationship with your spouse.

If you find your in-law situation is difficult, focus on the positive aspects of your spouse and remind yourself that he was raised by these people.

# Cha-Ching! You've Got It and Your Family Doesn't

When you have more money than others in your family, you may be looked upon as the family bank. Your niece comes to you to finance her car, while your cousin pitches his latest get-rich-quick scheme for you to invest in. And watch out for family holidays that you usually host, dinners out when you're always stuck with the tab, and special events you treat everyone to.

Only you can decide how generous you want to be with your family. Does it mean that you always have to come to someone's aid? When do people cross the line between genuinely asking for help and expecting perpetual financial bail-outs? And how do you tell your family enough is enough?

- **Let Go of "Having More" Guilt.** Notice the feelings you have related to being in the position you are in. If you are judged or criticized because you have more means than your family members, appreciate that this is their problem. It's not your issue that they have a hard time dealing with your success.

- **Don't Be a Loan Officer.** Be as generous as you feel is appropriate. Unless you are prepared not to get the money back, don't loan any money.

- **Pay Directly.** If you want to help out and feel it is appropriate, pay directly for the services that are needed (day care, help with rent or college tuition), or purchase what the person may need.

- **Go Out to a Crowd Pleaser.** When you go out, choose a place that is reasonably priced so you are not the only one picking up the check and others can chip in their share.

Understand that some people who are close to you may see your financial success as theirs. It's up to you to set boundaries.

## Too Many Celebrations . . .
## Too Little Time

Invitations to weddings, graduations, christenings, confirmations, and showers seem to arrive at the same time that Mother's Day and Father's Day pop up on the calendar.

For many of us leading busy lives, these joyous events can be difficult to schedule and become tedious to attend. How can we honestly be there for others when we have so much going on in our own lives?

When you are "there" for others, it means you care and value your relationship with that person. Making the effort to attend functions and events important to a family member, friend, or colleague acknowledges your ongoing relationship and the respect you feel for them. But if you're there in body only and not in spirit, are you really supporting that person and sending an encouraging and loving message?

If you hear yourself say, "I wish I didn't have to go," or "I don't have time for this," maybe it's time to reevaluate your relationship with the person being honored. Ask yourself in what ways is this person important to you, is attending worth the energy, and can you demonstrate enthusiasm? If not, consider whether this relationship is worth holding on to. If this is a person whom you really value, don your party hat and . . .

- **Stay Focused.** You have the ability to have a good time or not. As the old saying goes "Make the best of the situation." Talk to

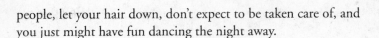

people, let your hair down, don't expect to be taken care of, and you just might have fun dancing the night away.

- **View It as a Mission.** Of course you have other things to do. Everyone does. In fact, each person at the function could be catching up on so many things instead of being there. Don't forget the reason you're present. Your mission is to support, love, and share special moments with the person who is being honored. Stay true to that mission and celebrate!

- **Go with Support or Go Alone.** Don't go to an event that you already have misgivings about with someone who will make you feel even more uncomfortable. If you are considering going with someone who complains or doesn't want to be there, this will only disengage you further, and you'll be preoccupied with his well-being. If there's no one else to go with, or if the person you would normally go with is a downer, why not go solo?

When people know you sincerely care
and receive your heartfelt warmth, they will
pick up on the message that they are important
and have value in your life.

## Sleep Well

Why is it that you just don't get enough sleep? Or that the sleep you do get is not restful or restorative?

Do you bring worries from your day into your bed with you or watch the TV news just before dozing off? Or perhaps you jump into bed after having a troubling conversation with your mom. Whatever the reason, lack of sleep plays havoc in your life. Your ability to function, to have energy, patience, and resistance, are all affected by a diminished night's sleep.

So how can you keep your sanity while trying to increase your zzzzz's?

- **Sleep When You Can.** Catnapping (otherwise known as power napping) can change your entire outlook and energy level. Give yourself the opportunity of shutting out the world from time to time and revitalizing yourself.

- **Shut Off the World.** Turn your TV set off at least a half hour before you want to go to bed and take a soothing bath with the lights low. Slowly drink a cup of chamomile tea and put a few drops of lavender on your pillow or sheets. Listen to some relaxing music, meditate, journal, read for pleasure . . . relax.

- **Put Your Worries and Thoughts in a Cupboard.** Mentally close the cupboard door and tell yourself you will deal with them from a fresh perspective tomorrow. Visualize a deep, restorative sleep and waking up refreshed to tackle whatever is on your mind in the morning.

- **Go Through a Progressive Relaxation** . . . as you lie in bed. Begin with your toes and move up to your head. At each body part, slow your breathing and feel yourself sinking deeper into the mattress and into a state of relaxation. If you wake in the night, do not look at the clock. Just tell yourself you need to go back to sleep, and repeat the progressive relaxation.

Sleep restores. Even when it is disturbed,
you can relax into it.

# Nurture Yourself to Nurture Your Child

When your child is upset, crying, and feeling afraid, think about how you were treated when you felt similarly at her age. Were you left alone? Were you expected to deal with everything on your own because the world is a tough place and you had better learn how to deal with it when you are young? Or were you held, cared for, and comforted through your fear?

Discovering what you needed and did or did not get is imperative so you can give yourself what you need (still) and then respond appropriately to your child.

- **Work on Your Calm.** If you are at your wits' end you will not be able to tolerate a frightened, crying child. Take some time to regroup within yourself at various times during the day so you have a reserve whenever your child has a mini-meltdown. Remember, your child is a sponge and learns positive and negative behaviors from you. Be a good role model.

- **Stay Balanced.** Giving away everything in your life depletes your energy for the person who needs it the most, your child. Learn to save your energy and restore it when it gets low so your supply is there when you need it. Learn to find calm by meditating, listening to soothing music, pampering yourself, or taking an aromatic bath. When you are balanced, you can help your child stay balanced.

- **Know Your Child.** Each child requires something different, and if you take care of yourself, you will be able to respond to each child's unique needs. Responding to someone (even yourself) in the appropriate way takes time and energy to discover. You need to be able to comfort your child in the manner he needs, not just in the manner that works for you.

When you do not care for yourself you will not appreciate what you must do for your children.

# Feeling Stressed and Old?
# Whistle an Old Tune

When you are overwhelmed and tasks keep building up, you feel stressed, and stress contributes to making you feel old. This cycle is important to break so you feel rejuvenated and young at heart no matter what's on your plate that day and no matter what age you are.

As you think about everything that needs to be done, use music to help reduce stress. Play tunes that bring you back to a time when you were free and easy. Think of songs, titles, and artists you heard back in your high school days or during your carefree summers.

For women in particular, hearing those melodies and feeling rhythms from earlier times in your life can bring you back to your basic, essential self. Dancing around the living room or kitchen re-membering a favorite dance partner can give you the energy you need to move forward and tackle the most foreboding task. In fact, listening to music lowers your blood pressure and heart rate as well as improves your mood.

- **Beat Stress Away.** Yes, drumming can bring a feeling of relax-ation, and for many its calming effects are immediate. Sign up for percussion lessons, join a drumming circle, or just buy a drum and start banging to the beat.

- **Sing Loud and Proud.** No one's around, so go ahead and belt out a tune. Just grab a hairbrush or wooden spoon for a micro-phone and sing along with your favorite CD. Maybe add in a few dance steps or grab your imaginary Fred Astaire and whirl around the living room. Express yourself through song.

- **Use Music in the Foreground.** Music does not have to be in the background. Focus on the sounds, melodies, lyrics, and rhythm. Get into the music, and likely you will be ready to begin your task. If not, transition into your task by keeping the music on and playing a game of solitaire, doing a crossword puzzle, or doing other mind-sharpening exercises as you focus your energy. Then approach the series of tasks you have lined up. One at a time, work and talk yourself through each task and remind yourself that you are moving forward. You will feel better when this work is behind you.

> Everyone has stress. It's not how much stress you have but how you handle it. Music is always available to "fill" you . . . and it's ageless.

## No Longer Friends

You and your friend just don't click anymore. She doesn't "get" you, is always trying to change you, cannot be supportive, is highly critical, or has become a downer. You just don't want to keep the friendship going.

It is your right, of course, to end your ties. Just remember that people go through periods in their lives when they are more available or in tune with each other than other times. Be sure you are not tossing out someone with enough positive aspects who has been there for you in difficult times.

So how do you let this friend know that you are no longer someone she can rely on?

- **Cut or Mend?** Consider whether you need to cut this person out of your life completely or shift your focus. Is there a new place for this person in your life?

- **No Answering Machine Good-byes.** Rather than not taking her calls or avoiding invitations, plan an uninterrupted conversation or write a thoughtful letter. Describe how grateful you are to have had her in your life. Recall wonderful times and memories. Let her know that you don't feel you can't continue to be the kind of friend you were in the past. Take responsibility because *you* are the one who is initiating the break.

- **No Need to Blame.** Let her know you need to have friends who share your vision and enthusiasm. Tell her you have a difficult time sharing your life because you feel she disapproves, judges,

or gets jealous. Be careful not to be critical of who she is. Wish her well. Let her know that she will always be in your heart.

Just as we change, so do our friendships. Some stay active with us forever while others come and go, receding to memory.

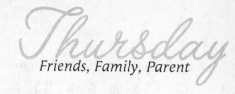
# When Mom Is Sick and the Kids Are in Denial

If your daughter, sister, aunt, or cousin gets seriously ill and her children are in denial, what, if anything can you do to help?

For many young children, teens, and young adults, denial is a way to keep the bad news at bay. The kids are likely thinking, "If I don't have to deal with it, maybe it won't be true." "Maybe it really isn't happening." "Maybe my life really is not going to be turned upside down and things won't change." Denial is a very common emotional response to life's challenges. But you know (and perhaps somewhere deep, they do, too) that by denying reality they are avoiding dealing with life.

- **Denial Should Be Temporary.** Denial can be a healthy initial response as children try to sort through things when their lives are turned upside down, especially with such unsettling news. It is a way to keep fear at bay. But being in denial for a long time isn't healthy. Children of all ages need to have loving people to turn to and talk with about the turmoil in their lives.

- **Get the Kids to Pitch In.** You may see that the mom needs help with some of the household responsibilities, and the children may be unwilling to do this if they are in denial. You can comment on how helpful it is (or will be) that they have contributed to the family to help out during this unusual and stressful time. Emphasize that whatever they do will be helpful to their mom and to the family, which will help them to see reality.

Denial initially helps children adapt to the thought that their life is going along a path that they know nothing (and want to know nothing) about. Help them to get on the path.

# Waiters Serving Crabs: Handling a Complaining Dinner Partner

What comes to mind when you've been at a restaurant with a friend or loved one who treats the waiter or waitress rudely? Even if there were wings sticking out of the mashed potatoes and the person had every right to be upset, the overall feeling you earned from the episode was discomfort.

You probably felt compassion for the waiter, just as surely as you felt embarrassment for your dinner companion. Many times you may feel that both parties were entitled to their opinions, no matter how poorly they were expressed. So how do you keep both your sanity and a seat at the table—if, in fact, you still have an appetite?

- **Diffuse the Tension.** First, take a deep breath and ask your friend to also. Let the complainer understand she has every reason to be upset because the service or the food is unacceptable, but that the method of communication is not the best one at hand. Ask if you can step in and help. Maybe the steak can be cooked to order if given a few minutes or another dish can be selected from the menu. Speak to a manager or simply announce that the service is beyond repair and you'd like to leave. Don't let the argument build and the tension to grow. No need to cross the line into insults.

- **Hold Up a Mirror.** When anger controls some people, even if it is an outburst that is out of the ordinary, common sense, perspective, and judgment all fly out the window. Sometimes, if

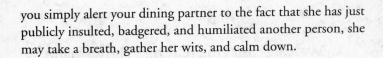

you simply alert your dining partner to the fact that she has just publicly insulted, badgered, and humiliated another person, she may take a breath, gather her wits, and calm down.

- **Helpful Suggestion.** Once you've left the restaurant, suggest that in the future, your friend send a note back to the kitchen and ask the waiter to read it before returning to the table. This avoids embarrassment and gives the restaurant staff a chance to remedy your dining experience.

> If being rude to waitstaff or people in service industries is something your friend can't stop doing, get together at your house instead and consider whether this behavior is a quality you want in a friend.

# Reach Out to Heal with Someone You Don't Like

You have in your life an in-law, a sibling, an aunt or uncle whom you have felt bitterness toward for years. Perhaps this person did not welcome you warmly into the family or barely gave you a nod despite your frequent attempts to reach out.

Realize this is his issue and not yours. He is dealing with his own life, feelings of self-importance or inadequacy, working the "social ladder" or whatever. You feel unrelenting resentment, bitterness, and anger. How can you save your sanity by not giving in to those feelings that are irrelevant to the other person's life but can so destroy yours?

- **Disconnect from Anger.** Determine why you are unable to cut yourself off from this person. Then try and slowly let go of the feeling of resentment or angst when you see him or hear his name. If you cannot release yourself from the bitterness that has become your emotional companion, consider taking an action that will help you to feel more at ease.

- **Take a Bold Step.** Extend an invitation that would include just the two of you. Do something "benign" like grabbing an informal bite of lunch or taking a walk in a park, away from family and work stimuli and distractions.

- **Tear Down the Wall.** Make this first attempt even if you are not even sure it's worth tearing down in the first place . . . and you

may be able to make mutually beneficial repairs to the relationship, and more important, to your soul and sense of self.

Harboring resentment only hurts
the one who harbors.

# Creating a Peaceful Workspace

With so many changes in the workplace these days, more and more people are working in physical environments that are quite challenging. The ability to have a private conversation, quiet environment to think or create, or view of the outdoors is becoming a thing of the past. Even if you like your job and enjoy your coworkers, your work environment itself may hamper your ability to operate at your peak capacity.

By working in a peaceful space, you can maximize your productivity. Take a cue from city cab drivers. They are in the worst traffic all day and yet their cabs are refuges from the stress and craziness. Dashboards often display photos of beautiful places, children, or a religious passage, while music drowns out horns, sirens, and jackhammers on the city streets.

You can enjoy work, too, when you are surrounded by peaceful pictures and mementos that really mean something to you and speak to your individuality.

- **Create a Space That Is Yours.** It does not have to be large but it needs to have something in it that reflects you. Even if you share the space with someone, personalize it by hanging a photo of your family, your pet, or a place that brings you a sense of peace and tranquillity.

- **Drown Out the Noise.** If you need to focus on your work and the din of the office is too distracting, plug in your earphones so you can hear music. If music doesn't do it for you, record nature sounds or use white noise to block out competing, distracting

sounds. Creating a calm work environment will enhance your productivity as well as your mood.

- **Take "Breath" Breaks.** At your desk, close your eyes and inhale deeply, visualizing yourself at a beach, in the mountains, or on the shore of a lake; somewhere in nature where you feel comfortable. Feel the calm come over you and restore your feeling of centeredness. Follow your breath in and out as you say to yourself, "My breath will guide my work."

- **Expand Your Workplace.** During coffee breaks or lunch breaks, try to go outside or look out a window and focus on a particular spot. When you return to work, bring that place with you in your mind's eye. Every day, focus on a different spot so that you bring a "new view" to your work. This can help you find a different perspective to a challenging work issue or give you a fresh way to problem solve.

We can always enhance our environment to reflect more of who we are.

*Parent, Partner, Family*

## You, the Kids, and Your Ex

It's a proven fact that children need to spend time with both parents. Even if you have not worked out all your issues with your ex-spouse, it is generally better for children when they are able to spend time with both of their parents. They especially need to know their noncustodial parent cares about them, appreciates them, and is interested in what they are doing and what their interests are.

As they grow up, it's important that they continue to identify with, love, and be proud of both parents. Save your family's sanity as you establish a new relationship with your ex-spouse and keep things as smooth and secure as possible for the children.

- **Inform Your Ex** . . . about everything concerning the kids. It is up to the parents (not the children) to know what is going on with school (a parent-teacher meeting, a change in a soccer practice), health (a sore throat or a curious rash), or family matters (a grandparent who is in the hospital). To stay in the loop, both parents should be on the contact list (via e-mail, telephone, or mail) for school and other activities.

- **Set Up Frequent, Predictable Visits.** Children need to establish a reliable pattern of life. The noncustodial parent connection should be present and consistent. This is especially true with young children, who do better with frequent but short visits. They have less difficulty separating if they know they will be seeing that parent again soon, and can rely on their vibrant memory in between visits.

- **Parents Are Forever.** You may need to say again and again that even though the marriage ended, the parent-child relationship will continue. Both parents need to tell the children that they will always love them and will never abandon them. Reiterate that the connection with each parent is forever.

Let the kids know that although you will now be a two-household family, you will always be a family.

# When Someone You Love Is an Alcoholic

Often it is difficult to come to terms and accept someone you love who is an alcoholic. You may make excuses, deny, pretend, and overlook what is obviously a problem. In fact, you may be exacerbating the problem by not accepting it.

Be patient and try not to interfere as they work on their issues. It's up to you to learn how to deal with alcoholism directly while saving your sanity in the process.

- **Are You Really Helping?** When you make excuses, understand that some of your behaviors and actions may in fact be contributing to and perpetuating your loved one's alcoholic behavior.

- **Change for the Better.** Although you may wish and pray that your loved one will change, you must come to terms with the fact that you are only able to change yourself. Investigate a support group (such as Al-Anon) for family members of people who have issues with alcohol and see how you can make positive changes in your life. Have a life of your own.

- **Live with Dignity.** Ask yourself if this is the life you feel you deserve and whether you can imagine living a life that allows you to live with more dignity.

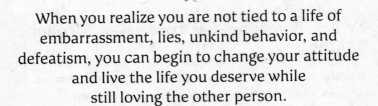

When you realize you are not tied to a life of embarrassment, lies, unkind behavior, and defeatism, you can begin to change your attitude and live the life you deserve while still loving the other person.

# Renewing Friendships

Even though you know the mental, emotional, and physical benefits of having friends, you may have difficulty keeping up with your friendships. Busy lives, family, work obligations, and trying to fit in that all-important private time often prevent you from nurturing those friendships. Sometimes it even causes you to be reluctant to reach out to old friends with whom you have lost touch or whose counsel or company you may have enjoyed in the past. For many reasons, cultivating friendships gets lost from your radar screen.

You can pick up where you left off with some friends; play quick catch-up and all is well. When you are with them you wonder where the time has gone. You miss being in their company and you know you are safe in their presence and that whatever you tell them will be safe, too.

But how do you do it? How do you reach out to someone from whom you have fallen away? Just pick up the phone? Send an e-mail? For some, yes, for others, no. Find what works for you and be aware of why you are contacting this person at this time. Maybe you need something. Your child wants to apply to her alma mater; your husband is ill and you need to have access to a hospital where she can be influential; you need a loan and she has money . . . whatever the reason, be up front about it.

When there is a warm place in your heart for an old friend, the years do not have to affect it. If you are somewhere that reminds you of your college roommate, why not reach out and give her a call? When you are in her city for a conference and think it would be good to say hello after all these years, go ahead and do it. Be clear

about what you want and why you are reaching out and see what happens.

- **Be Open to Her Memories.** Everyone recalls her past differently so be aware that you may learn something about yourself and your friend that you were not aware of. Your impressions and your memory may not jive exactly with your friend's. What was important to you may not carry the same significance to her.

- **Touch Her with How She Touched Your Life.** Was she influential in the way you approached your first job? Did she help you during a difficult time of your own life? "I remember after my mom died, you and I sat on the bed and cried and I felt that since you knew my mom you understood what I was going through." "When I think of you I recall how I looked to you as a model for how to parent my children since you had three terrific kids and I married late. You were my role model."

- **Understand Why You Connected.** Establish if there is something you are both experiencing at this time of your life that you can share or relate to. There may be a reason that you sought each other out now, at this moment of your life. Share what is important to you and how you spend your time. See if there are links from your past that help you to understand the choices you make now.

- **Something New from an Old Friend.** Maybe you'll discover that you have something to offer that you did not have before. You may have both had a similar health crisis and your experi-

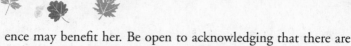

ence may benefit her. Be open to acknowledging that there are many reasons and benefits for reconnecting.

- **No Judgments.** If you seek out an old friend, give the encounter your best shot. Drop any judgment about your life path versus her life path. Be ready to see and hear and witness who she has become and is becoming. Maybe you shifted apart for reasons that are no longer valid (you did not like her husband and she is now divorced; her child who has extra needs is settled and she has more time and interest in things other than her family). She brought something to your life before, so give it your best effort to capture something in your friendship that has value today.

Friendships of long ago may stay as they were in our memory or may be revisited and rejuvenated.

## Sex at Midlife

Weren't you told that you were going to be at your sexual prime in midlife? With more confidence about who you are under your belt and a mature outlook on sex, why isn't your sex life at its peak?

Lots of things are going on in your forties and fifties and sixties. Guess what? Physical changes and aging are also happening to your partner. Problems related to maintaining erectile endurance are as normal for him as menopausal symptoms such as dryness are normal for you. And you might both be dealing with lower libidos and lots of stress.

Does this mean it's time to throw away your lingerie? Heck no. Save your sanity between the sheets and keep your sex life alive.

- **When Things Are Down.** If a diminishing testosterone level and daily stress is affecting his performance, don't take it personally. It's not about you. He still wants you but his manhood may be in an adjustment phase. It's about not being the virile twenty-year-old anymore, and his acceptance of that fact. Have patience and a willingness to talk about it. Bring this out in the open in a way that's comfortable so it's not something he has to harbor alone in the dark.

- **No Sex Intimacy.** When you're physically not in sync, plan an evening of togetherness without the expectation of sex. Light candles and give each other massages with scented oil. Take a soothing bath and lovingly wash each other. Cuddle and hold each other and talk about how close you really are. Find ways to

connect with your bodies, hearts, and souls and let sex happen when it happens.

- **It's an Opportunity.** Instead of bagging sex altogether and watching yet another rented movie to avoid being with your partner, find ways to be pleased other than the usual positions. Come on, you know what they are. Live out a fantasy or explore things you've been thinking of but haven't been brave enough to do. Find the nerve to ask him or show him something new. You now might have his attention, and since things take a bit longer, you have his time as well. Enjoy!

You don't have to be the couple with the bedroom door open because nothing is going on. Put more thought into intimacy and close those doors.

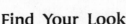

## Find Your Look

You may be basically content with the clothes in your wardrobe, comfortable in the belief that you've developed a style of dress that's right for you. But self-proclaimed fashion experts on television are telling you what not to wear (and what they're telling you what not to wear is what you're wearing!). And a nagging inner voice is telling you to rethink your sense of style.

If you've always been a person who's considered herself well groomed and attired and received consistent positive feedback, hearing something different from everyone from a talk show host to your office mate can be confusing and unsettling. It can certainly cause you to question your own judgment. But it can also open your mind to perhaps even enhancing the "together look" you've already self-designed.

- **Reassess Your Look.** What is it you like about it—what about it says so much about who you are? When you put these clothes on, are you projecting the image you want to project? If, for example, you love to wear solid, dark colors and your wardrobe is all about that, go through it carefully and remove items that could be considered out of style or a bit threadbare. They may be favorites in terms of fit, but you can probably find a more up-to-date version in the marketplace.

- **Try Someplace New to Shop.** Pay a visit to stores you've never considered before. Even if they're pricey and you can only window shop, a fresh place can give you ideas for creating new outfits out of some of the clothes you already own or spark your

interest for a new color, fabric, or accessory. And a little secret about stores you formerly considered prohibitive due to sky-high prices and exclusive clientele? You'll often also find in these stores several fellow shoppers just like you who are looking for something well made, simple, and stylish.

- **Know Your Style and Wear It.** So what to do when the TV tells you that wearing black makes you look "like your grandmother"? Or that you really can't wear a certain kind of shoe with that length skirt. Or when your friend comments that "Women over forty should wear little skirts over bathing suits that should only be brightly colored?" You should smile, think how much you really enjoy your clothes and look, and at your next pool party plan to wear that new black bathing suit you just bought on sale at that formerly forbidden elegant store and know how smashing it looks on you!

Feeling good in your clothes is all about feeling good about you.

Family, Parent, Midlife, Well-Being

# Loving People Whose Choices Disturb You

There are some situations that cause negative changes in your personality, making you feel sad, depressed, impatient, or anxious. When you analyze how you feel, you realize your emotional downswings are directly related to someone you love: your child, a relative, or a close friend.

You appreciate that almost everything else in your life works perfectly, except when you have dealings with your loved one. You get upset knowing that she does not take her university studies seriously, goes out late with friends, and often hangs out in unsafe neighborhoods, or gets involved in romantic relationships with someone who is clearly, and potentially devastatingly, wrong for her.

Living with this person's unhappiness and unconscious internal suffering contribute to your personal torment and worry. What can you do to save your own sanity while witnessing someone you love engage in self-destructive behavior?

- **Judging Doesn't Help.** Acknowledge the fact that at this point in the person's life, her priorities do not agree with what most people in your world consider healthy (God, family, work, college, friends). Talk to the person with an open heart, without judgment, sharing your concern about her choices and lifestyle.

- **Find Solace in Reflection.** Ask for support and pray to heal this person's emotional and spiritual wounds and scars, likely caused by situations in life that she has been exposed to. Meditate and focus on her well-being, sending thoughts and visualizations of health and safety.

- **Appreciate Your Wisdom** . . . which is an accumulation of years of experience and guidance, and be grateful for everything you have in life that helps you (food, friends, health, a home, a job). Even though you would love this person to have such wisdom, believe that in time she will grow, heal, and discover happiness.

Daily caring for yourself and focusing on the well-being of the person you are concerned about can help you diminish the negative effects of their choices on your health.

*Tuesday*

*Friends, Family, Well-Being*

## Responding to Friends with Your Difficult News

Thank goodness you have friends. Good friends. They are there for you and want to help while you are going through a tough time. But hey, you are exhausted. After coming home from treatments or taking care of your ill parent or going through an ordeal with your child, you just cannot have that "just fill me in" conversation with anyone.

Even though you're so appreciative of your friends' caring and support, how can you possibly keep your sanity while addressing their need to know what is going on in your life?

- **Telephone Chain.** It is not possible to tell everyone everything and you have to conserve your energy. Let your friends and family know you are going to post news with the people you are most in contact with and let them pass it down the line.

- **Create a Blog.** You or someone with computer know-how can prepare a blog or a newsletter that you send to friends and family at various intervals. By logging on to your personal website or reading the e-mail entitled, "Joe's Health and Status Report #6," you can satisfy your need to share and their need to know without repeating the same story twenty times each day.

- **Make a List.** You should have a list of names, numbers, and e-mail addresses of people to contact if news must be relayed

quickly. Keep this list handy so you can delegate this task to a friend or relative should the need arise.

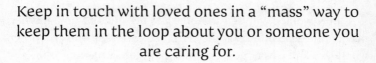

Keep in touch with loved ones in a "mass" way to keep them in the loop about you or someone you are caring for.

# Career Moms Running Their Kids' Lives

Career women who stay at home and become full-time mothers may "run" their children as they ran their careers. If you are a mom who plans and is very goal oriented, pay close attention to the fact that you may not be focused on your child and what he or she needs but on what you as a mom need.

A danger in running your kids' lives as though you were running a company is that not as much care is given to the process of your child's growing up and discovering and doing what comes naturally. More attention (and value) is given to the outcome. "How is your project going to come out?" rather than "What is your science project going to be about?"

- **Don't Grade Yourself.** Remember that kids get report cards, not you. If you did a great job in your career and don't feel you do as well as a stay-at-home mom, that is OK. Success as a mom is hard to measure. Work on raising happy kids.

- **Encourage and Support.** Children flourish with moms who allow them to be the unique individuals that they are. Let them progress at their pace, and don't have an underlying agenda that you impose, either consciously or subconsciously, for your own gratification.

- **Let Them Be Kids . . .** and let yourself enjoy playful time with them. If your son misses the sink and accidentally throws a sponge at your head, turn around, look at his fearful eyes, and

laugh. Humor helps take the edge off your expectations and can keep your home out of the boardroom.

A stay-at-home mom's job is raising children, not profits.

# Dealing with Differences

When we're overwhelmed by current events and all that we have to do, it's easy to become stressed and impatient with the people we live and deal with on a daily basis. Sometimes we snap more easily with family members and coworkers and are not as accepting of differences of opinions and different outlooks.

- **Don't Put Down Others' Opinions.** Try not to judge or criticize. Keep personalities and history out of it. Stick to the topic at hand.

- **Be Creative in Problem Solving.** Compromise is OK . . . even for parents!

- **Step into Their Shoes.** Allow yourself to see the other person's perspective and try something new. You do not have to agree. Even if the subject matter is difficult and clear answers are hard to come by, hang in there. Allowing others to be themselves shows you care.

- **Listen Better.** Do not interrupt or don't anticipate what the other person will say.

- **Be Patient.** Lay the groundwork for mutual respect and consideration when it's time to say your "peace."

Just because you have always looked at a situation one way, doesn't mean it's the only way.

# Being a Good Host

*Company!* Does that word direct a shock through your system? Do you conjure up images of yourself peeping through the curtains pretending you are not home or, on the contrary, are you eagerly awaiting the time together when you can enjoy your company?

Before you have people over, be sure you have what it takes to be a good host. That does not mean that you must work your tail off to prepare legions of gourmet food (although you may want to). It does mean that you make your guests feel as if you are happy they are with you, that you make time to be with them, and that you don't spend the time together feeling as if you are a servant. The whole point of having people visit is to enjoy their company, and sometimes the best way to do that is to plan activities that you enjoy (with and without them) so you have the energy and interest to be together.

- **Communicate the House Rules.** You can have expectations of how your guests will behave but unless you tell them, they may not know your guidelines. If you cannot have music blasting after ten, you need to tell them. If you don't want wet towels in the hamper, you need to tell them. It is all about what is on and off limits. If you live in an adult-oriented home, be careful about extending invitations to people with children.

- **Tolerate Normalcy.** You are not going to change someone's life-long habits, so be sure you are able to share a bathroom, a kitchen, or whatever *before* you extend an invitation. When people arrive with children, expect kid play. Maybe it's best to put away

your fine china accessories before guests arrive than to risk having them shattered on the hardwood floor.

- **Make Them Feel at Home.** When you open your home to guests, you also need to open your heart so they feel welcome. If the visit brings tension, make the best of the situation and see it through. If someone breaks something accidentally, be as gracious as you can. Accidents happen, and your guest will likely feel dreadful about what she did.

- **Who's on Vacation?** Sometimes when your guests are on vacation, they expect you to be, too. Entertaining while trying to keep up with your normal schedule can be overwhelming. Falling into bed exhausted because you are trying to be the best possible host can also breed resentment. Either take a few days off from your normal routine or make it clear to your guests that you have other obligations. If you are not going to be able to chauffeur, ask guests to rent a car; or hop a bus, train, or taxi; or bike or walk.

- **Plan Time Together and Alone.** Realize that the time will likely fly by if you are having fun with your guests while taking care of yourself. If you usually wake up to enjoy a quiet cup of coffee and read the paper, you may need to wake up earlier to have that happen. If your guests are early risers, then either read together or find another time of the day to be alone.

## The most valuable gift you can give to your guest is being a gracious host.

## Rituals

Rituals are important, helpful, and powerful. Performing a ritual is a small way of celebrating or honoring a bigger event in your life, and helps us gain insight when we are dealing with change.

Whether you perform an inner healing ritual, request a blessing, or engage in a special tradition for a special occasion, rituals can be encouraging, reassuring, and comforting. Holding on to our routines and rituals helps maintain our sanity and balance.

Before you begin performing a ritual, your heart must be open to the experience. Ask yourself, what is your intention? Throughout the ritual, allow yourself to be open to a different perspective. It is important when you perform a ritual that you suspend judgment and just allow yourself to "be."

- **Old or New.** A ritual is most effective when it has meaning for you. If you're performing an old ritual that isn't fulfilling, consider designing a new ritual to enliven a connection.

- **"Everyday" Rituals.** Morning coffee and reading the paper, walking the dog along a familiar path, calling a friend at the same time each week can be simple ways to ritualize a familiar pattern. Everyday routines can become rituals if you pay close attention to them and focus on the change you hope to experience.

- **Beginnings and Endings.** Rituals can help to bring closure. Tearing up a letter from someone who has hurt you and since died can be a freeing way to relegate them to your past. Writing your fears in the sand or on a piece of paper and lighting them on fire as you watch them burn can be amazingly liberating. Rituals can reflect a tradition such as a rite of passage or the naming of a child or the scattering of ashes.

- **Slow Down.** You cannot perform a ritual at accelerated speed. Where and how are you going to do this? Be sure you are not going to be disturbed as you begin your process. Allow yourself the time to do what you need.

- **Get Your Tools.** Collect whatever you need to give this ritual meaning—materials from nature, art supplies, old photos, magazine pictures, and fragrances.

- **Keep It Simple.** Rituals can be as simple as lighting a candle or filling a vase with flowers or thinking a special thought. The object is comfort.

Try this ritual when faced with a decision: Stand in the yoga "mountain" posture by firmly planting your feet on the ground, placing your hands at your side and standing tall. Visualize being a tree of your family—a family tree—rooted to your ancestors both in the ground and in the heavens. Listen for guidance from those in your ancestry.

# When Friends Part as Business Partners

Many friends go into business together and it works out well. Other times it doesn't.

A good working business relationship with a friend is one in which there is mutual trust, the workload is shared, each contributes what he or she does best, financial expectations are met, and both reap the benefits of working with and growing a business with a buddy.

But sometimes a good friendship closes after the "We're Open for Business" sign goes up. Maybe you felt you were doing more than your share of the work or perhaps your visions for the company diverged.

Whatever the reason, you probably now feel abandoned and betrayed, not to mention angry and hurt at the turn of events in your friendship. Dealing with this kind of anger can be a great challenge. And in the end, you may have to let your friend and business partner go from your life.

- **Accept Her Viewpoint** . . . although it's clearly not yours. Even if you know that you carried the workload and that your contributions to making your business work were not equal or fairly distributed, acknowledge that she is invested in her position and you will likely not change her point of view.

- **Do Not Ask Others to Take Sides.** Refrain from bringing other friends into the mix. As with a divorce, involving mutual friends could put you at risk for losing important people in your life as sources of support.

- **Don't Badmouth.** Your business partnership may be ending but that doesn't mean you have to make the details anyone else's business.

- **Move On.** Try to part on the best terms you can under the circumstances. Write a letter (that you will not send, especially if you are in litigation with your partner) about everything you did for the business and why you think what happened did happen. In your "testimony," take responsibility for your part in the breakdown of the business arrangement. Then put it into the past as quickly as you can, allowing for the appropriate time to heal. You will only keep yourself in the depths of despair if you don't allow for closure and continually revisit what went wrong.

Sometimes you think you know people when, in fact, certain circumstances can bring out aspects of them that you never knew existed. Prepare yourself for any eventuality.

# Selecting a Guardian for Your Children

Of course we all hope to live healthfully through our children's adulthood and enjoy all the predictable life passages with them. However, sometimes the unpredictable happens and someone else may be responsible for raising your children.

If the unthinkable happens to you (and the other parent), what thoughts have you given to providing for your children in the event of your untimely death or incapacitation?

- **Make or Revisit Your Will.** Hopefully you have written both a living will and a last will and testament naming someone you trust as guardian of your children. However, if you are like most people, you have put it away safely and have not revisited or revised it in some time. The single sister you may have named as guardian when you had twins is now married and living three thousand miles away with her own four children. Your parents, who at the time of your child's birth were healthy and vital, are now more frail or living in a retirement community. It is important to keep current.

- **Consider Your Choices.** Ask yourself about the people you are considering: Are they the kind of parents you would want to raise your children? Think about how well they know and like your children, their personalities, temperaments, parenting style, views on education and society. What is going on in their lives, and what are your concerns, if any, about financial and emotional security? Know that the perfect person is going to be hard to find. Pick the best available person for the job whom you trust

will make decisions with your intention and values in mind as they step up to the plate should they be called to do so.

- **Specify Concerns.** If you know that one of your brothers is better with kids and the other is better with money, you may want to divvy up responsibilities and make one the guardian and the other the trustee for the financials. If you can, specify that siblings stay together. When something happens to parents, siblings are more likely to depend on one another and feel more securely connected as they face the changes ahead.

Your children need you to plan for their welfare if the unthinkable happens. You will rest easier.

# The Partner-Parent Trap

Your partner doesn't like your parents. Whether it started early in your marriage or has been a slow-growing tumor, this can be a constant problem in your relationship.

Reference to your parents evokes rolled eyes, long sighs, expletives. When they are in the same room, he just cannot be civil. You have gone out of your way to plan their visits when he is out of town, but enough is enough. Keeping your sanity as you try to keep some sort of peace in your relationship with your parents and your partner is a contest that you sometimes feel you are not quite up to facing.

- **You're the Buffer.** Like it or not, you're in the middle of two sets of people you love. This can be a tough place to be, so manage it wisely. Instead of making up excuses each time your parents call and want to say hi to your partner, just say, "He can't talk right now but I will tell him you asked about him."

- **Accept the Disappointment** . . . that they will never be close. And let it go—just let it go and hopefully both sides will find their own state of existence.

- **Ask for Cordiality.** Share with your partner what you need and tell him his comments hurt you, so please keep them to himself. Be very clear that you are not saying, "Love me, love my parents." You are not even saying, "Love me, like my parents." You are, however—and this is the kicker—asking for "Love me, *be nice to my parents.*"

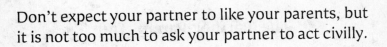

Don't expect your partner to like your parents, but it is not too much to ask your partner to act civilly.

# Empty Nester Mom

If you are a mother with a child who has just turned eighteen and is leaving for college, the military, or elsewhere, you might feel the pangs of loneliness creeping in. And if you are a single mom, or if this is your youngest or only child to leave the nest, the emptiness you feel can be overwhelming.

Pay attention to the fact that even if you have had a full professional and personal life, you may miss your child enormously because much of your life may have revolved around his schedule, studies, and friends. Mothers who have close relationships with their kids, single mothers, and mothers of only children also find that their child was probably the person who spoke to them most often, the one they planned life events with, and, in some ways, their companion.

- **Start Living for You.** Think of ways to fill up your life. Don't even try to fill the space in your heart that your child occupied; instead concentrate on filling the time. Discover things about yourself that have been dormant for eighteen years or so that you just now would like to discover. Enroll in a class, do something challenging (and possibly a tad daring) to develop confidence in doing things that are outside your comfort zone.

- **Think Good Thoughts.** Allow yourself to take time each day to think about your child and focus on his well-being. Write to him (try not to always communicate by cell phone or e-mail, which are very immediate and impermanent), and thoughtfully reflect on how your lives are positively progressing.

- **Enjoy Your Work.** Delve into that project you've been anxious to get to at work or at home. Volunteer for an organization that you can prepare for and look forward to doing at least once or twice a week. Being useful in a realm outside of day-to-day parenting can help take the sting out of not having your child around.

Your nest is empty to make room for you.

# Agreements and Disagreements with Your Partner

Many women are disappointed in their marriages and relationships because they feel they are neither known nor understood. However, all too often these women hide their true selves and avoid the risk of rejection or criticism. Because the image they portray to the world isn't real, it acts like a shield fending off connections with many people. When we're disconnected, it's difficult to be known or understood.

Often partners walk together on the road of least resistance, avoiding areas of disagreement. Sometimes this is smart when you get to a point where you can agree to disagree, with respect and compassion. Over time, however, if your true opinions, ideas, thoughts, and feelings become more and more private instead of more and more shared, you may be withdrawing from your partner and cutting off the chance to be open and known.

- **If You Want to Be Loved, You Must Give Love.** Stop expecting your partner to validate and agree with you. Rather, accept yourself for who you are, and you will do much better as a partner.

- **Invite Your Spouse into Your Heart** . . . and share your life. Sharing a life with someone who is different from you does not have to be isolating or lonely. Share your views and opinions that are based on your life experience and values. Do not be concerned about defending yourself but rather expressing yourself.

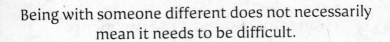

Being with someone different does not necessarily
mean it needs to be difficult.

## Letting Go of Your "Stuff"

Why is it so hard to give away the glass fish your favorite aunt gave you for a wedding present? Was it a special night when you wore your green dress that now collects dust in your closet? How long do you need to keep things that you no longer use, like, or fit you . . . either in style or temperament?

Sometimes you need to hold on to the past. Other times you feel you're dismissing someone's generosity or taste by no longer using her gift. When your things no longer bring you joy but rather evoke mixed or negative feelings, it's time to let go.

Save you sanity and find a new sense of freedom from things that are no longer pleasant, useful, or healthy, and create much needed space.

- **Focus on the Object.** What does this thing mean to you? Decide whether you need to keep it to retain the benefit or a memory. What do you need to do, think, feel, or say to let it go?

- **Your Things Put to Better Use.** Something came to you, you used it, and now it's time to let it go to someone else. Recall with good feeling the dinner party you had on this set of dishes and think of how nice they would look on someone else's table. Know the divine feeling someone will have wearing your suits at her new job.

- **Lighten Your Load.** When there is space, there are possibilities. Be open and let life bring you great joy, inspiration, and meaning in this next phase of your life.

Hanging on to things you no longer need or use prevents you from opening up to new forms, styles, and spaces.

# The Second Time Around

You've heard the stats. Second marriages have a higher failure rate than first marriages. There's enough doom and gloom information out there that makes you wonder how anyone can ever walk down the aisle again.

But you love this person. This is a good, healthy, solid relationship. Save your sanity by being aware of the mistakes of the past and make this one last.

- **Be a Realist.** You can be a romantic at heart, but when it comes to your expectations about marriage, remember, no marriage is perfect.

- **Do What Works This Time.** Did blaming, anger, and keeping score work in your first marriage? Bet not. So take the best from marriage number one and leave the rest. Be committed and flexible. Set aside special couple time. Listen carefully, make decisions together, and respect those boundaries. Don't forget your sense of humor.

- **Anticipate Differences** . . . lots of them. Second marriages are more complicated, especially if there are kids. Map out money issues, anniversaries, birthdays, holidays, and daily routines before you say, "I do."

*Flexible* is the buzzword for second marriages. You'll also need a whole lot of patience, and an open and forgiving heart.

# Tuesday

*Parent, Work*

## It's Easier at the Office

Did you leave your career to be an at-home mom and wish you hadn't? Can you admit that playing with blocks and doing loads of laundry are not your strong suits? Do you long for lunches with colleagues and stimulating business projects?

If you are considering leaving your at-home job and returning to "greener" pastures for your old job or career, let this be a personal decision for what is best for you and your family. Full-time motherhood may not be for you, and you need to make that OK.

- **Filter Out the Mother Guilt.** Leave open the possibility that your at-home job may not be what is best for everyone. You will be a better mother in the long run if you truly believe you can best serve yourself and your family by working outside your home. If you are fulfilling your needs, you'll be able to focus on your children more effectively and give them what they need from you. Allow yourself to seek out a nanny, arrange day care, or ask a willing family member to care for your kids and go and do what you do best.

- **Breathe Easier.** The safety precaution on airlines is to put your face mask on if you need oxygen and then assist your children. Same goes for your professional goals. Your oxygen supply just might be your work. When you are getting your daily dose you'll be able to give a breath of fresh air to your kids and everyone around you.

- **Make a Healthy Transition.** Maybe you need to get right to work full-time to restore what's missing in your life. Or working part-time for a while and creating a schedule that is good for everyone in your life is perhaps a better arrangement. Be realistic about what you can and can't do. Bringing work home at night might be more difficult with a baby or kids around. You may have to make some changes so your career and home life can successfully coexist.

> Going back to work is a whole lot better than expecting your child to be your work project.

# Interracial/Multicultural Children

If you are in an interracial relationship or involved with someone who is from another culture or country, it is essential to keep your children exposed to that other culture or race. It is a part of who they are. This is especially important if there is limited or no contact with their father because of death, living far apart, or any other reason.

How can you provide positive experiences and role models to your children when the other half of their gene pool might be a bit foreign to you?

- **Live in a Nurturing Community.** If you can, live in a neighborhood that is not homogenous. Mixed backgrounds, nationalities, and races will enrich your and your children's lives while allowing them to feel as if they are not "so different."

- **Seek Out Role Models.** Look for mentors from the race or culture that is part of your children's makeup so they can identify with that part of themselves as they develop their own identity. If there is a good male teacher in school that your boys can identify with, make sure they are in his class. Similarly, look for after-school sports, music, arts programs that have wonderful coaches and instructors from their father's culture, race, or religion. Find people who are accomplished in their fields and who will be people your kids will look up to. A guitar teacher who shares a common background with your children may teach them more about themselves than just music.

- **Find Other Ways to Influence Them.** Volunteer and introduce your children to as many people and families as you can. If possible, enroll your children in schools where they are not in the minority. Expose them to theater, music, and dance that is representative of their other parent's culture.

Your children deserve and need to have positive experiences with their heritage.

## Recovering from Sexual Abuse

You know you have been abused . . . as a child or as a young woman or an older woman. Whenever it happened, you may have put it aside, gone to the police/courts, told a trusted friend or family member, or kept it a secret. But you know all too well that some of the responses you have now, years later, are related to what happened to you.

Healing takes time . . . a long time, with support and openness and a direct desire to face what occurred in your past. The way to keep your sanity while coming to terms with what happened is to look at the world and yourself differently, to release the power that the abuse has over your life, and to regain control of your own life and the feelings associated with the sexual abuse.

- **Be in a Safe Environment and Share** . . . *only* with people you trust and who can relate to the devastation you experienced. You will realize a very important fact; you are not alone either in the experience or in your journey. This may be in a group therapy situation, an online support group, or an individual therapy situation. It may also be possible to invite someone into your life who can respect what happened to you. Through acceptance, empathy, and compassion, that person can assist you in your emotional healing.

- **Mourn Your Losses.** If you were abused as a child, allow yourself to grieve for the loss you experienced . . . the loss of innocence, of childhood, of trust, of protection from the adults in your world. Begin to take care of "that child" as if she was your

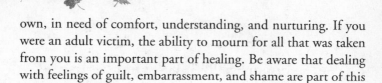

own, in need of comfort, understanding, and nurturing. If you were an adult victim, the ability to mourn for all that was taken from you is an important part of healing. Be aware that dealing with feelings of guilt, embarrassment, and shame are part of this rocky territory.

- **Reclaim *You*.** Believe that, in time—and it is a process—you will be able to regain a sense of yourself as a whole person; a person who has value and self-worth, who can begin to trust yourself and other people. Whether you decide to confront the person who abused you (and there are many ways to do this if you choose to, even if the person is dead) is a highly personal decision. Give yourself time.

As you recover and become who you were unable to become because of the sexual abuse, you may feel worse before you feel better—but you can regain your strength and your sense of self as a valuable person.

# *Friday*

*Well-Being, Friends, Family*

## Consider a Pet

You may wonder whether it is worthwhile to get a pet. You're not home all the time and a pet would be one more thing to think about, but floppy ears and a wagging tail to welcome you would be nice to come home to.

Whether or not you had a pet when you were a child, the returns can be beyond measure. Pets provide companionship; improved physical, emotional, and mental health and well-being; connection; security; playfulness; laughter; and exercise. And a pet helps you stay balanced as you learn the joy of taking care of another and being the recipient of unconditional love.

If you live alone, have an empty nest, or have recently retired, having the right pet companionship can save your sanity while enhancing the quality of your life.

- **Good for Your Health.** Walking a dog, laughing, playing, grooming, and petting an animal can improve your outlook, reduce stress, and add physical activity to your day.

- **Select Well.** Be sure you choose the right animal for you that accommodates your style, pace of life, where you live, and your habits. Keep expectations realistic, as it is a major commitment to take care of a pet. If you lead a get-up-and-go lifestyle maybe a smaller, more portable pet will be best. Or if you're the outdoorsy type, live in a warm climate, and love the water, a pet who loves to swim would be a great companion.

- **The Best Medicine.** Pets comfort us. Dealing with loss is more tolerable because you'll enjoy their company and feel less desolate. Older people with pets are usually less lonely and have fewer frequent doctor visits.

Companionship comes in many forms. Do not overlook the value of the human-pet bond.

## Your Heart Versus Your Head

What to do when your heart says one thing and your mind says another? Your heart may be tied to a particular place where you feel at home, connected, safe. But then you are faced with an opportunity to move elsewhere that may be better for you at this juncture of your life in so many ways.

You can either follow your heart or listen to your head . . . or maybe a little of both. Save your sanity by figuring out what part of your body is doing the talking at different times and let yourself move ahead and welcome the right changes into your life.

- **Focus on the Positives First.** Shut off the internal voice that accentuates the negatives. Have a virtual dress rehearsal in your mind without finding reasons that it will not work out. There will be plenty of opportunity to look at the downside, so first, consider the upside.

- **Something New?** If this change offers you something that you have longed for and that will help you evolve and grow, go for it.

- **Reserve the Final Decision.** Talk to those you trust but be aware that nobody knows what your heart feels or what your head is thinking the way you do. The best decisions are made when you can find ways to put both parts at ease. Do your research, but you make the final decision.

Sometimes our minds and hearts are at odds. We *think* we should do one thing but we *feel* we should do something else. See if you can find creative ways to comfort both.

## The Mother In and of Us All

Being late is one thing, but being late when you're a mom and kids are waiting at the other end is another.

Virtually every mother worries that something, anything, will happen during her well-planned day and cause her to miss the boat, literally and figuratively. The thought of having her kids wait aimlessly for a late mother or miss an opportunity because a mom couldn't arrange for transportation is a nightmare. And safety is at stake when children are left to wait for their ride at the movie theater or in the dark after dance class lets out.

Well, as we are often reminded, "It takes a village" to raise a child, and the comforting thought is that every other mother has these fears, is late at some point, and has bad days. Every mother also knows that moms help each other out.

So when you're due at school at two-forty-five, and at one-thirty your youngest shoves garbanzo beans up her nose, know that there is a friend you can call as you take your legume-stuffed child to the pediatrician. Develop a community around you so that you don't flip out when these things happen.

- **Team Up with Friends.** Plan in advance to rescue each other if you can't make bus pickup on time. Incorporate the buddy system and be each other's backups. Be careful not to overuse this system or heavily rely on it so your buddy is left doing all the pickups. Remember, knowing you have backup means peace; it also means commitment.

- **Team Up with the Team.** For after-school activities get to know the other moms and see if you can arrange carpooling or a sys-

tem that works. Don't wait until the last minute to introduce yourself and ask a favor. Soccer moms unite!

- **Stay in Touch** . . . with your friends and their lives and their needs, so you won't feel uncomfortable calling on them, asking for help, and helping them out.

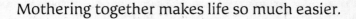

Mothering together makes life so much easier.

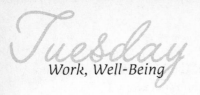

# Tuesday
*Work, Well-Being*

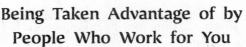

## Being Taken Advantage of by People Who Work for You

Your housekeeper, baby-sitter, nanny, assistant, or someone who makes it possible for you to work outside the home was once reliable and now she's not. She takes excessive time off, is often late, and leaves early. Her attitude is more take than give these days, and it's making you angry.

If you feel you are being taking advantage of, how do you stop it?

- **Be an Observer.** Take notes for a couple of weeks about how prevalent the problem is. Is there a pattern to her lateness? Is there predictability to the types of requests for time off that come your way? How long has this been going on, and how long has it been a problem?

- **You Won't Find Perfection.** The reality is that you will have to accept certain aspects of her behavior that you don't like or have difficulty dealing with. Decide what they are and honestly assess whether you *can* live with them or whether someone else will better serve your needs.

- **Go Forward.** If you feel you want her to continue working for you, make new parameters and let her know what they are. Offer a trial period, and after that time, get together again and see whether you are willing to proceed.

Someone whom you hire to make your life easier needs to do just that.

# Coming Out of the Closet That Your Child Is Gay

If you should learn that your child is gay or has other sexual-identity issues, the most important thing for you to do, first and foremost, is to come to terms with this news yourself. Truly come to terms.

Many parents are shocked to discover that they harbor homophobic thoughts and feelings, even if they've sublimated them successfully for years. Pay attention to your language, the jokes you tell or laugh at, and the stereotypes you keep in your head. It is troubling to learn that you have these feelings for your own child. What you must remember is that no one among your child's relatives or friends is likely to support and understand your child if you remain conflicted, defensive, or prejudiced. This announcement serves as a sharp adjustment for you as well as your child.

- **Take It in Stride.** There is no universal time frame for coming to terms with the fact that your child is homosexual. Take it easy and spend time with your son or daughter, learn what you can, and participate in a support group. When you and your child are ready, let others know where things stand.

- **It's Your Child's Announcement.** Although you are coming to terms with how this affects you, this is still your child's life you are addressing. If your son or daughter is not ready for you to tell the family, don't. It is your child's right to decide who knows about his or her personal life.

- **Open Your Heart, Others May Not.** Many people (and you may be one of them) are fearful and ignorant about homosexuality and homosexuals. You and others may hold religious or moral beliefs that homosexual behavior is wrong. There are some people who are not going to be able to hear what you have to say with an open heart and, in fact, it may be better not to tell them. Remember, you are not asking for your family's approval. You are telling them what you feel can be helpful to your child.

Other people will think what they think.
It is up to you to present yourself, your child,
and your family as whole.

# When Your Friend and Partner Clash

You had hoped that your dear friend and spouse would like each other. This wish is just not going to happen, and it hurts you to know that two of the most important people in your life don't see eye to eye—on anything!

Recognize that your wish to have those closest to you share experiences with you is just not likely to happen. Keeping your sanity while nurturing a good friendship as well as your marriage can make you feel as if you are queen of the emotional balancing act. With a little know-how, you can maintain both relationships for your own well-being.

- **Rethink Social Events.** If the dynamic of having these people in the same room is too taxing for you, orchestrate social events that don't involve getting everyone together at the same time. Don't put yourself in the position of feeling you need to "protect" your friend or always being on guard to be sure "everyone is having a good time."

- **Give Your Partner the Freedom** . . . to not like your friend but not the license to be rude or dismissive. Don't insist that they often spend time together in situations that will be unusually difficult for either of them.

- **Nurture Your Friendship** . . . on your own. Spend as much time with your friend as you can, doing things that you both enjoy and that are meaningful to you. When there's no way around getting together with the both of them under the same roof,

share with your partner why it is important for you as a couple to attend and spend some time with your friend.

Accept that your partner's absence is a gift to you to have enriched time with your friend. Save your requests to have your partner join you for those special times when you really want him with you.

## Spice Up Your Sex Life

What happened to your sex life?

It used to be several times a week but lately it's once or twice a month. Why remain unhappy? Why be in a relationship that is devoid of sensuous touching and gratifying sexual intimacy?

If changes in your body (or your partner's) or even in your attitude have contributed to waning interest, it may be time to begin to communicate honestly about what is going on. Without pushing, you can find subtle or not so subtle ways to get onto a track where you can express your desire for sexual intimacy in a way that is heard and will likely result in connecting with your partner.

- **Let's Talk About It.** Begin with a conversation. It doesn't have to be a deep, long-winded talk but maybe even a chuckle about "how it used to be." Opening up to your partner and getting out of denial is the first step.

- **Book Time Together.** After you open the book on your sex life, why not get a good book or two that you can read together (or on your own) and then talk about what you read that interests you.

- **Put Sex on Your To-Do List.** If you are on your computer till hours after your mate goes to sleep, it is likely that the signal you are sending is that you are not available for sex. If you wear the frumpiest flannels instead of sliding between the sheets in something a bit skimpy or nothing at all, you may also be sending a message that sex isn't important.

- **Create "Sexy" Rituals** . . . and your own private language that lead to sex. Ask him to join you for a sensuous shower or light a candle in the bedroom as a way to signal your mate that you are interested in making love.

You are never too old to have a great sexual life.

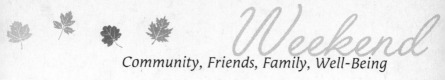

# Run for a Cause

You may have a friend who is battling breast cancer. Or maybe your mom has Parkinson's. Someone in your office has just been diagnosed with multiple sclerosis. And your neighbor's son needs a kidney transplant.

It seems as if wherever you turn or whomever you talk to, somebody is dealing with some major health issue, and there is just not enough money or awareness to deal with it. Raising the consciousness of a community takes time, energy, and stamina. Keep your sanity while you support your friends when they most need to feel as if they are part of a community of caring folks.

- **Do It.** Raise money in honor of your friend by running, walking, or bike riding and make donations to a particular organization or toward the payment for a specific medical procedure. After the event, keep donors posted on how you did and how much money you raised.

- **Do It with Family and Friends.** Enlist friends to be a part of the effort. If kids can't walk or run, push, pull, or stroller them. Spread the good feeling and educate as many people as you can to the importance of prevention, health, research, treatment, and awareness as well as "giving back."

- **Do It Again.** After the event, document what the experience meant to you and commit to participating again in events for causes that touch your soul.

There are many ways to participate in helping those you care about deal with their health challenges. Find the way that works for you and *do it*!

# Regain Trust of a Friend (or Not)

When someone you love betrays you, how do you regain the feeling of trust again? You may have a friend who doesn't tell the truth, and then returns to apologize and thinks everything will be all right. But after a couple of such betrayals, you may just not be able to trust her again.

You ask yourself if you are being fair, and how many chances a person should get before you just have to turn away.

Regaining trust becomes less and less possible the more someone continues to betray you. Unfortunately, part of the problem is that if they continue to engage in betrayal behavior, are consistently forgiven and are considered trustworthy, the more likely they are to continue along that path. Without consequences, there is little motivation to change.

- **Friends Forever?** Think long and hard about whether you want or need to continue to be in a relationship with a high likelihood of being betrayed. Consider whether you can imagine yourself in a friendship with someone who not only would not betray you, but would never even consider it. What type of friends do you want to spend time with? What values do you want them to have?

- **It's Time to Confront.** Share with this person your disappointment and frustration of having gone down the road of betrayal a few too many times.

- **No More.** Let your friend know you are not willing to put yourself at risk anymore. If it's clear she cannot prevent herself from

acting differently and you cannot rely on her to behave differently, then you may want to let go of the relationship.

- **Don't Be Vulnerable.** If you decide that you still want her in your life for whatever reason, it is up to you to change the nature of the friendship. Resist leaving yourself open or vulnerable.

Regaining trust takes time, consistency,
and a willingness by both parties
to relate to each other differently.

## Abortion

The at-home pregnancy test is positive. You're pregnant and will not have this baby.

Deciding not to carry a baby to term is a major decision. It must be made in as calm and relaxed a manner as you can. Hearing the news may cause you to panic, feel alone, and question your own standards and moral code. All that is a normal reaction. You may choose to speak to the father, friends, or family about your situation, or you may feel embarrassed that you became pregnant in the first place. (Why is it that women often feel embarrassed or ashamed when they certainly did not get themselves pregnant on their own?)

Only you know what this experience is like for you and only you can make decisions about your future with or without a child. You can enlist the opinions, advice, and guidance from others, but it is ultimately your decision whether it is the right time, situation, or circumstance for you to become a mother.

If you decide to undergo an abortion:

- **Go to a Reputable Facility.** Do careful research and get yourself to a clean and safe doctor's office, hospital, or clinic that is reputable.

- **Don't Go Alone.** Try to go with a trusted friend, boyfriend, husband, or member of your family who will support you and *not* condemn or disgrace you.

- **Take Care of You.** Now is not the time to rehash your sexual practices. Now is the time to stay present and take care of yourself. Tend to and restore your strength, energy, and health.

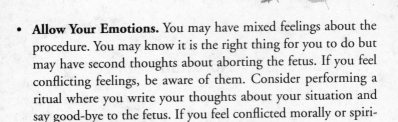

- **Allow Your Emotions.** You may have mixed feelings about the procedure. You may know it is the right thing for you to do but may have second thoughts about aborting the fetus. If you feel conflicting feelings, be aware of them. Consider performing a ritual where you write your thoughts about your situation and say good-bye to the fetus. If you feel conflicted morally or spiritually or religiously, forgive yourself and allow yourself to engage in a dialogue through prayer. Do not be afraid of your feelings.

You have a choice about what to do regarding your body and whether to have a baby.

## Cell Phone and Kids' Connections

If you are like many mothers, cell phones have changed your relationship with your child. Unlike days gone by, now children can reach their parents anytime, anywhere; and without giving it any thought, some do!

More and more children rely on their cell phone to call their parents (mostly their mothers) for help and advice, and to ask their folks to do things for them. Most of their requests are unwarranted. They are capable of doing it themselves, they need to do it to grow up and become independent, or they should rely on themselves to problem solve. Teens and young adults today think nothing of calling their moms for the slightest comment or question. This often prevents them from having their own life and figuring out everyday issues that come up. Self-sufficiency is not fostered.

True, most parents feel secure with their children having cell phones to use in emergencies. The social and political climate after September 11, 2001, increased the need for, desire for, and availability of cell phones, and as a result, most families have multiple phones. Sometimes parents encourage this intense phone connection by calling their children too much. But next time you find yourself speed dialing your kids, think again about whether you should make that call. Maybe it's best to have patience and let them come to you when they need guidance after they've thought about it for themselves.

- **Dialing Fingers Should Take a Rest.** Step back and take a deep breath every time you want to dial. It would be better for the children (and for you) to discourage cell phone use several times

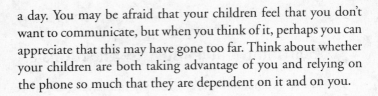

a day. You may be afraid that your children feel that you don't want to communicate, but when you think of it, perhaps you can appreciate that this may have gone too far. Think about whether your children are both taking advantage of you and relying on the phone so much that they are dependent on it and on you.

- **Don't Be Available 24/7.** Just because the phone rings does not mean you need to answer it. If there is an emergency, your child will leave a message and you can retrieve it. Judge for yourself and respond. Remember you are fostering independence in your child.

- **Let Them Make Decisions.** When your children do call, listen and give appropriate input. Advise less. Encourage your children to try to solve problems by asking probing questions, suggesting they seek out resources before dialing you up. Ultimately, rather than giving your children the feeling that you are not interested, this will help your children to develop self-confidence and self-management skills.

Everyone needs space in order to grow.

# Can't Get the Weight Off as You Age

There is no doubt about it, most women put on weight as they age. But wait, you say, you were always thin. Now that you are in your fifties, sixties, whatever, you have put on ten pounds and just can't get it off. Worse, when you look in the mirror (if you allow yourself to have a mirror), you don't even recognize the woman staring back.

You don't want to get used to your body as you age—and you don't want it to be the new norm. But, after a full day of eating, you feel so bloated and look pregnant. You could try to lose a little weight but that stomach roll may just be there to stay. And now you're even hiding your body from your partner.

- **Come to Terms.** Getting older means you have to deal with change, and having a tough time taking off a few pounds is part of that challenge. Your metabolism is slower, so it is more difficult to lose the weight and keep it off.

- **Accept a New Norm.** You have the power to change the shape of your body carefully, healthfully, and without injury—maybe not back to the same one you had thirty years ago, but you can reshape it through exercise and healthful eating.

- **Look at Your Body in a Different Way.** When you look at your stomach, legs, breasts, hands, pay close attention to all that they have gone through and appreciate what they have done for you. They have held and nursed your babies, carried you through your life, and endured much. If you look at your body through

the eyes of someone who has *lived* in your body, you are more likely to appreciate it differently.

You can mourn the loss of the body of your youth
while you welcome the body of a woman
who has lived fully.

# Terms of Endearment

Do you ever really look at couples who have good relationships and wonder what their secrets are?

One of the things you will probably notice is that there is playfulness about them—a privacy that is reserved just for them (which, however, you will probably not notice). They refer to each other fondly, use a few key words or phrases that only they "get," or talk with each other in playful voices, again reserved just for them. This lightheartedness allows couples to be youthful forever, have a sweet connection, and provide for unique closeness.

- **Sweetie Pie, Buttercup.** At times, communicate with your significant other using a pet name. Keep it in private conversation and say it with feeling and have some fun with it. Nobody else gets this name—it is for you and your partner's ears only.

- **Try It.** Even if you feel uncomfortable at first and have been together forever, it's never too late to use special terms of endearment for your mate. Use them as an enticement to revitalize your relationship. Everybody likes to feel special.

Special terms of affection and endearment can make you feel safe and special in a relationship whether it is one year old or fifty years old.

# *Weekend*
*Well-Being, Work*

## School Days Are Here Again

It's time to hit the books. Whether you are returning to school because of life circumstances such as job loss, illness, shift in family responsibility, divorce, or retirement, or because you were never able to enter or finish college, studying may be a bit more challenging than when you were fresh out of high school.

With many new fields emerging, there's good reason today to change or start a new career. Enrolling in classes now can not only prepare you for a new field, it can increase your self-confidence and help sharpen your mind.

- **Revisit and Restructure** . . . your impressions of yourself as the student you used to be. You are not doomed or programmed to keep the same assessment of yourself as a student based on how you did when you were younger.

- **Rethink and Rephrase** . . . your own or other people's comments about the type of student you were in elementary school, junior high, high school, and college because they no longer apply, and they certainly do not predict how you will do this time around.

- **Reassess** . . . your vision of yourself. See yourself as a student. Appreciate that you are open to learning and are motivated to enter a new field. Or just learn for the sake of learning.

- **Reengage.** Enjoy the fact that you can engage in intergenerational dialogue about topics of mutual interest, which will surely

contribute to keeping you young and vital. See humor in the fact that you will be older than your professors and most of the other students. Be a role model.

Engage in learning at any age in any way accessible to you.

# Monday
### Parent, Midlife, Family

## Allowing Your Kids to Grow Up

Some women find it very stressful to watch their children grow up. You want them to have friends. You want them to succeed. And then, somewhere along the way, you realize what you want for them may not necessarily be what they want for themselves.

This is when you need to examine why your agenda for them is so important—perhaps more important than helping them develop their own interests, talents, strengths.

Maybe you were an outstanding academic but your young son does not seem interested in books and is fabulous with his hands. Building things puts a great smile on his face and fills him with a sense of accomplishment. What do you do? Worry or celebrate?

If you feel he is avoiding dealing with developing an important skill or has a learning deficit, then you can work to remediate what is lacking. Worrying, however, will not help. Taking action will. Being preoccupied with the situation will get in the way of his self-confidence and may send the message that he is not good enough. The fact of the matter is, he *is* good enough and just hasn't yet mastered a skill he still has to learn.

- **Let Go of Your Image** . . . of what you need your child to be to make you happy and open up to possibilities based on who your child is and how he sees the world.

- **You Are a Guide.** Understand that you are there to guide your child and expose him to a world that has many possibilities that can reflect his talents, interests, and skills.

- **Your Child Is Not You.** Your child was not put on this earth to do for you what you could not do for yourself. There are plenty of unhappy adults who took a career path, married someone they did not love, or lived in places that were unsuitable because their parents needed them to do those things. Choose a different path as a parent and let your child choose his own life path.

- **Your Job as a Parent.** Tell yourself that your child is a unique individual and your job is to love and support him.

Our children are here to teach us what we need to learn about ourselves and about them.

## When You're the Breadwinner

Don't let money get in the way of your relationship when you earn more than your partner.

Not being the "norm" couple in your neighborhood, you've probably had your fair share of raised eyebrows and questioning about your way of living. Other people's perceptions and pressure for men to be the main provider can be intense, and that's the battle you and your partner have to confront and present a united front.

- **Honor Each Other.** Be sensitive to the contributions each of you bring to your relationship and your family. Define your roles in a manner that works for each of you.

- **Leave Your Ego at the Family Room Door.** Your family role is different from your role at work. Remind yourself that financial rewards often are unrelated to the importance of a job. Because you earn more, that does not mean that you or your job is more valuable than your partner or your partner's job.

- **You're Both Contributing.** Appreciate that you have reduced the financial pressure with household bills and can substantially provide for your partner or family. Feel good about affording your partner the luxury of pursuing work or study that may not be as financially rewarding but may be intensely gratifying.

Value and contribution to a relationship and a family are unrelated to money.

## Living with Just Guys

When you have sons there's a lot of testosterone flying around your house, as well as sports equipment, car parts, and high-tech gadgets. It's great learning what makes these guys tick, but you may miss having "girl time" and the chance to focus on being female.

How can you maintain your sanity when you're washing mounds of dirty sweatpants and listening to the pounding of a drum set at all hours?

- **Find Female Bonding Time.** Get a balance of female energy in your life. Invite your nieces, daughters of friends, and women friends to do things that allow you to enjoy your womanhood and femininity, like going to a day spa or seeing a chick flick.

- **Invoke Your Creativity.** When the guys are overpowering your world, bring space and balance in your life by doing things just for you, like painting, planting an herb garden, and creating memory books from your photos.

- **Ask Them to Do a Mom Activity.** Make a plan and put it on the calendar, to go to lunch with or attend a concert or a play with your sons. Getting some female energy in their life is a good thing, too.

By making sure your own life is in balance you will raise your son with an open and accepting heart— appreciating the differences.

# Gay Parents

Being a good parent has nothing to do with someone's sexual orientation. Since being gay or lesbian is much more about genetic predisposition than anything else, the ability to be a good parent rests in areas unrelated to sexuality.

If you know gay parents, are you uncomfortable with their sexuality? Do you discourage your kids from playing with their kids because they are not the norm? Are you worried that gay parents will foster gay qualities in their kids when they are old enough to become sexually aware?

- **Good Parents Are Good Parents.** Being a good parent is about possessing and expressing love, patience, affection, acceptance, good judgment. If the parents of your children's friends are gay or lesbian, it is important for you to understand that there are many more similarities than differences between children who are raised by homosexual and heterosexual parents. In fact, children who are raised with lesbian parents appear to be more tolerant of differences and more nurturing toward younger children than kids who are raised in heterosexual households.

- **Come to Terms with Your Own Issues** . . . and stereotypes related to gay parenting and be aware of what you are passing along to your children that will color their impressions of their friends and their friends' families. Think seriously about what you feel are the important qualities for being a good parent.

- **Reach Out.** If you don't feel comfortable with same-sex parenting, make an effort to go out of your comfort zone and get to know the parents of your child's friend. Ask them to join you for some social event with the kids, a picnic, ball game, afternoon movie, just to get to know them and feel more at ease.

Because parents are gay or lesbian does not mean their parenting skills are to be dismissed.

# Honoring Others Who Are Not Tops on Your List

Some relationships are strained while still being important to you. When you don't see eye-to-eye with someone in your life, attending an event in his honor becomes a challenge. Do you go or take a pass?

First, consider if you want to reach out and make an effort to be fully present at his life milestones. Will each of you gain from the experience, even if it may be difficult for the other person to acknowledge or express gratitude? Consider addressing any heated issues that may be resolved before the big event. Notice who else may contribute to any added friction and whether those other players will attend, and if their presence will perpetuate ill will.

Do a bit of soul searching and consider what is the best way you can attend, while staying centered and true to yourself. You may need to establish limits on what will be enough and what will be beyond the call of duty. An important consideration as you evaluate the relationship is how much of *you* are you prepared to give? Can you attend and put the past behind you, or set it aside for the event? Or maybe it's best to be at the ceremony and forgo the party, send a present in your place, or go and be just comfortably removed as you stay on the sidelines.

- **Will You Benefit?** Establish in your own mind and heart what is your place in the person's life and what is his place in your life (they are often not the same). If ultimately, you value this person and he values you (even if it's difficult for one or both of you to

express it), acknowledging your relationship by honoring the life event may be worth the extra effort.

- **If You Go, Be Present.** Before going, you can increase your energy and really "be there" for that person. He will feel this gift emanating from you.

- **Release Negative Feelings Beforehand.** If Mother's Day isn't easy for you, allow yourself to feel the sadness, disappointment, and anger over your relationship before your visit. Maybe you can journal or have a conversation with the mirror to release negative tension. Also, try and think back on some endearing memories. Remember, this is her day and you can show your mom you really do care by respecting her and sharing in the moment. You are not likely to repair a lifetime of hurt at one meeting, but you may be able to experience this day differently.

Even if another person in your life cannot fully
absorb your effort in sustaining a relationship,
you will know in your heart that you
are doing the right thing.

# Weekend
*Well-Being*

## Time Is Relatively Speaking

Can't relax, no matter how hard you try? Are you, like many young women, never sure you've done enough, never sure if you can handle all your responsibilities? Are your weeks growing busier and busier? Do you often complain that there is simply too much going on?

Are you someone who believes that if you aren't busy, you aren't doing anything?

- **Leave Your Watch at Home.** For one day, morning, or afternoon, let go of time and do not look at a clock on a building or in a restaurant, or at the watch of the person next to you. No peeking! Listen to your body clock and begin to do one thing. Then complete it to your satisfaction. When your mind wanders to another thing that needs to be done, tell yourself you are going to do what is at hand until you are no longer interested.

- **Don't Open Your Calendar.** If you do look, and it's full, don't stress out. Instead, focus on what needs to be done. You will be able to do it. Try not to plan too many things; just do those things you feel like doing, when you feel like doing them.

- **Let Your Body Be Your Guide.** Eat when you are hungry, sleep when you are tired, walk when you feel as though your body needs to move.

- **Give Yourself Credit for Slowing Down.** This alone may be relaxing. Pay attention to those things you normally ignore.

Not everyone relaxes in the same way. Find *your* way and practice to make it second nature to you.

# Asking for Help as an Alzheimer's Caregiver

You probably know someone who knows someone who has Alzheimer's disease. Millions of people have it.

Living with Alzheimer's and living with someone who has Alzheimer's is all about change and uncertainty and, sadly, stress. The one thing that does not ever change, however, is that the person who has Alzheimer's remains a person. After some time, people with Alzheimer's will act different, and eventually may look different, but they still deserve care, love, and respect.

Their lives are about dignity, adaptation, and change. If you are caring for someone who has Alzheimer's, you must remember that you need to care for yourself. Many caregivers feel disconnected from their former life because friends have fallen away or because they do not feel comfortable being with them. You wonder how this could have happened to you and your loved one, which can stoke the fires of anger, disappointment, depression, and isolation.

Talk with others who understand what you are experiencing through in-person support groups or online, or speak with a counselor. Getting time away from the person you care for is essential to your well-being. Exercise, good nutrition, and a hearty laugh all play an important part in living well with the person who is ill.

- **Ask for What You Need.** You need to ask for what you need (and you may not know exactly what that is until you need it). Most people want to be helpful but don't know precisely what to do. Ask people to do what they can reasonably do and what they

are good at. If you need help with insurance forms, bill paying, administrative work, ask someone who is reliable and good with numbers. Get help with meals from a friend who is a good cook. Get together with some friends and tell them what needs to be done and ask them to pick what they would like to do.

- **Be Direct** . . . when asking for help. Don't apologize. It is an honor to be able to help someone in need. "I could use a couple of hours to get my hair done, do some errands, or get to the gym, and could use your help in staying with Dad." If their schedule doesn't match yours, accommodate so they can be available and you can still accomplish what you need to do.

- **Appreciate Helpers.** Even if you think the people who help you *should* do what they are doing, let them know that you welcome their help. Everyone needs to feel appreciated.

- **Attend a Support Group.** Share your thoughts, feelings, and experiences with others who appreciate what you are going through. Sometimes your friends or family members cannot truly relate to what is happening in your life and will criticize you for your choices or for expressing negative feelings. Learn from others and be open to their support.

You will be a better caregiver if you accept help.

*Tuesday*
*Well-Being*

# When Your Counselor Makes an Error

One of the most difficult things to deal with in therapy is coming to terms with the fact that your therapist is human. Your therapist isn't perfect and will sometimes do or say things that will disappoint you.

You deserve to have this person's full attention during your time together. Also, your therapist should maintain professionalism by keeping the facts of your life straight and being there on time for your appointments so you don't wait.

How do you keep your sanity when your therapist does something that makes you question whether there is full attentiveness?

- **Let Your Therapist Be Human.** Recognize that your therapist will make mistakes. It is your prerogative to bring up what is bothering you so that there's something to learn.

- **If Something Bothers You.** If you raise an issue where you feel you were treated unfairly, dismissed, or not heard, or your therapist is defensive and does not assume responsibility for his or her actions and blames you for the problem, think seriously about whether this person is the right person for you.

- **Speak Up.** Allow yourself to engage in a discussion about how you felt when you arrived for your appointment and someone else was waiting to be seen. Or what it was like when your therapist referred to your children by the wrong names. Or how it felt when your therapist was preoccupied or looked exhausted. You deserve to have your therapist take responsibility for his or her

actions, apologizing and taking preventive measures so this does not happen again.

Every interaction in therapy can be therapeutic if
you feel as if you can trust your counselor
to be honest and take responsibility
for his or her mistakes.

*Well-Being, Family, Friends*

# Substance Abuse

You or someone you know may have a problem with alcohol, drugs, or even tobacco. None of these habits is healthy. With such easy access, it is difficult for someone to stop substance abuse on his own.

The familiar "triggers," such as places, people, and routines, all play into the habit. Breaking it is not only about stopping but about committing to dramatically changing your life. Concentrate on keeping your sanity as you or someone you love fights this battle.

- **Be Honest.** Many people who have substance abuse problems or are close to someone who does deny the problem. Now's the time to *stop* sweeping it under the rug. Covering up or making excuses never helps.

- **Be with the Right People.** Getting help from supportive family and friends, treatment centers, and rehabilitation professionals is essential to live a life substance-free.

- **Be Without Those Who Don't Help.** Changing friends and the people in your life who let you abuse your body is part of the challenge. Spend time only with those who support you through your detox.

Facing the demons that need to be covered up by substance abuse takes time and commitment.

# When Your Kid Doesn't Return to College

You may have dreamed about your child going to college. You visited campuses, helped with college applications, and paid tuition and room and board for one year. You thought your child was off to college and would begin the next stage of life, right? Not if he returns home after the first year and announces that he is not going back! If this is a surprise, or you were wondering whether this really was a fit, keep your sanity intact.

- **Be There.** Remain calm. You may have a hard time hiding your disappointment, but he'll need support from you now. Let him know that he is a successful person no matter what and that he always has been. Recognize his good points and the wise choices he makes such as saying no to drugs or other life-enhancing choices.

- **Listen, Listen, Listen** . . . to the reasons he is not going back and to what the college experience was like for him.

- **Set Standards for Living at Home as an Adult** . . . not as a child. Share what you expect in the household. Clear goals and structure are important since there may have been changes since he left. Sit down to talk on a regular, scheduled basis. This gives you all time to get your thoughts in order and reinforces the idea that you are all adults.

- **Make a Plan of Self-Sufficiency.** Decide if you are able to continue to support an education and not a lifestyle. Refer to it as

the "gap *year*" and together make a plan about where he goes from here. Discuss how he will find work in the interim and apply to the same or a different school next semester. The idea is how to move along with life.

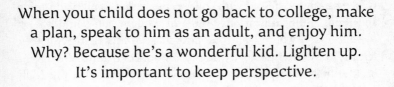

When your child does not go back to college, make a plan, speak to him as an adult, and enjoy him. Why? Because he's a wonderful kid. Lighten up. It's important to keep perspective.

## Compliment Your Partner

Everyone needs to feel appreciated. But giving out compliments is one of the first things to go in a relationship. You don't feel appreciated and likely don't let your partner know what you appreciate about him. After a short time, neither of you feels appreciated, noticed, or cared about by the other. And a vicious cycle gets set into gear and continues.

Rather than think about all the things you don't like about your partner, contemplate the qualities and things you do like, focusing on what you truly appreciate. Whether large or small, pay attention. Of course, some things about that person will always bug you. Guess what? Some things about you will always be irritating to your partner. Stay on track with the good things about each other and save the sanity of your relationship.

- **Compliment First.** You may wonder why you would tell your partner that you appreciate him when he doesn't tell you. Aside from two wrongs not making a right, isn't it better for you to take the risk and share what you like rather than what bothers you? The likelihood of someone paying attention to what you don't appreciate is increased if he feels he is appreciated and truly cared for and noticed.

- **The Family Benefits.** If you can hold your partner in high esteem and let him know, he will likely offer more praise to your children. It kind of works that way—when we feel we are valued in the eyes of another we want those we love to feel valued. (The

reverse is also true, so pay close attention to how you talk to your partner and your children.)

Appreciating others has a boomerang effect.
The good stuff comes back to you.

## Redesigning Friendships

The most meaningful friendships are often reciprocal relationships. You're there for them and they're there for you in times of need, loneliness, life milestones, celebrations, and defeats. But what do you do when you feel the scale is off balance and you're giving more than you are receiving? Some relationships are just like that, and you need to accept it, but others don't need to be, and examining them may help.

We all need to know that a good friend has our best interests at heart and that this feeling is mutual. It's important to rely on our friends who can help us tackle major challenges and changes and serve as our support systems. Without them, we know we could not make it.

However, sometimes your old friends may not know how to relate to what you are going through or may feel threatened or scared by your situation and either back off or become unavailable. Try not to take it personally, as people react to change differently. Rather than trying to change the friend to suit your needs, maybe you need to change the way you view the friendship.

- **Don't Look to One Friend.** Some people are there for your ups and downs and some are not. The people you can laugh with may not be the people you can cry with. Know who your supportive friends are and go to them when troubled. Maintain your social friends because it's important to enjoy life with others. You're truly blessed if you have thick-and-thin buddies with whom you can also share good times.

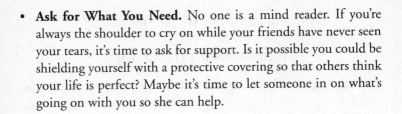

- **Ask for What You Need.** No one is a mind reader. If you're always the shoulder to cry on while your friends have never seen your tears, it's time to ask for support. Is it possible you could be shielding yourself with a protective covering so that others think your life is perfect? Maybe it's time to let someone in on what's going on with you so she can help.

- **Are You Really Giving More?** Be honest with yourself and examine your friendships. Have you truly been the one giving more? If you have, then this may be a good time to enlist a whole new group of people who also have similar issues, and with whom you can be vulnerable for a sense of safety, understanding, and nurturing. On the other hand, if you make time for friends only on your terms and schedule, your approach may be preventing you from experiencing that kind of nurturing and support you seek.

Redesign your friendships so you can give as well as reap the benefits.

## Relationship Tune-up

Have you ever wondered why so many couples are disappointed with their love life? Have you asked yourself, "Is that all there is?" or "Where has the romance gone?" If you have, it is quite possible that there may be nothing wrong with your partner, but it may be an indication that your relationship needs a tune-up to get back on track or to find a new track together.

Renew the spark in your relationship as part of your ongoing maintenance plan. With regular tune-ups, the partnership with your significant other can go the distance.

- **Reinforce Your Commitment.** Frequent, sincere, verbal re-statements of vows or promises keep the relationship at the forefront.

- **Carve Out a Time Together Every Day.** Turn off your cell phone, PDA, or computer and spend time together so that if you want, you can have a conversation, dinner alone, a short walk, and the opportunity to touch without interruption.

- **Respect Your Mate.** Sometimes we take our loved ones for granted and get too comfortable in our relationships. Use respectful language and actions. Be willing to see his point of view. Demonstrate appreciation not only for what each of you does but for who you are. A thank-you is always well received.

- **Try New Things Together.** Take a class, work together for a cause, do something you have never done before. Revisit some-

thing you both enjoyed that you participated in when you first met but that you have let slide.

- **Laugh and Have Fun.** Having a sense of humor is an essential ingredient to all good relationships. Playful openness can stimulate desire. Be careful that you do not use humor at the expense of your mate.

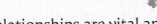

Relationships are vital and dynamic; they are not static. To thrive, they need attention, care, and nurturing.

# When Your Daughter Has an Eating Disorder

Most of the estimated five million people in this country who are affected by eating disorders, such as binge eating and bulimia, are young women and adolescent girls.

Many factors influence whether a young woman will go on eating binges and throw up her food. Among them are family dysfunction, personality traits, biology, and growing up in a media-dominated culture that promises happiness, desirability, and attractiveness as a direct result of being thin.

Bulimia often begins during adolescence and continues through adulthood. College women are especially susceptible because they experience an increase in academic demands, feel enormous pressure to fit in and be thin, and face many social stresses, while usually living away from home. In addition to contributing to a distorted body image, other problems, such as gastrointestinal, cardiovascular, metabolic, and endocrine issues, can arise.

When someone you care about has such an eating disorder, what can you do?

- **Focus on Healthy Living.** Even if you don't think so (because there is friction between the two of you), daughters model their mothers. Your behavior, habits, and actions count. Eating healthfully, exercising, and staying fit shows your daughter how to live a healthy lifestyle. Buying wholesome foods—fruits, veggies, grains, nuts, lean meats, and cheeses—provides growing teens with better food choices. Think about the message you

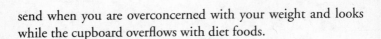

send when you are overconcerned with your weight and looks while the cupboard overflows with diet foods.

- **Express Concern Without Judgment** . . . about her health and eating healthfully. Challenge language such as "I'm such a pig" or "My body is disgusting." Pay attention to peer pressure your loved one is under to keep at a certain weight but be careful not to accuse, single out, or criticize friends, which will only bring up her defenses.

- **Visualize a Healthy Young Woman.** She's comfortable in her skin and at home in her body. Tell her you are picturing her content with who she is, inside and out.

When someone you love abuses her body, hold her in your heart to help her heal.

## Single and Being with Kids

When you are single and childless, you may feel a void when it comes to having a close and meaningful relationship to children. However, you can still benefit from some healthy kid energy in your life.

How? By being with kids in some way. Even though they are not your children and you are not with them on a regular basis, you'll save your sanity by welcoming someone else's child into your heart.

- **What Can You Offer Them?** What do you enjoy about being with children, and what can you do with them? Enroll as a "big sister" and help out a young girl who could use a role model and some good mentoring. Or take some neighborhood kids out for some fun and exploration at a fair, museum, or zoo. Do you like to ski, paint with watercolors, or cook? Invite children to do the things you love to do and open doors for them that they would never know existed.

- **What Can They Offer You?** Being around children can satisfy your desire to have laughter and lightheartedness in your life. By spending time with your sister or brother's children, you can develop a special relationship and take them on adventures as their "Auntie Mame."

- **What Can You Offer Each Other?** You both can have a profound influence on each other's lives. You will look at the world

through the eyes of a child again, and the child can learn from your vast interests, skills, and life experiences.

By living an intergenerational life, you keep yourself open to the wonder and charm of children, whether or not they are your own.

# When You Feel Old First Thing in the Morning

Some days you wake up, look in the mirror, and say, "Not bad." Other days, you wake up feeling some aches and pains in your body and notice the puffiness underneath your eyes or the way the pillow crease stayed imprinted on your cheek. Your mind immediately races to "I look so old."

- **Be Kinder and Gentler.** When you feel old first thing in the morning, give yourself a break. If you start the day feeling aged and decrepit, your whole day will be more of a challenge than it needs to be.

- **Awaken and Love the Skin You're In.** Instead of focusing on your image in the mirror first thing in the morning, don't even look into the looking glass until you slowly wake up each part of your body. While lying in bed, massage your fingers and your elbows. Slowly stretch your arms and legs and then bring your knees to your chest. Spend a little extra time on spots that may need a bit more attention. Gently stretch your arms and move your head from side to side. Roll your shoulders, move your back, legs, feet, and hands (make circles from your ankles and wrists) and be grateful that your body is in as good shape as it is.

- **Forget Your "Mirror Mirror on the Wall" Speech.** Before you look in the mirror, gently splash tepid water all over your face to help bring circulation to your skin. Once a week, apply an aromatic (menthol or peppermint) mask to bring life rushing to the surface of your skin and the feeling of youth and tightness. Spray your face with rosewater. Massage your skin with oil, taking time to focus on the area between your eyebrows, the temples, your jaw, and your neck. You can soften tension lines while invigorating your face—the face you present to the world. As you go through this routine, tell yourself that you are taking care of yourself and have a lot to offer. Be proud of the face you present to the world.

Be your body's champion, not its adversary.

# House Guests:
# Here Today, Gone Tomorrow

Everyone, at one time or another, stays in someone else's home. You may be on the couch in the family room, on an air mattress with the kids, or in your own beautiful guest accommodation. The blankets may be too many or too few, overly itchy or worn, the pillows puffy or flat; you may be sharing a bathroom with three teens or have the chance to soak in a sumptuous bath.

Wherever you are and whatever the circumstance, remember to be considerate because you are in someone's home. If you want room or maid service, stay at a hotel. The best guests are those who pitch in where needed and who stay out of the way when not. And remember, don't overstay your welcome. It's an old joke that guests and fish have one thing in common; they're both no longer good after three days.

- **Gifts of Thanks.** It can be food to share during your stay, flowers, or something unique that fits your host's taste. Offer to pick up the check at dinner, cook dinner, buy ice cream after the movies, or pay for pancakes at the local diner. After you leave, send a thoughtful note, preferably handwritten, in which you share some of the highlights of your time together.

- **If You Break Something, Own Up to It.** Whatever you do, don't hide it in the drawer and let your host find the pieces three weeks after you've gone. Don't throw broken items away because it may be a sentimental piece or repairable (even if you don't

*Week 42*

think so). Apologize sincerely instead of commenting, "This was sitting too close to the edge of the tabletop and was waiting for a tumble." Try to avoid repeated apologies. A better thing to do is offer to pay for the piece or help find a replacement.

- **Know "Sacred" Places.** Before you plop down on the comfy chair, ask your hosts if they are OK with you spending time in that space. You may unknowingly have chosen "Papa's" chair or an off-limits meditation corner. On a similar note, don't assume the phone is yours to use. Today we all have cell phones or phone cards. This is the time to use them.

A good guest is mindful of the host's needs.

# Living with Uncertainty and Anxiety in the World

How much more can you take? One more newscast of bombing or terror raids and you will just go through the roof!

When your tolerance level is low and current events get you down, save your sanity and give yourself a boost by taking a break from the news.

- **Put Calm in Your Day.** Post 9/11 we are all on daily heightened alert and awareness. Every day, find your calm and ground yourself, knowing you are secure and safe.

- **Control Only You.** Since you can't control the events that happen in the world, focus on what is possible and think about how you can control certain aspects of your life instead. Stay connected to people and things that interest you—this is important for adaptation and flexibility to new demands. Accept change but keep practicing your beliefs.

- **Sweet Dreams.** If you can't listen to the headlines without being upset, stay clear of the news before bedtime.

When dealing with the world's uncertainty, focus on what makes you have hope and feel resilient.

# Midlife Changes for Wellness

How did you arrive at midlife so quickly? Where has the time gone?

Going through midlife is all about loss and beginnings. Like many women, you may miss your younger body. It's scary to think that when you look in the mirror, you may see similarities to your mother. As a friend of mine said, the hairs on your face are harder to find and you need magnifying glasses just to tweeze your eyebrows.

Try to adjust to the changes as you transition through yet another stage in your life. Focus on the wisdom you've gathered over the years rather than what gravity does to your body. Shift your attention to the world you can contribute to now that you have lots of worldly experience. Let go of fears that creep into the crevices of your soul. A younger, more spunky person may, on the surface, look more attractive to your boss, but don't let your mind wander about being replaced when you know you have what it takes to get the job done.

Mourning what is no longer there gives you the chance to celebrate what is there. Celebrate!

- **Grow Older with Grace and Style.** Revel in the woman you are. Learn from life experiences and chart a course for this new chapter in your life. Keep blooming into the woman you are and the woman you will become. Are there goals you want to achieve or things you have longed to do? Now is the time. Keep growing.

- **Set Your Own Agenda.** Who says you have to do things a certain way? You know how you should be leading your life. Is it time to switch careers, take time off to write that book, or find your true calling? Listen to your internal voice as you make changes and adjust for the second half of your life.

- **Tap into Your Spiritual Side.** Whatever your belief system, know that we all come from a higher source. Take time to quiet your mind and go within. Pray, meditate, walk in nature, or journal. Ask yourself if you are living an authentic life. What's missing and what brings you joy? Get in tune with your soul so you can feel good about living your life.

- **Let Go of the Old, Welcome the New.** Have you been holding on to things or people in your life that you should release? Are you being held back in some way? Allow in new experiences by letting go of things that no longer serve you.

Remember, as you change, so will your relationships. Welcome the change.

# Tuesday
*Friends*

## No Time for Friends

You're buried under so much work and responsibility that you tend to lack time for your friends. And when you let too much time go before responding to their social entreaties and invitations, you dig yourself further and further into holes of unresponsiveness. Eventually you find yourself feeling everything from guilt to inertia, even resentment toward these friends, especially when they persist in attempting to engage you.

But what can you do to maintain and nurture these friendships even when you really don't have the time to "be there" for others?

- **Honesty Is the Best Policy.** Communicate your situation. Your true friends will understand. Call or e-mail your friends back, let them know of your responsibilities and inability to engage at that time. If possible, make a date to see them in the future and mark it in your calendar. Attempt to honor it, or reschedule it, if need be.

- ***Group* and Conquer.** If three or four of your friends are all acquainted with one another, suggest that you meet for dinner together, or plan on casually entertaining the entire group. No, you don't have a lot of time, but you just might have enough for one relaxing, fun night out with this group—and they are likely to be delighted to be with each other, too!

- **Brief Encounters Can Be Satisfying.** Strive to steal a little time back for yourself out of your busy workday, and arrange to meet friends for brief shared breakfasts, lunches, or cocktails. Or, if

possible, arrange to walk together in the early morning. Sometimes spending an hour with each other is all that each of you may need.

Friendships need to be flexible
and friends forgiving.

# Learn from Your Son

Raising a son teaches you much of what you need to know about the world through different eyes. Sons raise your awareness in ways that do not focus on the obvious.

Get in touch with that other side of yourself by learning things from the boy you are raising. He can help you save your sanity by teaching you a lot about the opposite sex and, most important, about yourself.

- **Learn Connection.** You know how your twelve-year-old son winces when you give him a hug? Where girls show their connection to each other by hugging, many boys punch each other on the arm, shifting the focus to the physical rather than the emotional. When you're with people or in situations where warm and fuzzy won't work, you can learn how to connect to others by how you connect with your son.

- **Learn Adventure.** Finding things that you have in common (love of the sea?) can find you deep sea fishing but not in that stylish navy and white sailor outfit. Or how about sharing a glider ride since he's into flying? Seeing the world through his eyes can open yours to wonderful explorations.

- **Learn Creativity.** You have to talk and interact with your son differently than you do to your daughter or others, and he'll teach you how you can be a part of his world. Find the right approach. Too many questions and probing won't work, and don't expect him to give you glowing thanks (or any recognition, for

that matter) for showing up at his soccer games. Learn to have a creative approach with him and you will learn how to relate to all sorts of people.

All boys are not alike. Get to know *your* son for who he is and learn from him.

## To Tell or Not to Tell About Her Cheater

You are mortified to discover that your very dear friend's partner is cheating on her. You are absolutely sure. No doubt.

You're in a tough situation. If you tell her, surely she will be devastated. If you don't, and she finds out that you knew, she will feel doubly betrayed. How do you keep your sanity and do what is right for your friendship?

- **No Hard and Fast Concealing Rule.** Just because you know information does not mean you must share it. Every friendship is different, based in its own unique history, with its own values and rules. Only you can decide if it is better or worse to share this information. Bear in mind that she may already know, consciously or unconsciously, but has not shared her fears or any information with you.

- **What's Her View.** If you decide that you have the wherewithal to tell her, find a place where you can sit together, quietly, and tell her you have a moral dilemma. What would she do if she were in the position of knowing personal information that's difficult to share and difficult to hear? What would she do if she knew of a husband who was cheating? Then go a step further and ask if she would want a friend to tell her if it were her own husband.

- **Proceed or Not?** If she has a no-tell viewpoint, maybe you want to stop there. Her negative response signals that she may not be able to handle this news. However, she may be able to read be-

tween the lines or start to tuck it in the back of her mind. Either way, you've planted a seed, whether or not she acts on it.

- **Telling.** If you go into details, back it up with accurate facts and tell her you will be there to support her through whatever she chooses to do.

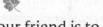

Your commitment to your friend is to be there for her in ways that work for both of you.
Find that way together.

*Partner*

# Read Together

You know the classic scene of two people at the breakfast table buried behind their morning newspapers? They don't talk, and they leave for the day without really connecting.

Very often couples read books, magazines, articles, and journals and never discuss what they read or share their feelings about how they were moved by the material. Continuing on without sharing experiences and feelings promotes distance and disconnection. Here's how to foster intimacy if you both love to read.

- **Read the Same Stuff.** Try and read the same book or article together to create a shared experience. This will give you insight into your mate's responses, attitudes, and perceptions. Reading the same book at the same time can also serve as a common bond, as can playing a challenging video game together. You can talk about the characters and have a similar frame of reference, and stay interested in the storyline by predicting what might happen, planning your strategy, or sharing your perceptions about the writing, the characters, the tone.

- **Read New Stuff.** Find a book or game that seems to be new for both of you or reflects a common interest. Read together or sequentially so you can talk about your perceptions and experiences and get your significant other's point of view.

- **Read Together and Alone.** Recognize that only the two of you are "invited" to participate in this exercise because it is about

the two of you sharing something that is unique for you as a couple.

A sense of intimacy can be created by sharing almost any experience in which you are learning together, experiencing each other's perceptions and perspectives, and finding out more about who you are.

*Weekend*
*Well-Being*

## Balance Posture

One of the best ways to balance your life is to balance your body.

Stand on one foot and focus yourself as you feel the energy come up from the earth through your feet. Let an imaginary string extend out of the top of your head, keeping you straight and tall. This is called the "tree posture" in yoga, and you can increase your balance and focus on your ability to achieve your goals.

At first you may tip back and forth, reaching out for something to steady you. When your mind is all over the place it is nearly impossible to keep your body in balance. But over time, you will be able to achieve the pose and hold it for a few minutes. By practicing this posture, you can start overcoming obstacles in your mind that prevented you from being in balance. This is why yoga can be so helpful when you feel stressed.

- **Focus on Your Breath.** Don't worry about whether you are "doing the posture," whether other people are looking at you, or "why can't I do this today since I did it last week?" The internal chatter is hardly constructive. Bringing together your mind and body is most easily accomplished by focusing on your breath.

- **Don't Look Around.** Fix your eyes on a specific point (not a moving target) and hold it there. If you practice this posture in the same place each day, you may wish to look at a tree across your yard or some other fixed object as your focal point. Over time, you will notice the small changes that occur to that tree. Anchor yourself to your position and say you are tall and straight as a tree.

*Week 43*

- **You Are a Tree.** If you do not have a tree to relate to, imagine a tree. Feel as if you are a tree and allow the image of roots to go deep into the earth. Let your mind just be. You may find that in such a position you feel connected to your ancestors, strong and stable.

Balance yourself through posture and imagery.

Work

# Firing Someone

Firing someone is never easy. And when you're a woman, sometimes the task is harder. You may have helped this person become a better worker and tried to nurture her along and now find it difficult to accept that she is not working out.

It's uncomfortable for both boss and employee to be in this predicament, and sometimes it's easier to avoid the situation altogether. If you find yourself giving the employee one more chance (yet again), compensating for her mistakes, or compromising on the quality of her work, it may be time to let this person go.

Remember, you are setting a standard for your company, so keep your sanity as you do it. Even if you are upset with a person for lack of commitment to work, she deserves to be fired in a humane way.

- **Do It in Person.** Arrange to meet the person face to face and do not allow interruptions. Stay off the phone, computer, or PDA while you have this conversation.

- **Be Direct.** Review with the person why she is being let go. Be specific and stay focused on the facts.

- **Give Helpful Criticism.** Give feedback that will be helpful to her when seeking another job. Chronic lateness, inattention to details, and neglecting confidentiality issues are aspects of work that need to be addressed. Also mention positive qualities.

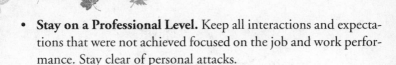

- **Stay on a Professional Level.** Keep all interactions and expectations that were not achieved focused on the job and work performance. Stay clear of personal attacks.

When you have to fire people, guiding them to do their best in whatever they do next is the considerate thing to do.

# Tuesday

*Parent, Family*

## Leaving Dad Out of the Picture

You had good reasons, and you decided to raise your children without their dad being a part of their lives. In fact, you never encouraged the relationship between them and imparted lots of your negative feelings onto your children.

As they grow, they harbor resentment toward your decision and feelings. Will they ever forgive you, or can you forgive them for not understanding your personal choice?

- **Accept Their Blame.** Being on the defensive and fighting will only add fuel to the fire. Own up to your decision because you can't change the past. If you did the best you could, let them know. Whether you like it or not, you are a sum of all your experiences and this one won't go away, so confront it.

- **Know Their Point of View.** See what their anger is all about. Did you leave their father for another man? Did you move the family away so they could never see their father again? Get to the bottom of their feelings, accusations, and fears and be aware of what they are thinking. Saying you're sorry doesn't mean you didn't make the right decision, and it's never too late to do so.

- **Move Forward.** This is about forgiveness and moving on. To begin to build a good relationship, both sides have to open their hearts. You are responsible for your end. Know that having a relationship with their father is a normal request for any kid, even if he isn't a good candidate in your eyes. Hopefully, they'll

come around if you truly forgive them for being angry with you. It may be time to work this out in family therapy.

Your children do not have to like the choices you made for them, and now that they are older, you may need to deal with the feelings they have about your choices.

# Getting the Kids Prepared to Go Back to School

No matter how many summers you go through it, the process of readying your children to return to school in the late summer or early fall is often stressful. But why? Is it just because there are so many things to do, items to buy, meetings to attend, classes to prepare for? And if your kids are new to a school, there are the extra challenges of a different school culture, friends, schedules, administration, and personalities to negotiate for both the children and their parents.

Summertime usually is a time of slower pace, relaxed schedules, and reduced pressure. Giving this up for a more regimented (predictable in some ways and often mysterious in other ways) routine of schoolwork, reports, obligations, car pools, homework, friendship cliques, and teacher concerns is often hard to do. But with a little sanity-saving know-how, you and your kids can make an easy transition.

- **Prepare Your Kids in Advance.** Help your child become as familiar as possible with new buildings to negotiate, teachers, courses, reading assignments. Purchase as many things as you can online with your children, and have them participate in selecting their own school supplies and school clothes. Talk with them about what else needs to be done to prepare for the beginning of a new school year. You may be surprised how much of their own preparation they want to be responsible for.

- **Relax and Enjoy the Rest of Summer.** Do as many fun things as you can as the summer winds down. Watch silly movies and engage in activities that allow you to be free of time pressure. Relax and enjoy yourself with your children as you begin to prepare for the school term. Keep some of that joy and calm as you shift gears.

- **Take Interest.** When you are talking about school with your children, tell them you look forward to hearing about their teachers, the subjects they are taking, and what is going on as they get into their year. Let them know you have confidence in them to do their best and get a lot out of this year's school experience. Kids need to know their parents believe in them.

- **Monitor Your Anxiety Level.** Your children will pick up on your level of anxiety. If you keep it managed, they will look forward to beginning the school year with reduced tension and pressure. Everyone will benefit.

Let your children know you believe in them and their ability to do their best in school.

# Thursday
### Partner, Midlife

## Retired without Driving Each Other Crazy

You've just retired and your partner has been retired for years (or vice versa). So it comes as no shock that one of you has developed a life apart from work and your relationship, while the other hasn't a clue.

You and your partner each need to get used to the idea (and the reality) of the shift and change in your lives, attitudes, roles, and schedules. Settle into this new lifestyle and help both of you save your sanity.

- **How Much Is Too Much** . . . togetherness, that is. Be respectful of each other's needs and schedules. Try not to look to the other as the activities coordinator or always available playmate. And don't expect that your every need or desire is now your partner's problem. It's more important than ever to have your own separate interests, activities, and friends. But check in with each other and keep each other informed.

- **Be a Responsive Partner.** Work on making yourself an even more receptive and approachable companion. You now have time to listen to each other and reconnect in ways that you both find meaningful. Find *that* time and use it well.

- **Planning Recreation Time.** When planning your days and nights, be aware of the need to have space, and build that space into the overall scheme. Vacations, once needed to reduce every-day stressors, will now take on a new form and will be more about sharing and developing a leisure life together.

Take your retired life together in stride
and see how it can grow.

*Friday*
*Family, Parent*

# Family Vacations

Some people look forward to the whole intergenerational clan experience as a great opportunity for everyone to get to know each other in a relaxed and easy manner. Others think that those two words, *family* and *vacation,* cannot coexist happily in the same sentence.

To up your odds and have a great trip, think about all the people and personalities involved and how everyone can interact best. Plan ahead and discover what is available at the place you are going (activities, proximity to religious institutions, parks, restaurants, etc.) before you book those reservations.

- **Who's Paying for What?** Decide before the check comes what is being paid for and by whom.

- **Recharge.** That long solo sunrise walk along the beach may be worth getting up for.

- **Stay Connected to Your Mate.** Sometimes it is difficult to demonstrate your loyalty when you feel torn between your parents, siblings, and spouse. Take time to be together, alone.

- **Share Child Care.** Make it a win-win for both kids and parents. Take a siesta while your grandchild naps. Spend time with your nieces and nephews and explore an interesting site. Swap kids between two families and go on separate adventures.

- **Commemorate the Event.** For fun and a sense of camaraderie, offer T-shirts or hats with the family name. Designate one person as the family trip chronicler/photographer. Send CDs with everyone's best pictures or duplicate a memory book for everyone that you created from an online site.

Pair up with family members who have similar interests to yours but remember to enjoy the group experience.

# Weekend

*Well-Being, Friends, Family*

## The Need to Be on Time

Were you raised to always be on time? Or were you always waiting for your mom or dad who were never ready, and your family earned a reputation for always being late? Did you become determined to always be on time?

If you value punctuality, what happens when you find yourself in a situation in which you are unable to be on time? Living in today's world with unpredictable traffic, train, or bus patterns, and last-minute things taking longer than the last minute, you may be late some of the time.

Everyone is late sometime. Rather than fall apart, understand that from time to time, you, too, may be late.

- **Desensitize Yourself.** Arrive late a number of times, on purpose. It doesn't have to be that late, but enough to deal with the anxiety it creates. And when you are going to put yourself in this stressful situation, make sure it's with people who have a history of being late or who understand. Being late does not mean that you do not value the person or the event or the appointment you are late to.

- **Avoid Berating Yourself.** Stop the negative self-talk. When you hear yourself say, "I am ruining their dinner by being late," "I'll miss my appointment," or "The person I am meeting will think I don't take the meeting seriously," stop those thoughts.

- **Calm Down.** Here's how: (1) Breathe deeply and slowly. (2) Appreciate that the situation was unavoidable (e.g., the traffic pat-

500

*Week 44*

terns were extra challenging and you had no control over them).
(3) If you left late or tried to do too many things at the last
minute, admit it and recognize that next time you will plan more
time to give yourself more wiggle room. (4) Tell yourself you are
no less a person because you are late—you are not dumb, stupid,
inconsiderate, or undependable. (5) Try to reach whomever you
are meeting and let them know what's happening, to give them
the option of using their time more wisely.

When controlling your time is out of your control,
remember that the second best thing is to be
"fashionably" late.

# Monday
*Friendship*

## When Your Friend Uses Your Professional Services for Free

Do you feel that your friends have open access to your professional abilities? Are you constantly giving your time and resources away for free? Do you feel you never leave the office even when you're out with friends?

Free educational, medical, business, counseling, legal, decorating, or insurance advice does not necessarily come along with the territory of friendship. Certainly, for some relationships it does, and there is no ill feeling attached either way. However, when you have ample work and want to donate your pro bono expertise to causes that you choose rather than to everyone who asks, helping a friend can be awkward. Exercise your right to choose who gets your services for free and for how long and who doesn't.

- **You Don't Have to Give It Away.** Just because someone believes you are a friend, he shouldn't have complete and total free access to your professional expertise. You are under no obligation to comply.

- **If They Know They Shouldn't, Why Should You Let Them?** If a conversation begins, "I know I shouldn't ask you for your advice," or "I'm probably overstepping the boundaries," or "I don't want to take advantage of your expertise, but . . ." be prepared to respond kindly and with conviction.

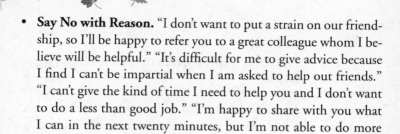

- **Say No with Reason.** "I don't want to put a strain on our friendship, so I'll be happy to refer you to a great colleague whom I believe will be helpful." "It's difficult for me to give advice because I find I can't be impartial when I am asked to help out friends." "I can't give the kind of time I need to help you and I don't want to do a less than good job." "I'm happy to share with you what I can in the next twenty minutes, but I'm not able to do more than that. I hope you understand."

When you feel taken for granted and put into a situation where you are giving away your professional advice and resenting it, boundaries need to be set.

# Tuesday
*Partner*

## Money and Marriage

For many couples money is a touchy topic. There is no one right answer or formula. When you're ready to walk down the aisle, hopefully you've both discussed money and are on similar footing. But what if you and your partner are not aligned about the finances now or in the future?

For a really strong relationship to thrive, the focus should not be about money. The balance of the relationship—rather than the balance sheet—is what is vital to a flourishing marriage. When things get out of balance, trouble brews. The key to saving your sanity is to resist outside pressures, stay in balance, and create what works for you.

- **Talk It Up.** Can you talk about money issues? How about starting with designating income, savings, and debt that is "ours," "yours" and "mine." Determine if you'll have one budget (sharing all income and expenses) or several (household and individual). How will you pay for travel, gifts, and charitable contributions? Discuss what happens when circumstances change and you are planning for a family. And are you equal partners regardless of who makes more? Make a plan to achieve financial and lifestyle goals.

- **Focus on Financial Strengths.** Build trust in each other's ability to make sound financial decisions. One of you might be a "numbers" person and can balance the checkbook, while the other may be better at overseeing financing and investing decisions.

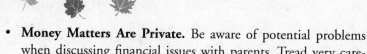

- **Money Matters Are Private.** Be aware of potential problems when discussing financial issues with parents. Tread very carefully about revealing how you spend your money when getting advice.

The goal is not that you and your partner agree on everything involving money, but that each feels valued, heard, understood, and appreciated.

*Parent, Family*

# Stop Battling with Your Teenage Daughter

Life with a teenage daughter has quite a reputation! There are lots of books and movies written about both sides of the equation, and anyone who has raised a teenage daughter will tell you to be patient, keep your wits about you, and have a sense of humor.

Some of the time your daughter may not like you at all. Guess what? At times you may not like her, either. Your job is not to have her like you but rather to show her how to be a successful person now and when she becomes an adult. If you rise to battle at every turn, you will not be teaching her the best way to deal with the world and you will surely be having a hard time yourself.

Remember that much of what you are dealing with is hormones and emotions. Don't lose sight of the fact that the two of you are both female and share a lot of the same chemistry and personality traits (even though it surely doesn't seem like it).

- **You Are the Female Role Model.** Your daughter will watch you and how you handle stress. So if you are constantly in battle mode, she will likely be, too. Listen to her and be engaged but be *calm*. By example, show your daughter how to deal with feelings that may overwhelm her. Keep the door open to talk about whatever she needs to talk about but realize that you are not going to fight with her. Understand her upheaval but don't join in.

- **Use Empathy.** If you see she is pouty or upset, handle it with care. "Looks like something's going on. I'm around if you feel like talking." Or don't say anything but acknowledge that you see she is upset and offer a hug and a cup of tea instead of "What's

with your pouty face?" When she is ready she will come to you for advice or to just have an empathetic ear.

- **Be Her Sounding Board.** Give her the chance to talk about alternative ways to think about and handle things that are bothering her. Sometimes she will be overwhelmed with emotions. Let her vent and then help her regroup.

- **Compromise.** When you establish rules, share the reasons behind your thinking, based on safety and good sense. Listen to her point of view and see if there is room for compromise. There usually is.

- **Love Unconditionally.** This does not mean you have to like her decisions, the way she dresses, how she combs (or doesn't comb) her hair, her taste in music, or her role models. But you can still love her with all your heart and accept her for who she is now (which will probably change as she changes).

Give your daughter the impression that no matter
what she is dealing with, you will be available
to her to help her through it.
Remember, unconditional love.

# Putting Your Kids on Hold

Why does this always happen? You're freaking out at work, your boss is being a beast, and then your daughter calls you ten times to beg, plead, whine, share a long story about what happened after school, or enlist you to help make some *major* decision in her life that *must* be made *right now*. While you want to hear what she has to say and you want to help, you also need to get your work done. (And keep your boss or coworkers from begging, pleading, and whining.)

It's hard to juggle work and kids, so understand that this is really a tough problem to handle. Doing both things, however, is impossible, so let yourself off the hook.

- **Is There Something Else Going On?** If your child is calling you ten times to keep you informed, maybe something else, something bigger, is going on. There might be something that's upsetting her at school or something on her mind. You might want to take the time to find out what's going on if you can find a few minutes at work or bring the matter up when you get home.

- **Foster Independence.** On the other hand, your children might be so connected to you that every decision they make has to go through you. Depending on their age, maybe it's time to help them problem solve some matters for themselves and only call you when they are really stuck. Teaching them to think on their own and be self-sufficient is a gift you can give to them and to you.

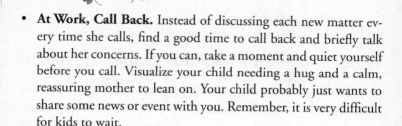

- **At Work, Call Back.** Instead of discussing each new matter every time she calls, find a good time to call back and briefly talk about her concerns. If you can, take a moment and quiet yourself before you call. Visualize your child needing a hug and a calm, reassuring mother to lean on. Your child probably just wants to share some news or event with you. Remember, it is very difficult for kids to wait.

- **After Work, Focus.** When you call back, tell her that you look forward to talking with her more about it when you get home. After work, sit down with that child, look her in the eye, and tell her you want to hear the whole story.

- **Explain Your Situation.** Even though it is easy to lose control, don't scream and tell her never to call you at the office. Calmly explain that it is tough for you to be interrupted at work; tougher still to really help her or hear her with all your job distractions. Ask her to please have patience until you can give her your full attention.

Giving your all to your work makes it hard to give your all to the kids. When you have a lull during the day, give a holler and just say hi.

*Friday*

*Single, Midlife*

# Being Single and Meeting People Creatively

You're single and are interested in meeting someone, but you don't want to advertise the fact. It's not your style to march, all alone, into a bar or a singles event, and you surely don't want to surf on-line dating sites ten times a day. Actually, you're OK about being single, but not so OK about being identified as single by family, friends, and peers.

You are not alone. No one wants to attend something that she fears will label her as desperate. So given this, how do you keep your sanity as you go about exploring programs and events and meeting people?

- **What Are Your Interests?** Attend events with a strong theme that is compelling, no matter who shows up. Essentially, you are there because you are interested in the topic. Whether or not you meet someone, you will have learned something, expanded your world, experienced something or someone new, and had a good time.

- **What's Your Thing?** Consider what appeals to you, and if you have not addressed whatever it is in a while, begin right away. Think about whether listening to someone discuss unusual and exotic destinations stimulates your passion to travel or not. Or you may want to become involved with a non-profit support group or participate in charitable fund-raising activities for a cause you believe in. Discover something that stimulates you.

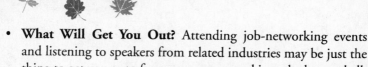

- **What Will Get You Out?** Attending job-networking events and listening to speakers from related industries may be just the thing to get you out of your apartment and into the lecture hall. How about taking the time to learn about estate or financial planning by joining an investment club? Or you may gravitate toward topical current-events speakers, high-profile authors, or journalists. Find art and cultural events to attend.

Being single does not define who you are. Actively engage in life, exposing yourself to new knowledge, new people, new experiences.

# Weekend
### *Well-Being*

## Traveling Healthfully

Going away on vacation is all about renewal and restoration of the body and soul. But coming down with a virus while away from home or breaking your arm while windsurfing can cause you to have an adventure of the type you were not expecting.

Among the many tourist attractions, you don't want to have hospitals and pharmacies on your list of "must sees." Even though I received great care in a hospital in Austria when I broke my leg, it was an awful way to prematurely end a vacation.

It's a good idea to save your sanity by knowing the health risks of the places you are visiting and being as prepared and as sensible as you can when traveling.

- **Plan Ahead.** If you're traveling overseas, you may need immunizations in several rounds. Check out the Center for Disease Control website and talk with a doctor or nurse at a travel clinic at least two months before departure.

- **Personal Health History List.** Travel at all times with your medical history and information about your allergies, as well as a list of medications you take on a regular basis. Bring all medicines in their original containers with the prescription label affixed.

- **Don't Take Chances.** Having an intestinal bug can "cramp" your style. Open sealed bottled water at your table and stay away from ice and uncooked fruits and veggies in less developed countries, unless you know it's OK. Don't brush your

teeth with tap water in places where the safety of the water is questionable. Why visit someplace at peak mosquito season if there's a high risk of malaria?

When traveling, take care of your health to maximize your ability to absorb as much as you can from the experience of being in a different place.

# Monday

*Family, Friends, Partner*

## Surviving When Someone You Love Takes His or Her Life

Someone takes his or her life, and survivors often blame themselves or wonder if there wasn't something they could have done, should have noticed, helped out with more, or done differently.

These feelings are often present with any death of a loved one, regardless of circumstance, but are particularly intense when people try to come to terms with suicide. Because suicide is more often whispered about than openly discussed, there is the added dimension of shame and embarrassment that attaches itself to the survivors.

Friends who want to be a support are often uncomfortable, not knowing what to say or do. Not knowing how to deal with your sorrow, they may stay away. As a mourner you may feel shunned and abandoned; you may feel that something is wrong with you and your family because someone dear to you took his or her life. You or others may feel that suicide is an unstated accusation that is directed at you, and you wonder why you don't have quite the same right to your mourning as someone else.

What makes this even worse is when the leader of a religious community does not comfort but rather condemns the person who took his or her life and prescribes a type of mourning that is neither appropriate nor compassionate. How do you maintain your sanity with so many loose ends?

- **This Death Is *Not* About You.** You should repeat this over again until you truly understand it and know this to be true. If some-

one is intent on taking his or her life, you will not prevent it. And you cannot make someone happy who is severely depressed. Try to accept that the death was a result of what was happening within that person and was *not* about you.

- **This Death Is *Not* a Reflection of You.** Do not accept other people's definition of you or your family as "less than" because someone you love took his or her life.

- **The Person Loved You.** Understand that when someone takes his or her life, it does not mean he or she did not love you. It may mean he or she could not bear the thought of living in such a state of pain and did not want to bring that to you. Often when people take their lives, their thinking and their perception of the world is different from yours. They do not see another way out from dealing with their intense emotional pain.

- **Honor the Memory.** Mourning can occur and rituals can be followed to allow yourself to fully feel what has happened and to open yourself up to moving forward. No matter what others say, listen to your heart and honor the loved one's memory. When you are able, talk about the person and keep the positive memories alive in ways that are helpful to you.

- **Get Support.** It can be very helpful to go to a suicide survivors' group for support. Nobody understands what it is like unless she went through it.

Forgiveness is a major element in moving forward;
forgive yourself for not being able to prevent
the death and forgive the loved one
for leaving you in that way.

## Not Wanting to Be Close Friends

Friendships are indeed precious. You may find, however, that someone in your life wants to have a closer relationship with you than you are comfortable with. Maybe having her as an acquaintance is OK, but she wants to get close to you, asking you to join her to do things, come to dinner parties, etc. Even if she is a nice person, you simply may not have time for or interest in developing a friendship.

In a world in which you are very busy, you may feel that you don't have enough time for the friends you want to spend time with and whose friendships you want to nourish—much less for those people who simply don't have that priority in your life. It can be uncomfortable to repeatedly give excuses or decline invitations, and after some time she may give up. But it is uncomfortable.

- **You Are in Charge of Your Life.** Recognize that you have the right to spend your time with whomever you choose. Take responsibility for planning how and with whom you share your time and your life.

- **Be Truthful.** You may have feelings of discomfort about telling someone you are not as available as they would like to pursue a friendship, but it is significantly kinder to communicate directly and from your heart than to consistently turn down invitations. Your indirect rejections can be very hurtful and perhaps make her wonder what is wrong with her or why she is not good enough for you. Everyone deserves to feel valued for the person she is.

- **Set Your Boundaries.** If you want her in your life at all, explain to her what you can and cannot do. Offer your concern that being unavailable to her will be hurtful. Tell her that you put a lot of time and energy into friendships and that at this point in your life, you cannot foster that type of friendship with her and don't like to do things partway. Communicate how you appreciate her desire to include you in her life, but you cannot hold up your part of the relationship.

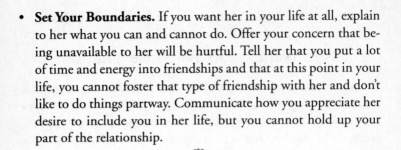

It is important that in not accepting the friendship you are not diminishing the person.

# Visualize as You Embrace Change

Some people like change. Others don't. Or you may like some change but not a lot. Everyone is different and everyone handles changes in their lives differently. But one thing you can bet on will be a constant in your life is change.

A change in life circumstances, whether positive or negative, is something that initially knocks you a bit off-balance as you wonder how you are going to adjust. When something comes your way that you didn't foresee, get back on track and save your sanity.

- **When There Is Change There Is Loss.** Know that you'll experience feelings of loss. Try not to make assumptions about the future and how things will be. Instead, move through the loss to see positive possibilities.

- **Call on Your Buddies.** The support of your friends and family is critical as you go through change. But if the people you thought you could count on are preoccupied with their own lives, seek other forms of support, such as counseling, coaching, support groups, women's organizations, on-line forums, or chat rooms. You don't have to go through this alone, so don't.

- **Visualize and Adjust.** Breathe deeply as you quietly visualize yourself adjusting through the change of circumstance. Create a comforting mental picture to help you embrace this change. Although it's been around for ages, visualization is a powerful and effective way to face your fears and become balanced. By

calmly visualizing yourself handling change, you will more likely succeed.

Remember the 3 Bs when you face challenges brought on by change: 1) Breathe 2) Become Balanced and 3) Bounce Back.

*Parent, Community, Family*

## Mainstreaming with Muscle

You've tried to mainstream your child into the school system but there are so many struggles and challenges. Other kids tease your son, and you secretly wish that he was just like all the other kids. But, once again you're questioning why the world will not see beyond your child's disability and focus on what a great, determined, sensitive kid he is.

Your frustration sometimes gets the better of you as you advocate for your child in the face of adversity and small-mindedness. Keep your sanity as you try to help create a welcoming educational environment for your child.

- **One at a Time.** Even though people tell you the opposite, you can change the world—one child, one teacher, one parent, one bus driver, one cafeteria helper at a time.

- **"Introduce" Your Child** . . . before anyone even meets him. Talk about his interests, his talents, his likes and dislikes. Focus on his strengths and what makes him unique.

- **Minimize Discomfort** . . . by answering questions, and emphasize how we are all different and all the same.

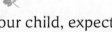

When mainstreaming your child, expect judgment
because before you were the mother of this child
you were uncomfortable with kids who were
"different," too.

# Friday
*Partner*

## Renovating Your Home Together

Few things can tax a relationship more than renovating your living space together. There are multiple decisions, countless disruptions, financial constraints, dependence on other people's schedules and trusting service people whom you just met, not to mention that nobody really honors a deadline. And how *do* you come to terms with the fact that you both have such different taste and sensibilities?

For some people renovating their living space is a mutually satisfying project that brings them closer together as they envision the changes that will benefit them. For others it is a nightmare. Know your strengths and play to them.

- **Dream Together.** Talk extensively before beginning any project. Each of you needs to share your idea of your "dream" space. Create plans together and discuss as many details as is appropriate. If you are into doing this project yourselves, wander around with a tape measure before beginning, to make sure you feel comfortable with sizes, scaling, and details.

- **The Road Ahead Will Be Bumpy** . . . and so might the floors. Know ahead of time there will absolutely, positively be many problems and aggravations. When the project starts, try to go with the flow. Know to give each other space and time when necessary.

- **Designate Your Jobs.** Who will be the overseer and who will make the calls to the service people and keep track of progress?

Check all decisions with each other. Try to keep surprises to a minimum.

- **Keep a Sense of Humor.** Know that *your* "story of the renovation" will be told for years to come.

Renovating your home may or may not mean renovating your relationship.

## It's More Than Meatloaf

Someone in your community, whom you may barely know, lost his wife and is dealing with being a single parent. Or a father at your kid's school died, and the mom is trying to pick up the pieces.

Everyone rallies to help them. But, as time marches on, fewer and fewer folks ask if there is anything they can do. Everyone's routine has settled in and yet this family is still grieving as school is starting and the holidays are looming in the near future.

Let's face it, this family could use some tender loving care to save their sanity.

- **Love Them, Feed Them.** After someone in your community dies, the queue for the casserole brigade shouldn't cease to exist. Organize neighbors and cook meals, maybe to be delivered two or three times each week for several months after the death.

- **Caring with Care Packages.** Place a refrigerator box or cooler outside their home or arrange to drop the food at the same time each day so family members will know it is there and can receive it. With simple instructions taped on the container the family will unpack some great and healthy food and know they are remembered and are part of a community.

- **Helping to Heal.** Sometimes a simple act of kindness shared among neighbors makes the world of difference to someone struggling in a new situation. Make sure all the neighbors understand their role and the rules. No chit-chat unless requested—

cook, deliver, and leave the food, and that's it. This is not the time to visit unless you are invited to do so.

Go beyond what you think is reasonable and help heal the suffering in your backyard—one person or family at a time.

*Monday*
*Well-Being*

# Nature as Teacher

The ultimate balancing act is performed by Mother Nature. She tries to stay in balance no matter what is thrown her way (quite literally as people continue to pollute). Try to be in nature every day and learn from her.

Discover how you can balance your life by using metaphors from nature. Visualize your life as a flowing river. What can you learn? Is it rushing or trickling? Are there paths that have been forged due to the constancy of the same flow, or are there new paths that have formed because of a storm or a fallen tree? What obstructions interrupt the flow?

Or put yourself in the forest. If you are saddened over losses and feel adrift, allow the trees to embrace you with their strength, their power, and their roots. There is life; constant, regenerative life. Learn what you need to do to restore your own power and recharge your life. Some paths are open, sunny, and welcoming. Others are shaded and somewhat scary. Realize that even in the darkest places there is life and hope.

Or walk up a mountain. Keep your eye on the summit. Remember the value of stopping and looking around to notice how far you have come on your journey. Bring enough supplies so you maintain yourself along the way. Shift your pace; adapt your clothing as you feel you must. Approach the mountain with respect. It is your partner.

- **Engage All Your Senses.** See, hear, taste, and smell. Walk barefoot in fresh-cut grass, along a sandy beach, on stepping stones. See what it feels like to become grounded and connect to the

earth. Notice the wind. Focus on subtle changes as if you are looking through a camera lens. *Really* look. Glance at the variations of the shades of green in the forest, the hues of blue in the sky. Observe both the majestic and the minute.

- **Know Your Place.** Be in awe of the trees, the plants, the rock formations. See how nature portrays the cycles of life and death. We plant, harvest, and then replant. Nature renews itself and so can you.

- **Appreciate the Seasonal Changes.** Notice the flow of nature and how there is momentum toward constant growth. Experience the withering of winter and the rebirth of spring. Revel in a new seasonal palette every few months to add different color and a fresh outlook to your life's canvas.

Appreciation of nature's balance is what allows us to keep balance in our daily lives.

# Tuesday
*Parent, Family*

## Making Stepfamilies Work

Two families coming together as one is a challenge. Realizing the time it takes to become a family; keeping the children out of the interactions between the adults who are no longer married; navigating adult alone time while also spending much-needed time with the children to build a family; appreciating the past connections and honoring them while moving forward are just a few of the issues facing new stepfamilies.

Too often, the couple or the children have a timetable about when they think they should jell as a family. If the buzzer rings and the family is still dealing with the delicate job of integrating all these new people, personalities, habits, expectations, hobbies, likes, dislikes, fears, desires, hopes, and dreams, some members of the family might get frustrated.

Allow the family to bond at its own pace. With each passing day, you'll integrate more and more and with time find that you've built a loving family connection.

- **Encourage Family Members to Be Themselves** . . . and to be their best selves. Be accepting of each other's styles and habits, and focus on strengths and positive qualities. Don't try to change anyone to fit into a specific mold.

- **Hold Back.** Allow the parent spouse to be the primary person in charge of the children (discipline, boundaries, limits), and don't undermine his or her authority.

- **If Your Partner Is Forced to Choose, You Lose.** Avoid situations where your new spouse must choose between you and the children.

- **Plan Family Time.** Encourage participating in family activities that reflect both the kids' interests and your interests (as long as they are age-appropriate). Not everything you do is going to be a home run.

- **Be OK with Mediocre Responses.** Remind yourself that you are a person in your own right and that what you bring to the family may or may not be appreciated by your stepchildren. They do not have to be your cheerleaders.

Navigating a stepfamily relationship requires you to be open to adults and people who have different ways of dealing with the world than you do. You are there to learn as well as influence.

## Discovering You Have Alzheimer's

Becoming aware that you no longer remember things the way you used to may be a sign of stress, fatigue, or inattention. But for many people it is one of the early signs that they have Alzheimer's disease.

Being aware that you are slowly losing your ability to reason, think, remember, recognize, and function independently is not only shocking, frightening, and sad but can also be overwhelming. All you think about is your future, and the inevitability is exactly what you don't want to see.

When you are in the early stages of Alzheimer's, it is essential that you recognize that you are still able to function in many of the ways that you did before your diagnosis. It is important to keep yourself actively involved in life in ways that you enjoy and that will enhance your skills and abilities. You may have to rearrange your activities and schedule to rely on others to help you or keep you company. Keeping physically active with exercise and being involved in a regular, calming activity, such as gardening, or creating art, can reduce anxiety and depression that accompanies this diagnosis.

Sometimes what you are able to do changes from day to day. Or some tasks are easier at certain times of the day or with certain people or in certain environments. You need to figure out what works best for you and who is your support system.

- **Educate Yourself and Loved Ones.** Find out for yourself, family and friends what is happening and what assistance you will need. Let them know that many of your behaviors have nothing to do with you but are the result of the disease. Talk together

about the concerns you face either in a support group or with a social worker who specializes in Alzheimer's.

- **Get Support.** Attend a support group with other people who have Alzheimer's so you can be yourself and not worry about forgetting something or repeating yourself. Suggest that the people you are close to also attend a support group to help them deal with their own issues.

- **Document What Is Important.** Write or dictate things you feel are important for your family and friends to know or remember about you and your life. Include your perceptions about things and your wishes for others. This will be a guide for people to know about you when you are unable to express yourself in the ways you would like.

- **Keep Active.** Plan to spend time doing the things you enjoy and being with people you like. Retain your self-respect and your personhood. You may find that you develop interests in new things (painting, houseplants, clay modeling, puzzles, playing with children).

- **Live for Today.** Stay as present as you can and don't dwell on the future. Blaming yourself for becoming ill or becoming a "burden" is unproductive and unnecessarily creates anxiety.

Even as your mind fades, you are still a person who deserves love and care and can give it in return.

*Family, Parent, Friends*

# Being with Family at the Holidays

In your mind is a Norman Rockwell picture of the "quintessential" family as you envision spending the holidays with one another.

Even though no holiday has come close to that image, you say once again, "This year will be different." Maybe, but not likely. Guaranteed, someone will say something that offends someone between Thanksgiving and New Year's. And somehow you have to survive another telling of how you were so cute when you had braces, pigtails, and freckles, or, worse yet, how you were so smart and promising in school and nobody knows what happened.

- **Avoid Trouble Spots.** Make efforts to avoid troublesome yet familiar communication patterns. Remember, it takes two to tango, and if you don't dance, there is no chance to do the old steps.

- **Do What You Feel Is Right** . . . and appropriate regardless of what family members do. Avoid playing games, and then you will avoid keeping score.

- **Getting to Know You.** Inquire about family members and be interested in getting to know their histories. Ask key family members to recall times in their lives when they were the most content or the most interested or the most happy. Discover aspects of these people that you never knew.

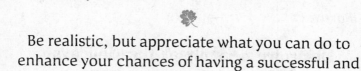

Be realistic, but appreciate what you can do to enhance your chances of having a successful and warm holiday.

### Parent

# Difficulty Attaching to a New Baby

Women react to pregnancy and giving birth differently—physically, emotionally, and mentally—from one pregnancy to another. The exhilaration of first-time motherhood can dissipate after a fourth child is born. Or a young mother who feels her loss of independence may welcome another child later in life with open arms. While everyone thinks that a new mother should be filled with joy and excitement, the reality is that some mothers are left feeling overwhelmed, burdened, and unhappy. And this can affect how moms bond with their babies.

It is a proven fact that infants who are securely attached to their mothers early on do better in life overall. They develop a sense of trust with people who are in their worlds and who care for them in a loving and responsive way. They understand, very early, that they are worthwhile and valued. They depend on those who care for them because those who care for them are consistently there for them in a loving and accepting way.

When babies and young children do not have their needs looked after and experience rejection or negative caregiving experiences, they can come to understand that they are not worthy, and will have a hard time trusting people. They may spend much of their lives trying to gain acceptance from others in a never-ending battle to find love and reassurance that they are valuable and worthy of love. To help care for your baby when you're not up to it, you can:

- **Find a Temporary Surrogate.** Ask your mom or someone you trust to take over while you are not emotionally or physically available to your baby. Your child needs to have a supportive

and consistent person who smiles and appreciates that this innocent baby is a blessing. Getting yourself in shape physically is only part of the challenge. It would be good to focus on getting yourself in shape emotionally so you can accept and enjoy your new baby.

- **Explore Why?** Do you feel overweight and not good about yourself? Do you quietly resent making some lifestyle changes to have this baby? Are you afraid that you won't be a good mother? Are the demands of work and your job pulling at you? Is your partner missing in action when you need help? Find out the real reasons you are feeling the way you are and work through these issues so your mind and heart can open to your new baby.

- **Seek a Counselor.** Even the best of mothers can detach from their newborns for short periods of time. Some experience postpartum depression, whether mild or severe. If you think this is happening to you, seek a mental health counselor to help you deal with fostering your mother-child bond.

Sometimes it takes time to connect to your baby. You can figure out what keeps you from feeling close so that you can become available as a mom in your heart as well as in your mind.

## Eating Out for Health

You never cook. You're not fat, but you haven't had anything healthy to eat since you went off to college (twenty years ago) and you feel guilty all the time.

As you get older you see it is not so easy to keep your shape, especially since you eat out all of the time. Those health reports are finally sinking in, and you think it's time to start eating right. But you don't know how. Here's how you can eat out and eat healthfully while keeping your sanity.

- **Health in a Hurry.** Why not get three meals out of one when you eat out? Ask for a side order of steamed veggies. Toss them into your order of Kung Pow Chicken, Pad Thai or whatever saucy meal you order and coat them in the sauce. Divide the meal into thirds and ask for a doggie bag with two containers for the other two-thirds. One is for lunch the next day and the other goes into the freezer.

- **Eat Colorfully.** Add to the green in your salads every day. Always order a salad and eat it before the entree comes. Order the most colorful salad on the menu. A diet rich in a variety of fruits and vegetables can help reduce risk of heart disease, stroke, and some cancers. Baby spinach, garden lettuces, strawberries, grapes, grated carrots, red and yellow bell pepper are almost a day's worth of fruits and veggies.

- **Kid Yourself.** If you don't want to give up on drive-through fast-food places, first stop at a gourmet grocery or deli that has

prepared meals. Get something healthy and then go to the drive-through and order a kid-size meal. This way you can satisfy your craving for fast food and your craving for good health.

- **Trade Up.** Upgrade the quality of protein you consume. Lean cuts of chicken, pork, fish, turkey, ham, and beef go a lot further toward good health than high-fat cuts such as some beef, sausage, and bacon, which, ounce for ounce, are more calorie-dense and higher in cholesterol.

- **Soup's On.** Visit restaurants that have at least two or more soups on their menus. Piping hot soups loaded with vegetables and legumes take a long time to consume and satisfy your need to nosh.

Take charge of your health and well-being
as you experiment with food and portions
when you eat out.

# Dealing with Sexual Harassment

Sexual harassment has nothing to do with sex and everything to do with power.

If you believe you are being sexually harassed, you can think about whether you want to confront the perpetrator. If this is a friend, an acquaintance, or a colleague, you may need the support of someone you trust to talk with confidentially to help you.

Generally it is better to confront directly. If you don't, you will be sending a silent message that this is acceptable to you and to society. And the harassment behavior will likely continue. Whether it is verbal, nonverbal, or physical, it is important that you say no in a very emphatic way. Your sanity is at stake.

- **Speak Up for Yourself.** If you are uneasy about addressing this person, relax and focus entirely on what you are going to say. Keep it short and to the point. "Your comments are offensive. You need to stop and stop now." Be sure you practice saying what you intend to say several times so the words do not get stuck in your throat. Even if you feel uneasy about being near this person, desensitize yourself by practicing.

- **Write It Down.** Review what you told him and immediately write it down. In the note, describe what he said or did and briefly state why you find his behavior objectionable. Keep a copy for yourself, at home, and send a copy to him.

- **Keep Recording.** In your journal, record what happened, when it happened, and where it happened. If there were other people

who witnessed what happened, mention that in your notes so you have documentation should you need it.

You need to stand up to whoever feels it is OK to try to demean you or your womanhood.

# Tuesday
*Parent, Family*

## The First Holiday Alone with Children

Immediately after you experience the death of a spouse or a divorce, your children will undergo many transitions. Life as they know it changes, and you are all unaware of what life will be like. There will be waves of turbulence, unrest, and confusion.

Soon after a death or divorce, children ask questions that require answers, and the answer is often "I don't know." "We'll see." "I'm not sure." "This is all new to me, too." Parents (and kids) are surely angry, sad, disappointed, confused, and sometimes somewhat relieved but on shaky ground. Their holidays are now going to be different, and they don't know in what ways. They only know that one of their parents is not here.

During the first year, it is important to know that the holidays this year may not be the way they will be in the future, will likely be highly emotional, and may or may not be spent with people you feel close to, and memories of the way things were will be prominent in the minds and hearts of each person in the family in a different way. The dream of what the holidays should be (and often were) is now up for grabs.

- **Give Them a Hopeful Future.** It is important for the children to see that you have confidence in the future. Keep the what-ifs and "How did this happen?" or "It was long in coming but it still feels awful" at bay.

- **Allow Them to Have Mixed Feelings.** Keep in mind that in a divorce situation your children may have ambivalent feelings about being with you and guilty that they are not with their

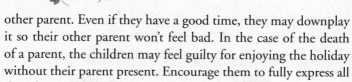

other parent. Even if they have a good time, they may downplay it so their other parent won't feel bad. In the case of the death of a parent, the children may feel guilty for enjoying the holiday without their parent present. Encourage them to fully express all that they are feeling whether positive or negative (excitement, reservations, nerves).

- **Be with Others.** Accept any and all invitations for dinner and invite a bunch of people (not just one or two) over to your house. Encourage the children to participate in preparing some special holiday food for the meal and serve it to guests.

- **Don't Shield Them.** Receiving a call from your deceased husband's sister who lives far away can give you and your children a feeling of love and connectedness that will help to buoy you. Let them have a good cry. Don't bury the past but don't dwell in it, either. Ask the children to think about some way they would like to celebrate the holiday and see if you are able to accommodate them. They will feel heard and they will feel as if they have some influence in a situation that is clearly not within their control.

Firsts for you are also firsts for your children—
but they are not always the same.

# Wednesday

*Friends, Family*

## Comforting Someone

Most people don't know what to say or do when friends are grieving. Do you try to cheer them up? Reassure them that things will be all right? Pray with them? Tell them about your own similar experiences?

If you're not comfortable with what they are going through, it will be difficult to be a source of comfort for them. So first come to terms with their predicament and then reach out. You can and will make a difference and help save their sanity.

- **What's OK to Say?** In my psychology practice, people want to know if they should ask questions. I know all too well that the best thing you can do is listen. It's healing for someone to know you are really hearing what they are going through. It is not wise to ignore the whole matter and act as if nothing has happened because resentment can build. If you say anything, first ask if it's OK to offer your experience or thoughts. If they don't want to hear about what you have to say, you'll know.

- **Don't Let Them Lose Face.** People who are grieving must not lose their dignity. They might be dealing with fear, anger, disappointment, betrayal, hopelessness, sadness, grief, and perhaps guilt or shame. They are vulnerable. Let them know you have their confidence.

- **Don't Have an Agenda.** Just be there. Take their cues and get a feel for their receptivity for some cheering up or diversions from

their suffering. If they want to wallow, let them. Have patience and compassion.

Instead of saying, "Call me if there's anything I can do," check in with them and let them know they are in your heart.

*Parent, Family, Midlife*

## Let Them Leave the Nest

When your kids go off into the world you may not feel you are finished parenting. The truth is you are *never* finished being a parent. You just become a parent in a different way. You'll always be Mom, but you may have to redefine your role in your children's life now that they are away.

Feeling lonely is part of the process. Now that you have an empty nest, you may question your life and your purpose. It may be time to examine your own relationship more carefully since you don't have your children to take the focus off of it.

You and your partner, if you have one, may experience this loss differently from each other. For one of you, having the child out of the house may help the relationship, and for the other it may exacerbate difficulties or it may just be too tough—the sadness too excruciating.

- **Roots and Wings.** You gave them roots (good values, ethics, and standards) and now are offering them wings to fly on their own. It is important that children leaving home not be burdened with the guilt that they are abandoning you. Let them go and be responsible for your own happiness.

- **Connect on a Regular Basis.** Stay in touch via cell phone, mail, e-mail, etc. Be careful not to have too much contact or be intrusive so your children can gain independence and develop a healthy self-image apart from their life at home. Allowing for separation and privacy will help these young adults to become more of an adult on their own. Also listen to what they are expe-

riencing instead of starting off phone conversations with twenty questions. Give ample time before the first visit.

- **Let Them Go over Time.** Once they leave, be conscious of the different changes you will make. Some kids go to college and their parents are eager to turn their rooms into an office, a sewing room, a den—and the kids feel unwelcome. The kids were in your life for eighteen years or so, so everyone is in transition. Help them sort through some belongings before leaving, and maybe when they return in summers from time to time. This way you can both let go a little at a time and no one is jolted.

- **Use Your Time Wisely.** Do the projects you have been unable to do because you were so busy being a mom. Fill up the time you used to spend with your child or for your child with things that interest you. Reconnect with your partner as a couple again.

Your role is changing to become more of a mentor than a manager. You are still and will always be Mom.

*Friday*

*Parent, Single*

# Dating When You Have Kids

Making the transition from parent mode to date mode can be a challenge. Just remember that many single parents have fulfilling social lives, and you can, too. Whether you're involved in an established relationship or are dating several people, here are some basic sanity-saving suggestions for dating when you have children.

- **Introduce a New Love When It's Time.** Keep your romantic life separate from your family life until you know you're ready to introduce your new love interest to your kids.

- **You Don't Need Permission.** Your children may have a hard time adapting at first, but you don't need their permission to date. Tell your children who you are going out with, but don't discuss the details with them when you return. Remember, be honest, because kids are smart. They'll recognize you are dating rather than just going out with friends. They'll also know when a "friend" is more than just that. You need not discuss details about your dating, but you should be honest that you *are* dating. Where you are going and with whom may be all that children need to gain a comfort level and take the mystery out of your private life.

- **It Is OK to Have a Social Life.** Allowing yourself to be an adult on "your time" is an essential part of maturing into your single life. Ease your mind by making sure your children are properly cared for and supervised by someone who knows them well and

enjoys being with them, and whom they look forward to being with so you can really enjoy yourself when you are out.

- **It Is OK to Recognize Your Sexual Needs.** If you are involved in a sexual relationship, limit the encounters to times when you can be totally alone and your sexual relationship can remain private. *Do not* have sex in your house if the kids are there or could come home.

- **Act Responsibly.** You're an adult, so act like one. Coming home at three A.M. when your baby-sitter or teens thought you were returning at midnight will raise lots of issues. They'll know when you're out of sync, either dating too frequently or spending too much energy with the thought of dating. Save a good part of your energy source for your primary responsibility, parenting; save lots more for your work; and have fun with the rest.

You deserve to have a full life that encourages the many sides of you to flourish.

# *Weekend*

*Community, Well-Being*

## Teach and Expand Your World

You daydream about traveling to other cultures and exotic sites but don't have the opportunity to do so because of the job, the kids, the lack of time, or the lack of funds. By tutoring an adult ESL student, you can expand your world. You'll meet people from other lands and help someone else feel more comfortable in their new homeland.

If you are frustrated and stuck in the same old place, preserve your sanity as you reach out to someone who comes from a different country. You can make a difference in the world, one person at a time.

- **Connect One-on-One.** As you tutor, open your mind to diverse traditions and ways of life that you can experience through your students. Even though you are the teacher, so are you also the student.

- **Be a Link.** As you develop relationships with people you probably would never have met before, assist them in developing a sense of belonging in a place where others perceive them as different.

- **Develop a Partnership.** Focus on the progress your students make. Reflect on your own life when you learned something you wanted to know and the gratification you and your teacher felt.

As you help someone to learn the English language, appreciate that your pupil is not the only learner in this partnership.

*Monday*

*Friends, Family*

## Now You Are Caregiving

You may feel as if it is a tremendous imposition to be a caregiver. If you do, this attitude will make your role much more difficult. It will impact not only the quality of care you offer but also the nature of the relationship with the person for whom you are caring.

Consider seeing this role as an honor, perhaps a privilege, as well as an opportunity to discover aspects of yourself that you may not have developed in the past, as you preserve your sanity.

- **Expect the Unexpected.** You might learn something you never knew from this experience. Cultivate patience, a sense of humor, and flexibility.

- **Demonstrate Affection.** Appreciate the person you are caring for and really open up to her. Be willing to try it her way.

- **Communicate Respectfully.** Encourage and *model* a respectful attitude. Expect to feel isolated and misunderstood at times, but nonetheless keep the connection open.

Expect at times to feel incompetent as a caregiver and take time to do things that you enjoy and make you feel competent.

# It's None of Your Business

Your friend is cheating. She is fooling around with someone who is highly inappropriate and you want to help her call off this ridiculousness because her marriage and her life as she knows it is in jeopardy. Or your adult daughter is dating a creep and she seems to be blinded by the love light. You are unsure whether you should say anything to her to help open her eyes. How about knowing that your neighbor is doing something illicit in her apartment and you wonder if, as a good citizen and friend, you have a responsibility to talk to her?

In order to keep your sanity, how and where do you draw the line regarding when to get involved and when to stay out of it?

- **There's a Fine Line.** Sometimes "none of your business" is your business because you care about the person. Knowing where to draw the line between being helpful and being intrusive is different in every situation and depends, in large part, on your relationship and the personalities involved.

- **The Important Question.** Assess if getting involved could put your relationship with that person at risk. If so, decide whether that's a risk you're willing to take (pushing for an intervention is a good example).

- **Are You Too Involved?** The best lessons are learned by our own experiences. Sometimes someone will wake up if we heighten their awareness, but many times they'll just ignore good advice. They may know deep inside that what they are doing is not right

for them, but will have to find it out for themselves in their own time. Try and keep your personal agenda out of this and determine if you can let them learn life lessons on their own even if it causes them pain.

Nobody will get help until they are ready. But oftentimes, changes can be made when the right person, in the right way, encourages and supports them to do so.

## Anxiety

You may wonder why lately you're breathing quickly and have sweaty palms, a fast heartbeat, the shakes, and a queasy stomach. Of course, you should see a doctor, who just might determine that your symptoms are from excessive worrying and being on edge all the time.

If you have been feeling anxious for some time, saving your sanity is about dealing with the stress.

- **Your "Hakuna Matata."** Depending on a variety of factors, anxiety can be reduced by therapy, relaxation techniques, biofeedback, and medication. Learning how to breathe deeply (rather than short, shallow, scary breaths) along with simple progressive relaxation of your muscles can assist in feeling less anxious. The key to effective relaxation techniques is practicing them two or three times each day for about fifteen to twenty minutes each time when you are not feeling anxious, as well as when you are.

- **Balance Your Energy.** Consider whether the pace of your life is benefiting you in the long run. If you are busy, busy, busy, your anxiety may be tied into not being able to see an opportunity to stop the rat race. Where do you need to put your energy or reduce it so that you can feel more relaxed?

- **Challenge Your Belief System.** It is possible for you to think about situations differently so they do not raise your level of anxiety or worry.

When you change the way you see the world, alter your belief system, and learn and practice techniques for relaxation, anxiety can become a thing of the past.

## Secrets Are Not for Children

Picture this: two schoolchildren whispering in each other's ears and giggling about something that was just said. Seems innocent and cute and, well, no harm done. But as adults we know that telling secrets may be harmful not only to the person about whom the secret is said, but also to the people who tell someone else's secret. Encouraging secret telling among our children can teach them more than mistrust. It can encourage them to conceal or alter information, and it can promote exclusionary cliques as well as enlisting allies to impart power over others. Is this what we want to teach our kids about social behavior? I think we can do better in the life lessons department.

On the other hand, when children are told to keep secrets it is often in the context of a problematic or threatening situation. For instance, a parent might want her anger to be kept under wraps or may want to hide a shocking family truth from coming out. Often children who hold secrets, such as family embarrassments, tend to grow up with shame and confusion. All children need to know that they can always tell a trustworthy adult what is happening to them or what they have witnessed in their family.

How and when do we adults keep secrets from our children? Many of us wrestle with the issue of whether we provide important information that is potentially hurtful versus protecting them because they are children and not saying anything. It is essential to know whether your decision is made because you are uncomfortable discussing something, you don't know how to talk about it, or you really do believe your children would benefit from knowing or not knowing the information.

- **Age Appropriate.** If you feel it's important to tell children information that may be painful, you can present it in stages. Use discretion in providing details and just reveal information that is appropriate with their stage of development. Adult situations and certain concepts can be complicated. Just focus on what needs to be said now and remember that you can wait to give information (particularly details) until they are able to understand more.

- **Some Matters Are Private.** If your children find out something they should never have known, you may wonder if you can ask them not to tell. If it doesn't involve something that they can attach shame or confusion about themselves, and is related to your personal privacy, then the answer is yes. If your preteen accidentally finds your birth control medication when she wasn't allowed to go into your drawers, you might want to ask her to keep your personal business to herself. Explain the situation to her as best you can for her age—why a single mom would need birth control—and request that she not announce it to the world. Then let it go. If she has the need to discuss it with her friends, she's going to do so anyway, and you can't monitor her conversations. On the other hand, if the secret your children discover would cast shame or guilt on them, seek out a professional who can work through this issue with you and them as a family.

- **Secrets Versus Surprises.** Unfortunately, there are abusive people who can cause harm to our children and ask them to keep it a secret. That's why it's so important for kids to be told not to keep secrets. One of the only secrets we can ask our children to hold is in relation to a celebration—say, asking them not to blow

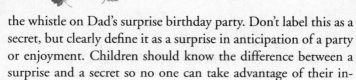

the whistle on Dad's surprise birthday party. Don't label this as a secret, but clearly define it as a surprise in anticipation of a party or enjoyment. Children should know the difference between a surprise and a secret so no one can take advantage of their innocence.

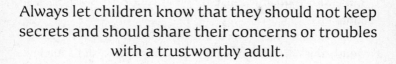

Always let children know that they should not keep secrets and should share their concerns or troubles with a trustworthy adult.

## Newly Married with Adult Children

Some newly married women in their fifties face the challenge of their adult children not liking or being nice to their new partners. Dealing with your adult child as well as your partner can be challenging.

If you have decided to take a chance on another marriage, then obviously this relationship is important to you. But your adult children may not think this person is so great or they may just feel they have no responsibility or benefit in being nice to your new partner. For whatever reasons, they may not be ready to reach out to another father figure. On the other hand, your children are adults, and you may have the expectation that they will behave in a respectful manner to all other adults. You may even feel protective of your kids and understand the difficulty they are having warming up to a new stepparent.

Think quietly about what might be upsetting your children about your partner. Be open to whatever comes into your mind and your heart. Whatever it is, tell your adult children that you are interested in hearing what their objection is to your partner. If they do not tell you, offer what you think may be impeding closeness and ask if you may be on the right track.

- **Alone Time.** Spend as much time with your partner and with your children alone as you can. Although you may want to, your role is neither as referee nor mediator. Have a conversation with your children in which you tell them that they do not have to like your new partner but that you and he are very happy and you would appreciate your children treating you both respect-

fully. You can also tell them that you hope, in time, they will get to know this new person through your eyes and like him or her. If that will not happen, you will be in the awkward position of having to spend time with each of them, separately, which will be stressful for you.

- **Parenting Goes On.** Let your children know that you love them and will be there for them as their parent. This does not mean that you will not be able to live your life with this new person. Tell your children that you will not allow yourself to be in the position of taking sides or of defending either your children or your partner to the other.

- **Be True to You.** Tell your children you feel they have put you in an unfair and untenable position and you will do your best to be true to yourself and work it out.

- **Negotiate.** Establish the minimum that you would want from your children when they are with your partner (a greeting, small talk, and avoiding insults). Get agreements about treating your partner with respect.

You are entitled to love someone.
When you remarry, your adult children
may have a tough time.

*Weekend*
*Community, Well-Being*

# Be of Service in Times of Crisis

In recent years, this nation has dealt with the unthinkable events of September 11, the devastation of Hurricane Katrina and the tsunami. At times like these we're forced to reflect on our own lives and what is meaningful. Is our life in balance? Are we off track from that which is important? Is it time to start to be of service?

If you're left with feelings of loss, sadness, and helplessness when disaster strikes, commit yourself to some kind of service for others. Contributing is good for you and helps you to heal. Save your sanity by helping others and yourself.

- **Where to Begin?** Let the crisis be a catalyst for getting out and giving even if unrelated to the current event. Start small with something that sparks your interest, keep it simple, and let your charitable nature evolve.

- **So Much To Do, So Little Time.** Write a letter to an inmate in jail, help in a local library, get involved with a cause or political campaign, be a baby rocker in the hospital, play the piano at a nursing home, rake leaves or shovel snow for a home-bound elderly person, cook a meal for your local shelter, help teach children to read. Get the idea?

- **You'll Reap the Rewards.** Sow seeds of contributing to your community and grow. Make a difference; be a role model for kids; feel involved; improve your outlook as well as your physical, mental, and emotional health; and touch others' lives.

Unglue yourself from the news. Don't obsess over situations beyond your control. Maintain your balance and contribute to repairing the world.

# Feeling Overwhelmed at the Beginning of the Day

Sometimes, when you wake up, you may feel overwhelmed. Not depressed, just tired from all you have to do. You *think* you are organized. You *think* you can take on more. But perhaps you are wrong on both counts, because you really don't want the day to begin and just want to stay in bed.

There are so many phone calls to make, people who count on you to respond to their needs, errands to run, plans to make. When did life get so complicated? Maybe you used to be an optimist who bounded out of bed. Now you just can't seem to face the day.

- **Begin and End Your Day with a Smile.** Before you get out of bed, instead of thinking of all the things waiting for you to do, take a moment as you lie there. Breathe deeply and think of two or three things that make you smile that you are grateful for. Before you go to bed, give yourself credit for what you did rather than worrying about what needs to be done tomorrow. Think of something pleasant, again that makes you smile, as you doze off to sleep.

- **Embrace the Day** . . . rather than dread it. Pay attention to the fact that you are alive and able to do something to change your (or someone else's) world today.

- **Break Down Your List.** Tell yourself that everything does not need to get done today. Pare down to the basics and focus on the

errands or tasks that are essential. If you know you are in for a long, potentially harrowing phone call (or series of phone calls) to figure out an insurance claim, be sure you do something pleasant just before and after the call to prepare and reward yourself.

Optimists who feel discouraged can find their way back to their former view of life.

# Tuesday

*Friends*

## Forever Friends

As the saying goes, some people are in our lives for a reason, a season, or a lifetime. A friend may have been there to teach you a valuable lesson, and when the lesson was learned, was gone. At other stages in your life, someone may have been there to see you through a transition. With her support you landed in a better place while she may have remained back where you started. And then there are those friends who are with you from your school days to your golden years. Their presence in many situations may not have been apparent, but they were with you in spirit always.

Friendships need not be established from childhood for someone to be a lifelong buddy. A "keeper" is someone you can rely on to be there in the way you need as your ally or partner, and someone with whom you can share your innermost thoughts, feelings, hopes, or fears. An everlasting friend is one with whom you are your true self and who is in your heart as you are in hers.

Even though you may not interact on a day-to-day basis, maintaining long-term friendships is healthy. Studies show that people with friendships are less likely to develop physical impairments as they age. Social ties reduce our risk of disease by lowering blood pressure, heart rate, and cholesterol. Quality friendships add to our overall sense of well-being.

- **Friendships Go Through Transitions.** Remember, friendships can go through periods of closeness and distance. Sometimes it is important to put up limits or boundaries, and other times there

need to be no restrictions. As we go through our own life transitions, so will our friendships ebb and flow.

- **Give Breathing Room.** Old friendships survive because each allows for the other's growth. The friend you knew when you were a teen may be much different from the one you know now as a mother at midlife. Embrace each other's changes and celebrate each other's accomplishments. You may have watched each other from afar over the years, but the people you have both become may draw you closer in friendship through mutual respect and admiration.

- **Acknowledge Loved Ones.** Have you made an effort to know your friend's children? Seen their photos? When you talk, do you ask about her significant other even if the two of you never hit it off? If the miles or different lifestyles separate you, have you kept your friend in mind when her son got married or when her first grandchild was born? Just because you didn't send cards or gifts through the years doesn't mean you can't start now. The biggest gift might just be getting to know the people in her life by asking about them, even if you'll never really get to know them in person.

- **Reminisce but Don't Regress.** Recall good times and laugh over great memories. Give thanks to your friend for times when she was there for you, and hopefully she'll do the same. Pull out the yearbook and remember years gone by. Use caution trying to recreate the "good ol' days" and instead expand your relationship to how it can grow from where you are now.

- **Plan an Outing.** Whether it's lunch, a vacation together, or e-mailing once a month to check in, plan something to maintain the friendship. You don't need to celebrate every birthday with each other, but one every few years may bring you right back to the feeling of connectedness you once had.

There is no statute of limitations on friendship.

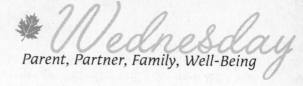
# Miscarriage

When you discover you are pregnant, your world changes dramatically. If you were trying to have a family, the news is nothing short of overwhelming joy.

So when, for whatever reason, you miscarry, your life changes as dramatically as it did when you found out you were pregnant except in the opposite direction—there are likely feelings of sadness, worry, guilt, mourning.

For a while, people close to you will share your sadness. Often they will say things like, "Oh, it is nature's way or God's way," or "Something was obviously 'wrong' with the baby, and it is for the best. You'll be able to get pregnant again." And then they will expect you to be back to your old self within a couple of weeks. Even your partner may not want to talk about it or dwell on it or obsess about it because it is too painful or because "we have to move on." But you are still experiencing feelings of loss, not only of the fetus but of the dream for the future of this baby and you as its mother.

When you have had a miscarriage it is difficult to get the kind of support and sympathy you need. It is neither unreasonable nor unlikely to be feeling the immediacy of the loss for weeks and months. Even if you have other children and believe you can get pregnant again, there are often feelings of sadness that overwhelm and overtake you.

- **Give Yourself Time to Heal.** Know that we all recover emotionally in our own time. Early on you may be in shock and feel confused. Connect with people (online or referrals of other women

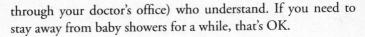

through your doctor's office) who understand. If you need to stay away from baby showers for a while, that's OK.

- **There's No Reason.** Not knowing the reason for a miscarriage can haunt you if you let it. Recognize that it was not your fault and allow yourself to appreciate that there are some things in life that happen that we don't have control over.

- **Create a "Space"** . . . where you have whatever memorabilia you have collected that is related to the baby. It could be a place for the sonogram pictures, the baby names book, booties that someone gave you, sympathy cards you may have gotten from friends and family. Give yourself the time to be in this space whenever you need.

- **What Have You Learned?** Understand something about yourself and your partner if you have one. See how you both handled this and what it takes to recover. Recognize that you managed to get through something so negative that promised to be positive.

Thoughts, feelings, and reflections on the baby who miscarried can remain with you for your lifetime. And even though they are initially negative, they can transform.

*Well-Being, Friends, Family*

# Gaining Weight and It Is OK

You have gained weight. Although you have tried to lose some pounds, you have settled into your body and accept that it is no longer as easy as it once was to maintain a thin figure. This is not an unhealthy weight, and you're getting used to the way you look and have found flattering clothes. In fact, you even think you look pretty good.

But you find that other people in your life are fixated on your weight. They can't seem to see that you are OK the way you are. Even though they may not mean it, they are constantly hurting your feelings. You've heard, "I am sure you can lose the weight if you try hard enough," or "Bet you're disappointed that you can't get into your clothes anymore."

When other people's assessment of you focuses on your weight, you need to keep your sanity and your ability to talk about other things.

- **Comfortably You.** Understand that you, unlike most women, actually like your body. *Brava*! Because so many women are obsessed with being thin, your comfort with "extra weight" challenges their own sense of what is acceptable, attractive, and healthy. Their comments may not at all be about you but rather about them and their inability to be comfortable with themselves if they are not skinny.

- **Love Your Body** . . . and have a positive sense of self. Celebrate being healthy, fit, and comfortable.

- **It's Not Up for Discussion.** When other people comment, kindly let them know you are feeling better than you have felt in ages. With so many wonderful things to talk about, you are no longer going to discuss your weight.

When others feel the need to comment about your body, lead them on a different track to keep yourself in balance.

# Jury Duty

As a citizen you have a responsibility to perform your civic duty as a member of a jury. However, when the notice arrives, you dread opening it, convinced there is no good time to serve on a jury.

Of course, becoming a member of a jury requires you to suspend your life as you know it and enter a world that is closed but relies on your ability to judge based on fact and fact alone. You are needed to share your opinions based on your common sense and life experience. It is also a great opportunity to put your own life in perspective—just think of the origins of the system and how important the process is. So, after you have arranged for child care or your colleague at work to cover for you in your absence and while you are waiting in the jury assembly room, contemplate:

- **What Is Your Duty?** Although demanding, the process can be rewarding if you allow yourself to learn about these other aspects of life and the world at large. Contemplate what you would want from a juror if you were a plaintiff or a defendant and attempt to be that person. If you are chosen to be a member of the jury and have served, allow yourself to feel pride that you performed a vital public service and your civic duty.

- **What Can I Learn from This?** Bring an engaging book, as well as paper and pens to record your thoughts and observations. You may even be allowed to bring a laptop to jot down your experiences as you wait and think about this unique event. Consider how you can use the skills of listening and sorting through facts in your life outside the court experience.

Serving on a jury is time-consuming, intrusive, and inconvenient but try thinking of it as a right and privilege that many people in the world would die for (as many do).

## Ditching the Rat Race

You want to get out of living life in the fast lane. The rat race may have served you well for a period of time but now you notice you just are not getting the "high" from it that you once did.

It's time to make a major change, or else your health, relationships, and well-being will suffer. Save your sanity by investigating other opportunities that reflect your true calling.

- **Ditch That Commute.** If commuting is contributing to premature aging and an aching back, explore opportunities in and around your hometown. Or consider moving to a place that is closer to what you want to do or will offer you an easier and more manageable lifestyle. Re-pot yourself and see how you can grow when the pressure is off.

- **Ditch Your Unserving Lifestyle.** Because you lived one way for a long period of time does not mean you need to continue to do it. It's never too late to change a way of life that doesn't serve you anymore.

- **Ditch Competition.** Maybe you can find a more relaxed way to live and stop keeping up with everyone else. The casual age is here, so having the best crystal, the latest high heels, and a formal home may be out of line now.

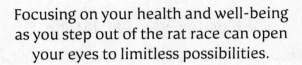

Focusing on your health and well-being
as you step out of the rat race can open
your eyes to limitless possibilities.

# Whenever You Feel Afraid

Whenever you feel afraid you can whistle, as the popular song suggests, or you can breathe deeply and calm yourself.

Breathe deeply and bring yourself back into balance and save your sanity.

- **Don't Feed the Fear.** Breathe deeply from your belly. If you stay in your mind, you will run a few not so pleasant scenarios through your head and fear will grow.

- **Get a Handle on It.** Instead, feel the energy settle in your feet and feel yourself grounded to the earth. Visualize roots growing from your feet, holding you firm. Keep your breath steady, going in and out from your abdomen. Before long, you will have a handle on your fear.

- **Tell Yourself You Are Dealing** . . . with whatever it is you are afraid of by slowly monitoring your breath and feeling secure and at peace. This internal message will help to override your scampering, fear-filled mind.

Breathe slowly, deeply, and with purpose to curtail and manage your fear.

*Midlife, Family, Parent*

# Being a Grandmother When You Have Never Been a Mother

There is a saying, "If I knew how much fun it would be to be a grandmother, I would have done this first!" Well, you may be that person.

If you are like me, you married someone with children and never had any of your own. You love those children, and when they have their own children, you become a grandparent!

It can be thrilling and exciting and wonderful and maybe a bit scary. Keep your sanity as you learn how to change diapers, decipher the different cries and what they mean, and fall in love with the bundle of joy as if the baby was your own grandchild.

- **Your Very Own Grandchild.** Look at this baby as your own grandchild and be open to discovering who the baby is. What is your grandchild going to teach you about life, love, and the wonders of childhood?

- **Appreciate Your Gift.** You have been given the opportunity to be in the company of a baby—with all the innocence, joy, and delight that is humanly possible. Open your heart and learn everything you can so you can help the baby and the baby's parents.

- **You *Are* Grandma.** Know that you are the child's grandmother and can be very involved. Step up to the plate on birthdays, holidays, and when your baby-sitting services are called on. Love

this child as your own and he or she will never care if you share genes or not.

There is enough love to go around, so shower your grandchildren with love as you learn about the life of babies.

# Become a Cyber Sister

Too busy to spend quality time with your friends? Wonder how or when you will find other women with similar interests to have a cup of tea and just sit back and share with?

Although it may seem strange, that you can *really connect* with someone without ever having met her in person, in fact, you can forge friendships online that will serve you well. And you don't even have to dress up or comb your hair, but just connect and help preserve your sanity.

- **Let's Chat.** Log on to a chat room to find ideas for how to handle a particular issue your child is dealing with or to find a friend who has a similar diagnosis to yours. Commiserate and brainstorm ideas for coping and healing with someone who is long on empathy.

- **It's Sisterhood.** Appreciate that you are reaching out to others, as well as being available to them as a source of support, encouragement, and creative ideas for dealing with what is on their mind and yours.

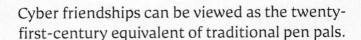

Cyber friendships can be viewed as the twenty-first-century equivalent of traditional pen pals.

# People's Responses to Death of Your Child

People don't know how to react when there's a death in the family. It's even more difficult for people to relate when you lose a child.

Going through the death of your child is painful enough, but to feel alone or unaccepted by your friends or family makes the process worse. Because parents are not supposed to outlive their children (in the world of the way things are supposed to be), some people will feel so uncomfortable with your grief and pain that they will not be able to be with you. They cannot deal with their own feelings and fears and may be afraid of death in general. Or they may be too frightened to even think about losing a child.

Others feel it isn't healthy to "dwell" and will want to change the subject. Still others will say, "It was for the best." Know that they don't want to upset you but think they are saying something helpful. Try to let go of their comments, insensitive as they may seem, rather than get bogged down in anger.

Allow these people to process your loss in their own way and rely on the people in your life who are your real supporters. These are the friends who will be with you for the long haul and who will look to you and take your lead. They will be there in ways that work for you; will understand when you need to be alone, when you want company, when to talk about your child and when not to talk about your child. They will not judge and they will not avoid you or your family.

When people are either silent or ask probing questions, how can you respond?

- **Talk When *You* Are Ready.** Talk about your child and remember your child in conversation, even if it is years later. Allow and

welcome your friend's questions if they are appropriate. When people ask how many children you have, you can say, "I have a daughter and I had a son who died." "I feel particularly sad today, it would have been my daughter's thirty-second birthday."

- **Keep *Your* Needs in Focus.** If someone inquires about your child or the circumstances of the child's death and you do not feel like sharing, you are under no obligation to. "I appreciate your concern and interest. I'd rather not talk about that." Other people may feel uncomfortable and you may accommodate them without paying full attention to your own needs. If you do this, you may feel as if you have to hide the fact that your child lived or keep your mourning (or the joy of remembering) to yourself. Instead, be with those who comfort you when talking about your deceased child.

- **Grieve in *Your* Time.** Other people may think you have had "enough time" to get past your grief. People grieve differently. Our memories are jarred by various stimuli. You never know what will trigger a poignant memory. It may be an odor, a place, a person, someone's walk, or the sound of a voice. Allow yourself to be comforted and not judged.

Friends are people first. Sometimes, because of their own life experience or view, they cannot be there in the ways we need when we are in mourning for our children.

# Robbed by Your Employee

You have someone in your employ whom you trust implicitly. He or she does your books, takes care of your children, or helps you with housework. You are decent, kind, and honest, and believe that this person is, too. It never occurs to you to keep a close watch.

Then one day you discover money is missing or a piece of jewelry is gone. You question whether you misplaced it and think it is probably your mistake, but deep down, you know that is not the case. How do you keep your sanity when you know someone you trust is cheating you and maybe has been doing it for some time?

- **Gain an Understanding.** Many people who steal from people they work for do not hate their employers. However, they may feel entitled or jealous, or tell themselves that you have enough and won't miss it. Once they begin to justify their illegal and immoral behavior, they no longer feel they are in the wrong.

- **Be Sure.** Double check before you confront. Was anything dismissed for reasons that you now, upon reflection, feel was questionable? If you're not sure how much money was in the drawer (or your bank account) to begin with, count what's there now. Document it. If a later recount doesn't add up, you'll know why.

- **Confront and Seek Retribution.** Call the person on his or her actions and enlist aid (the police, a banker, your attorney). Construct a payback plan that can work for both of you. Be certain this person has no further access to your assets and information,

change the locks, and protect yourself from being vulnerable again.

When faced with someone who works for you for whom "Thou shalt not steal" means nothing, proceed with recovering your losses and firing the person so you can move on.

## De-Clutter Your Life

To allow for growth, women especially have to feel their home and life are in order. When you're bogged down with lots of stuff and things to do, you close the door to welcoming in the new.

Allow your spaces and yourself to truly breathe. This is more than just cleaning closets, but a whole new way to simplify life, lighten up what's weighing on your mind, and save your sanity.

- **Take Care of the "Externals."** Home, finances, and some relationships need cleaning out every so often. Vacuum out your car, organize the garage, simplify your daily routine, let go of burdensome relationships, and spend less time with those who drain your energy.

- **Take Care of Those You Care For.** Make sure those you are responsible for (children, spouses, parents) are taken care of so you can make room and space for new things in your life. When the people you love are tended to, you can breathe easier.

- **Take Care of You.** Don't feel overwhelmed, because you're starting to tackle the pile. Know you're chipping away at your to-do list and feel good about it. Let go of worry about sundry concerns because you'll always have some. Start to feel lighter and now focus on you and your internal process of change.

Free yourself from that which has weighed you down, and give yourself the opportunity to be open to transition.

*Single, Parent*

# Single Motherhood

Being single and deciding to become a parent is a serious decision that takes enormous thought and planning. Many celebrities make it look so easy because most of them have several people on the payroll to help them care for their children, their households, their food preparation, their bodies, hair, you name it.

If you are like most people, you don't have that kind of checkbook or entourage. So if and when you consider becoming a mom on your own, think about the commitment to your child and the dramatic change in your lifestyle as you contemplate remaining sane in the process.

- **Raising Kids Is Great . . . Sometimes.** They'll challenge you beyond your dreams. But they'll also reward you with their love. Don't take on the role of mom unless you are willing and able to learn about children and child development. It takes time to know your child.

- **The Essentials** . . . are patience, a sense of humor, and good judgment. And a lot of sacrifice. If you don't have the stamina, stay away from the parenting role.

- **Dating Takes a Backseat.** You'll be busy working and raising your child. Your child comes first. Expect times when you are at home and your friends are doing the town.

Being a single mom takes a huge amount of
courage, but the rewards can be phenomenal.
Are you up for the lifelong job?

# Lingering Grief

When someone you love dies after a long illness, you may hear people telling you how "lucky" you are because the recently deceased is "no longer suffering."

While it may be true that suffering has ended (for the deceased, at least), you still miss him, and may think that you would give anything to have some more time with him. This hoped-for but impossible barter of anything for your loved one will inhabit your imagination for some time, and even when you eventually get back on track, you will find lingering grief that hangs over you and fills you.

Your days will be up and down, which is to be expected—the grief can be very intense one moment, and then manageable the next. Understand that these aspects are out of your control, and be gentle with yourself.

- **Go at Your Own Pace.** Be careful about how much you push yourself each day. Honor your feelings on those days when you feel ready to tackle the world, as well as on those when your energy fades. Take time to consider how you go back to work or begin projects that were left during the time of the protracted illness of your loved one.

- **Help Yourself Heal.** Consult with a grief counselor, who can be helpful during this time. Honor or construct rituals to keep the memory of your loved one alive. Don't burden yourself with guilt or remorse.

- **Grieving Is a Process.** Focus on all your blessings and be grateful—and give yourself space to grieve.

Grief is an honest and valiant emotion. Embrace it as a sign of your love for your lost one, and allow it to honor him and strengthen you.

## Best Buddy Then, Alien Being Now

You and your cousin were connected at the hip when you were little. But you're both adults now and grew up very differently. Her lifestyle, belief system, values, and most everything else bug you. You have a really hard time spending time with her now and you move at an entirely different pace. Actually, the way she lives tends to drive you nuts.

But you still love the person she was and still is deep down inside even though she's the carnivore city dweller and you're the vegetarian who lives in the country. She devours fried chicken and you just cannot make a case for tofu no matter how hard you try. Is there a way to be with this person you love without losing your mind or sanity?

- **Take a Cue from *Star Trek*.** That's right. Trekkies know the golden rule when visiting alien planets is to observe and never interfere. So when you go to visit your cousin, pretend you are on her alien planet and you have no control over anything. Enjoy her the way she is.

- **Why Disagree?** Don't get into discord when she says something that you feel is just not the way you believe it to be. Who's to say who is right? You just know how you choose to live and leave it at that. So eat what she serves and marvel at the bustle of the city!

- **It's a Lifetime Connection.** The relationship obviously has something in the root or you would not still love this person,

so stay on that level of relating—it may only be a shared history, but your connection to her can still be worth a lot.

Even though you both walk to the beat of different drums now, throw out judgment, don't question why you still want this person in your life, and enjoy your time together.

# Only the Lonely

Sometimes when you feel lonely you don't quite know how to deal with the blues. You think about everyone else in the world having a great time but you. You pout, cry, or watch too much television. You are stagnant, but there is a way out.

- **Get Up.** Get out of bed, out of that chair, or off your bottom and get motivated to do something. Is there a project that's long overdue to get started? Tackle organizing your photo album and connect to your loved ones in the pictures. Sort through your e-mail inbox or go through items in your closet to donate. When you feel productive, you're moving forward and away from the "lonelies."

- **Get Out.** Staying in and feeling sorry for yourself isn't helpful. When you are feeling really lonely and losing your mind, don't stay inside. Get dressed, put on something uplifting to wear or your favorite lipstick, and pick a destination. How about the grocery store? Ask every question you've ever wanted to ask of the butcher, the produce guy, and the person standing next to you who's trying to decide which brand to buy. Ask why she's choosing that brand. These are not intimate conversations, but contact conversations that stimulate healthy interactivity with others. It's also called schmoozing, and it's a good way to practice connecting. You'll find a lot of people just like you, hungry for neighborly contact.

- **Get Going.** And when you're really feeling all alone, it's good to contact the outside world. Don't, however, call friends who

might not be home and end up talking to answering machines. Also don't set yourself up for disappointment by calling your soccer mom friend on a busy Saturday when you are upset with your single life. Unless, of course, you are truly ready to let go of feeling lonely and want to drop over and enjoy time kicking the soccer ball around with her kids.

There are lots of positive ways to deal with loneliness. Staying home alone and feeling sorry for yourself is not one of them.

# Raising Sons to Be Proud Of

The mother-son connection serves as a foundation for that little boy to develop a healthy sense of himself. By your nurturing nature, you teach him that the world is a place where he can feel safe and that he can trust.

And raising your son could be one of your greatest contributions. Surely the world's sanity would be saved if more women raised caring, sensitive, and responsible men.

- **Teach Him About Women.** Scary thought, but he'll compare all women to you. Show him how to respect you so he'll respect all women. Let him know that old-fashioned chivalry isn't dead and have him pull out the chair for you (or any older person), open the door and go through it after you and everyone else, and help you put on your coat (however, laying his coat over a puddle for you is taking this point too far). Be his guide and show him that communication is not only about the facts but also about emotion.

- **Teach Him to Connect to the World.** Participate in community-based activities together as he matures and begins to go out into the world. Volunteer on specific projects sponsored by schools, religious organizations, or community or political organizations.

- **Teach Him Through Positive Male Role Models.** Even if your partner is a great guy, encourage other wonderful men who have different interests and personalities to spend time with your son to cultivate his various interests and talents and to show him the different ways of becoming a man. If his father needs some pointers himself, it's doubly important to get uncles, teachers, coaches, and friends into his life who can give him the values he lacks from his primary source.

Boys with healthy upbringings have terrific opportunities to grow up to be wonderful men.

## Create Calm

We all have tumultuous times in our lives. You may not believe you can create calm in the midst of such chaos. But you can.

Quiet yourself and find a way to solve the problem. If you can't figure it out, quiet your mind again and come back to it later. While being realistic, you can face a challenge and give it your best shot.

- **Relax Your Mind** . . . and tell yourself that you will manage to get through whatever is troubling you or whatever obstacle is in your path. If you need a plan, tell yourself you will find it rather than saying, "I'll never do it," or "I can't find a solution." Allow yourself to imagine yourself doing whatever it is you need to do.

- **Repeat a Positive Phrase** . . . in your mind as you breathe slowly and deeply.

- **Remember Your Triumphs.** Remind yourself that you have faced challenges before, perhaps not exactly like this one, but you have prevailed, and you can again.

Bring attention to your ability to focus on your inner strength when facing difficulty.

# Acknowledgments

Dr. Dale Atkins wishes to acknowledge . . .

I would like to acknowledge every person who is a sanity saver in my life, as well as those whom I met as a result of my involvement in this book. The list is too long to include, but I say thank-you to each one of you.

I am grateful to my dear friends—Laurie Witkin, Janet Weathers, Annie Gilbar, Maggie Kneip, and Nancy Miller—who offered invaluable encouragement, creative ideas, and editorial advice. My daughters-in-law, Tracy and Yael Rosen, and my niece, Amanda Salzhauer, took time they did not have to be available to me and to enlist their friends and colleagues to gather sanity-saving situations unique to young women.

I am particularly appreciative to my family, friends, colleagues, clients, students, and the many people who shared their personal challenges with me for inclusion in this book. Some hosted opportunities for women to get together and talk about the kinds of things that concern them and for which they need sanity saving. Others sent letters and e-mails to their friends who contacted me about particular issues. The circle widened to include women of all ages, backgrounds, cultures, and lifestyles. I am unable to mention everyone as the list, happily, is too long to include in these acknowledgments, but I will mention some of the extraordinary folks who helped to make this book happen and whose support was invaluable: Barbara Frumkin, Barb Kimmel, Barbara Lane, Barbara Orenstein, Bob Danuszar, Brenda Johnson, Brooke Stewart, Brooke Suhler, Carel Ristuccia, Carissa Smithem, Carol Abrams, Carol Levy, Charlene Dunagan, Charlotte Schoenfeld, Claire Ciliotta, Connie Silver, Dana Lipman, Dana Manciagli, Dana Witkin, David Carmel, Debbie Hoffman, Deborah Phillips, Diane Bliss, Diane Browne, Diana Muller, Dianne Wallace, Edie Mencher, Emily Glassberg, Eileen

Blank, Elise Meyer, Elizabeth Axel, Fatima Hortelao, Gary Stolzoff, Georg Anderson, Gerald Post, Guita Wainberg, Helen Lasershon, Ilene Dixel, Irene Kent Smith, Jane Schoenberg, Jeannette Dussell, Jennifer Ancker, Jennifer Marrus, Jennifer Witkin, Jeri Bilus, Jill Cohen, Josh Lachowicz, Judith Fein, Karen Simon Farrell, Kathleen Daelemans, Kathy Kennedy, Kim Phillips, Laura Rothschild, Laurie Woods, Lee and Rona Javitch, Linda Abramson, Linda and Harvey Meranus, Lisa Gilbar, Lisa Napoli, Lisa Osta, Liz Reuven, Lorraine Allen, Lynn Gold, Marcella Raymond, Marie Gaworecki, Mary Fawcett, Mary Foss-Skiftesvik, Maureen Marwick, Megan Garufi, Melissa Zaluski, Michelle Danuszar, Mickey Murray, Mickie Baldwin, Mike Visnicky, Mimi Merton, Miriam Sumner, Nicole Rabner, Nicole Witkin, Nikki Keldsen, Norma and Sy Feshbach, Orna Stern, Pamela Hadden, Pat McCain, Patti Altman, Patty Abramson, Perry Adato, Rosie Morgan, Roy Witkin, Ruth Herzel, Shelly Kassen, Sherry Halperin, Sue Smith, Susan Millar Perry, Suzi Alexander, Suzy and Elihu Rose, Teri Errin, Terri Childs, Vanessa Brenes, Virginia Haynes Montgomery, and Virginia Waters.

An extraordinary woman, Barbara Scala's, creative contributions to this project went beyond what either of us thought would be required at the outset. Working together was always fun as she kept her own sanity, sense of humor, and perspective during the entire process.

Jim Grissom's wit and appreciation of the nuance of sanity saving and finding the perfect title never fails to save the day.

My literary agent, Christy Fletcher, is a caring, imaginative partner who understood and shared my vision for *Sanity Savers*. Liate Stehlik and the incredibly welcoming group at Avon Books, HarperCollins, particularly my editor, Sarah Durand, enthusiastically embraced this book from the beginning and encouraged me to address multiple aspects of women's lives.

My mother, Sylvia Atkins, is an inspiration for us all. I learned about the importance of balance as she tried to retain her own sanity during the challenging years when she lovingly cared for my father, Jerry. My beloved sister, Daryl Roth, and her family, Steven, Amanda, Michael, Rebecca, Abigail, Emily, Jordan, Richie, and Jackson continue to support me, and during this project, encouraged me to tap into the various ways we all create balance.

My husband, Rob Rosen, is my whole heart and personal sanity saver. His humor, generosity, support, love, and devotion make it possible for us to constantly create our own sanity savers to enrich our lives together. He has transformed my life. I am eternally grateful for our two magnificent, caring sons, Jono and Josh Rosen, and for Tracy and Yael, the wonderful women they brought to us as daughters. They, together with our grandson, Ross, are the true blessings in my life. My family and friends regularly contribute to helping me remember the importance of a balanced life.

And to Miles, whose undying spirit and loving companionship remain with me forever.

To all of the people in my life who have helped me stay balanced through thick and thin:

To Dale, for your gift of putting balance into my life and for having faith in me.

To my lasting friends—Diane, Lisa, Brian, Renee, Lee, Deanie and Mary Hope.

To my loving family—Mom, Joe, Keith, Abby, Ken, Sherry, Tori and Honey.

To my love, Billy.

And to the greatest balancing acts of all time, my children—JoAnna and Robbie—who have guided me and will continue to guide me to be the best mother, woman and person I can be.